The Make-Believe Space

Yael Navaro-Yashin

THE MAKE-BELIEVE SPACE

Affective Geography in a Postwar Polity

DUKE UNIVERSITY PRESS   DURHAM AND LONDON   2012

© 2012 Duke University Press

All rights reserved

Printed in the United States of
America on acid-free paper ∞

Designed by C. H. Westmoreland

Typeset in Chaparral by Keystone
Typesetting, Inc.

Library of Congress Cataloging-in-
Publication Data appear on the
last printed page of this book.

The frontispiece and
all other photographs were
taken by the author.

for Ayshe-Mira

Contents

Preface

MY FIRST CONNECTION WITH CYPRUS was not through research but through kinship. It may also have had something to do with *kısmet* (luck, destiny). Soon after I met Mehmet Yashin in Istanbul in 1995, he took me to Cyprus, his homeland, and to the childhood home left to him by his deceased mother. Little did I know then, on this first trip, that this, one day, would also be one of my homes.

The Cyprus we were visiting in 1995 was carved in half, with a border of barbed wire running right through its middle. We were on the "Turkish side," but the "Greek side" was visible in the distance. As evening fell over the Mesarya (Mesaoria in Greek) plain, one could distinguish the electric lights on the other side from those on ours, as they glittered in a different color. Crossing to the other side was forbidden. The border was heavily guarded. On my first visit, I was struck by the bullet holes in the side of a hotel building in Mağusa (Ammochostos in Greek; Famagusta in English) and discovered that it had previously belonged to a Greek-Cypriot and was now empty. Southward along the Mağusa seashore was an entire city of high-rise apartment blocks and hotel buildings that looked like a ghost town: broken windows, dangling gates, decrepit stairs, decaying walls. I was to learn that this city, to which no access was allowed, was Maraş; for the Greek-Cypriots, Varosha. It was a thriving tourist destination in the 1970s, until the war of 1974 and Turkey's invasion of the north of the island, including the town. The Greek-Cypriots of Varosha had escaped from the invading Turkish army, and the town was blocked off from habitation after the war. This is where the seashore of Mağusa stopped. Running across the end of a beach facing Varosha was a barbed-wire fence and military signs forbidding access and photography.

After Mağusa, we were to visit Lefkoşa (Lefkosia in Greek; Nicosia in English), which is Mehmet's home town, both his parents being original

Nicosians. We first drove through erratically erected low-rise cement buildings on the road leading to (north) Lefkoşa and then turned inward towards the walled city. The home where Mehmet was born was in a neighborhood called Yenişehir (Neapolis in Greek and English), just outside the walled city. It was built in the 1930s, when Cyprus was under British rule. The land, which used to be Turkish-owned, had been bought by an Armenian real-estate agent who developed it into a complex of suburban houses with gardens in the colonial British architectural style of the period. When Mehmet was born in 1958, Cyprus was still under British sovereignty, and this neighborhood was cosmopolitan. On the same street lived Mehmet's mother and his two aunts, who had bought separate homes there as young women by working as primary-school teachers. They were Turkish-Cypriots, but the neighbors in the houses with gardens on either side were Greek-Cypriots who often came for home visits, while those across the street were Armenian-Cypriots and other Turkish-Cypriots. At one end of the street was a Greek Orthodox church, which was now being used as a mosque. Mehmet told me that the house across from the church belonged to the priest and that the one next to it used to be inhabited by a Maronite-Cypriot family.

I heard many stories about the house and read Mehmet's poems and novels about it. In 1963, three years into independence and the foundation of the Republic of Cyprus as a bi-communal state, the house was set on fire by the Greek-Cypriot neighbors, whose son had become a member of the Greek-Cypriot fighter force EOKA (National Organization of Cypriot Fighters), which favored *enosis* (union with Greece). At the time, an EOKA team under the leadership of Nikos Sampson had begun to attack Turkish-Cypriots who lived in the nearby neighborhood of Küçük Kaymaklı (Kuchuk Kaimakli in Greek).[1] The entire neighborhood of Yenişehir/ Neapolis was also being claimed by EOKA, and the Turkish-Cypriots who lived there had to flee for their lives to enclaves that had been designated for them. Mehmet, his mother, and his aunt were among the victims of these attacks and the displacement that ensued. They had to live away from their home between 1963 and 1974 as refugees in the Turkish-Cypriot enclave of Lefke (Lefka in Greek and English). In the same period, Mehmet's aunt and grandmother were held as "prisoners of war" in the Kykkos Monastery. Close relatives were killed or made to "disappear."[2]

In 1974, after Turkey invaded northern Cyprus, Yenişehir/Neapolis remained on the northern side of the border. Mehmet, his mother, and his aunt could then return to their original property, but they could not live in it immediately, as it was in a burned and decrepit state. The repair work took more than two years. When they eventually moved back in, their neighbors were different. With Turkey's claim over northern Cyprus, the Greek-, Armenian-, and Maronite-Cypriots of this neighborhood had escaped to the south. Their homes had been allocated for the inhabitation of Turkish-Cypriots who had arrived in the north as refugees from the south. To this day, most of our neighbors on the street are Turkish-Cypriots originally from villages of the Baf (Paphos in Greek and English) region of Cyprus, people who lost their own houses and belongings in the south. Some homes in the neighborhood have since been rented by the Turkish-Cypriots to settler families from Turkey.

I first arrived in Cyprus not only as an anthropologist but also as a relative. I was an Istanbuli of Jewish origin who was Mehmet Yashin's partner, Mehmet being a very well-known poet and author who was in the public eye in Cyprus. So I was recognized as well as accepted. In time, people came to know me for who I was, where I came from, how I spoke my thoughts and politics, how I related, and what I did professionally and to incorporate me in that way. For many of our Turkish-Cypriot friends, my "minority" status in Turkey helped them converse and speak more freely and comfortably. It was through the positionality developed by these Turkish-Cypriot friends—their critical reflections on the actions of the Turkish army in its invasion of northern Cyprus, their mention of the bodies of Greek-Cypriots they remembered seeing on the shores of Girne (Kyrenia in Greek and English), the crosses on the road sides they remembered being removed, their remarks on the administration in northern Cyprus as a state of loot (*ganimet*) built on the expropriation of Greek-Cypriot property, and their actions geared toward the opening of the border with the Greek side—that I developed my understanding of Cyprus. It was precisely this ground of friendship, kinship, and intimacy that allowed me a closer understanding of and access to discussions among Turkish-Cypriots that no unrelated anthropologist could have had.

We were to settle down not in Cyprus but in England after getting married in 1996. From 1998 onward, as we visited Cyprus from England on short as well as longer trips, I started conducting fieldwork in northern Cyprus. I was to find my relationality vis-à-vis Cyprus and my subjectivity, as well as my background as perceived by Turkish-Cypriots, to be resources rather than hindrances to research. Being "related" meant being affectively attuned to the environments and history that Cypriots (both Turkish and Greek) had experienced, if only vicariously. Being a non-Cypriot who had married in allowed a good inside-outside position, an ability to "relate" as well as to "reflect." Being a minority also meant being positioned both inside and outside, a way to perceive and look from more than one angle at any one time. Being an anthropologist (who thought through comparative analytical and theoretical frameworks) entailed a methodological distancing, as well, which any healthy research would require.

The anthropologist's imagination is never simply a product of her or his professional training. Nor is the ability to relate in the field. Against a colonial conceptualization of research in which students of anthropology assume that the world is a laboratory from which they can pick and choose sites for fieldwork, I would argue that only certain spaces and themes make themselves available and accessible for study by certain people. The people whom we call our "informants" always study us back, allowing certain engagements and blocking others. A positivist imaginary of research, which still survives in certain areas of anthropology, would only conceive of our informants as "objects of analysis," rather than relate with them as subjects of their lives and of narratives about their lives. Here I take a different route, suggesting that anthropology is fruitful only insofar as the anthropologist is able to establish a relationality with the people whom she or he is studying. This is not possible just anywhere, for any one person or with any other person. The world does not wait for us out there to be the object of our science.

Northern Cyprus triggered my imagination as it resonated with experiences in my own personal history. Little had I realized at first that the story of my birthplace, Istanbul, where I grew up in a Jewish family in the 1970s and 1980s, was so intrinsically tied to events in Cyprus. In my childhood, I heard stories from my father about the events of 6–7 September 1955, when Turkish nationalist youth rampaged through neighborhoods of Istanbul inhabited by the "non-Muslim minorities," especially the Greeks, breaking shop and home windows, attacking members of the minority communities, and looting.[3] My father's family had escaped being a victim of these attacks by putting a Turkish flag on the street window of their home, as did many other minority families, in order for the nationalist youth to pass them by. The 6–7 September events, which only in the last decade have been marked by Istanbul's intellectuals as a major event in the city's declining cosmopolitanism, were directly linked with events in Cyprus. At the same time that Istanbul's Greeks and other minorities who lived in nearby neighborhoods were being attacked, Turkish nationalist youth were chanting slogans in favor of the "partition (*taksim*)" of Cyprus. Slogans such as "Cyprus Is Turkish (Kıbrıs Türktür)" and "Partition or Death (Ya Taksim Ya Ölüm)" were being chanted by thousands on the streets of Istanbul in the 1950s. Therefore, what is called the "Cyprus case (*Kıbrıs davası*)" in Turkish nationalist discourse is a political imagination intrinsically linked with the last attempts in the twentieth century to empty Turkey of its non-Muslim minorities.

In 1964, as the Greek-Cypriot EOKA (as well as the National Guard of the Republic of Cyprus) continued its attacks against Turkish-Cypriot civilians in Cyprus, the Republic of Turkey announced that all citizens of Greece would be officially deported from Turkey.[4] This deportation decree, which targeted the Greek community of Istanbul, was intended as a reprisal against the EOKA's attacks on the Turkish-Cypriots. In other words, events in Cyprus that were perceived as being linked with one of Turkey's so-called ethnic minorities received a response from the Turkish state in the form of threats against this minority community in Turkey.

My grandfather on my mother's side was originally from the town of Didimoticho (Dimetoka) in northern Greece.[5] Having migrated to Istanbul in the early 1930s, he escaped the Nazi occupation of Greece. He was a Jewish citizen of Greece, and although he married my Istanbuli grandmother, with whom he conversed in Ladino (Judeo-Spanish), he never became a citizen of Turkey. When the deportation decree was announced in 1964, my grandfather, being a Greek citizen, was targeted. My mother remembers this as one of the most traumatic events in her family history. My grandfather was in fact able to remain in Turkey through the help of a Turkish judge who classified him as a "Jew," not a "Greek."

The wave of the war of 1974 in Cyprus was to hit the shores of the Bosphorus and the Marmara Sea in Istanbul. This is a time I remember from my childhood, when we spent summers on the island of Büyükada (Prinkipo in Greek). Our neighbors at the time were Istanbuli Greeks. As threats against the Greeks of Istanbul mounted once again during and in the aftermath of the Cyprus conflict, we watched one family after another pack to leave Istanbul permanently and move to Athens.[6] Though each classified minority in Turkey had its own configuration of fate, the non-Muslims always experienced each other's discrimination by the Turkish state, as they were similarly categorized as "non-Turkish" or "foreigners" in popular discourses.

So events in Cyprus were intricately linked with every wave of migration out of Istanbul by the city's last remaining non-Muslims. Each displacement of the Turkish-Cypriot minority in Cyprus by the Greek-Cypriot majority would receive a *revanche* in Turkey through the displacement of Turkey's own Greek (and other non-Muslim) minorities.[7] Therefore, growing up in Turkey I learned to perceive the spaces and environments around me from the point of view of "a minority."[8] Büyükada was full of houses left behind by the Greeks, whose numbers had dwindled through several currents of out-migration. My mother's childhood neighborhood of Şişhane-Galata was likewise full of flats and buildings evacuated by their Jewish, Greek, and Levantine owners in the course of the twentieth century. Yet although we experienced our surroundings through the lens of a minority, we were Turkish, as well, giving us another outlook at the same time.[9] Living and growing up in Turkey gave one the ability to experience the world and view it through Turkish eyes, too.

Entering Cyprus as a relative, as well as an anthropologist, I was therefore able to engage with both the Turkish-Cypriot and Greek-Cypriot experiences at the same time. Though opposed in intercommunal conflict and war, the Turkish-Cypriot and Greek-Cypriot experiences coincide in shared spaces and materialities. The objects dispersed over the landscape of Cyprus in the aftermath of war and displacement bear the fingerprints of members of both communities, containing both viewpoints at any one time. This ability to co-view or co-experience, to see from both inside and outside or experience any given situation in a double, triple, or multiple manner, came to Cyprus along with me. Although it was fed by my anthropological education, where one is trained to perceive radically "other" points of view, it did not singularly emerge from it.

From 1995, when I first visited, until 2005, or two years after the opening of checkpoints to the Greek side for access, northern Cyprus was administered under the leadership of Rauf Denktaş, the nationalist president of the 'Turkish Republic of Northern Cyprus' (TRNC) recognized as the long-term leader of the Turkish-Cypriot community. This was a distinct period to be conducting research in Cyprus, one marked by excessive repression on the part of the regime, as well as by antigovernment protests on the part of the Turkish-Cypriots.

In 1996, the journalist Kutlu Adalı was assassinated in front of his house by an unidentified gunman. Adalı had been publishing columns in the newspaper *Yeni Düzen* criticizing the Denktaş regime and Turkey, which supported it, and favoring the unification of northern and southern Cyprus.[10] Turkish-Cypriots were alarmed by the killing of Adalı. Hundreds walked in protest on the streets of Lefkoşa demanding that the murderer be identified. The assassination of Adalı resonated for Turkish-Cypriots with the repression they felt they were experiencing, at the time, under the Denktaş regime in northern Cyprus. It therefore became a turning point in the resistance against it. Trade unions, which previously had struggled independently against aspects of the regime, unified, calling themselves the Trade Unionists' Struggle Platform (Sendikal Mücadele Platformu).[11]

In the years to follow, the repressive political atmosphere in northern Cyprus continued. In the summer of 2000, Şener Levent and other journalists who worked for the newspaper *Avrupa*, which was critical of the regime, were arrested. The offices of the newspaper were sabotaged more than once. When a high fine was levied on the newspaper's publisher, *Avrupa* was shut down, and a new paper under the name *Afrika* began to be printed in its place, signifying the repressive measures of the administration, which resembled, according to the journalists, that of "third world countries."[12] Meanwhile, the headquarters of the Republican Turkish Party (CTP), which was in opposition in the northern Cypriot Parliament at the time, was sabotaged. Members of the CTP gave accounts of hand grenades being thrown over their garden gates. Repression was similarly experienced by members and supporters of other opposition groups, including the People's Liberation Party (TKP) and the New Cyprus Party (YKP). Villagers as well as town dwellers spoke of being able to speak their minds only in their back gardens (*avlu*) out of fear of surveillance. Many suspected that their phones were being tapped. Critics of the regime checked under their cars for any suspect item before they got in. Columnists in nationalist papers and magazines, such as *Volkan* and *Kıbrıslı*, who were spokespeople of the Denktaş government and Turkey, published articles full of slurs and slogans against anyone they identified as a critic of the regime. People feared being on the assassination list of Turkey's "deep state."[13] More mundanely, supporters of opposition groups or parties experienced grave difficulties getting jobs in the civil service or getting promoted in it. Only supporters of Denktaş's ruling government, under the Democratic Party (DP) and its partner (and rival), the National Union Party (UBP), appeared to have peace and prospects. They were informally criticized by members of the opposition for collaborating with the regime.

When I arrived in northern Cyprus for a year and a half of fieldwork in 2000–2001, discontent with the administration (and with Turkey's sovereignty over it) was mounting and widespread. The *Avrupa/Afrika* newspaper, which published articles exposing the corruption of the administration, was being sold and read in the thousands. In almost every home I visited, people spoke of their unhappiness. Many described their experience as "a sense of suffocation," attributing this to their prolonged living in a bordered territory in divided Cyprus, with identity papers that were not recognized internationally. A common phrase used by Turkish-Cypriots in this period to describe their experience of living in northern Cyprus was "an open-air prison *(açık hava hapishanesi)*." Numerous such metaphors described the affects of living in northern Cyprus in that period. Turkish-Cypriots spoke of being "enclosed inside this place *(bunun çinde kapalı olmak)*," of feeling as if they were "being strangled by our throats *(boğazımızdan sıkılıyormuş gibi hissetmek)*." And many spoke of experiencing "*maraz*," a state of deep melancholy or depression. In everyday conversations, Turkish-Cypriots gave political interpretations for the maraz they said they were feeling, attributing it to their repression and discontent under the northern Cypriot administration. Some put meaning into their serious illnesses, linking it with their maraz.

So profound was the discontent with life under the governing administration in northern Cyprus then that criticism had been turned mainly toward the Turkish-Cypriots' own polity (the TRNC) and toward Turkey more than toward the Republic of Cyprus (effectively on the "other side"), which had been de facto taken over by the Greek-Cypriots. At the time, I remember being astonished by the critical self-reflections of Turkish-Cypriots: about their administration, about northern Cyprus, about Turkey, about the settlement of immigrants from Turkey in northern Cyprus, about their own collaboration in the system of looting and expropriation, about those who had benefited and acquired wealth from it by exploiting patronage networks. In reflecting on the homes they lived in, many of those who inhabited Greek-Cypriot property obtained after the war spoke almost with a sense of warmth about the Greek-Cypriots who had owned it, expressing some sort of feeling of empathy with them for having lost their homes, if not a sense of guilt for having acquired them.

In referring to the "Greek side (*Rum tarafı*)," Turkish-Cypriots spoke with longing, saying they "would not die before seeing the south again (*güneye bir daha gitmeden ölmeyiz*)." Trying to imagine what life for the Greek-Cypriots might be like at the time, many asked me if I had visited the Greek side. Aware of adults' curiosity about the south, children would ask questions, wondering whether the sky looked the same to children in the south or whether they wore similar kinds of T-shirts.

There was a widespread wish for a solution to the Cyprus problem in this period. Many expressed their desire for reconciliation with the Greek-Cypriots in saying, "If they [the leaders of the two sides] could only put down a signature! (*Bir imzacik atsalar!*)." Turkish-Cypriots spoke of the border with the south through metaphors of "closure" and of their wish for its "opening." Those who had received permission to cross to the "Greek side" were questioned by curious friends and relatives about what it was like. Refugees from the south who now lived in the north watched the lights twinkling on the Trodos (Troodos) Mountains or in villages across the Mesarya (Mesaoria) Plain, saying they longed to revisit their ancestral homes on the "other side." As BRT, the state television of northern Cyprus, broadcast programs that tried to remind the Turkish-Cypriots of their suffering at the hands of the Greek-Cypriot fighters of EOKA between 1963 and 1974, and as Denktaş appeared on television every evening giving speeches about the rationale for a divided Cyprus and a separate state, Turkish-Cypriots mostly listened with nonchalance and cynicism. Such television programs, as well as newspapers and other tools of state propaganda, were received by most Turkish-Cypriots, at the time, with irony and critical distance. In spite of the domineering and pervasive aspect of such propaganda, Turkish-Cypriots expressed a widespread desire for a solution to the Cyprus problem that would have northern Cyprus unify with the south.

The various repressive events, including the arrest of *Avrupa*'s columnists in the year 2000, led to the formation of a joint movement on the part of forty-one organizations and trade unions under the name "Bu Memleket Bizim Platformu" (This Country Is Ours Platform). The movement started to organize significant protests against the Denktaş regime, calling for an end to the division of Cyprus and the unification of the island under one governmental roof. The first took place on 18 July 2000, when 15,000 workers and civil servants took to the streets demanding that the *Avrupa* journalists be freed.[14] Around the same time, and due to

an economic crisis in Turkey, numerous banks in northern Cyprus went
bankrupt, swallowing the accounts of about 50,000 Turkish-Cypriots.[15]
This great economic blow drew a huge number of those struck by the
bankruptcy (*mudiler*) to storm Parliament on 24 July in protests against
the Denktaş administration. In the year to follow (2001), every month
was marked by demonstrations and other protest events on the streets of
Lefkoşa and other towns of northern Cyprus, attended by two thousand
to three thousand people in each instance.[16] People in the streets called
for an end to Denktaş's rule. They chanted in favor of the opening of the
border for access to the Greek side. Organizing around the This Country
Is Ours Platform, Turkish-Cypriots were saying that they wanted to rule
themselves rather than be governed through orders from Turkey.[17] In
demonstrations, which I participated in as well as observed, Turkish-
Cypriots cried for peace and called for the unification of the island. In
many such events and in nighttime demonstrations, those attending
marched toward the border, with candles in hand, chanting for it to be
opened. Between November 2002 and February 2003, "four major rallies
took place in Northern Nicosia the last of which was attended by an
estimated 70,000 people, an extraordinary number, given that the 'official' population of Northern Cyprus is around 250,000."[18]

The public protests in northern Cyprus were likened to a "social revolution," a complete grassroots formation.[19] So effective were the protests
that, in the round of municipal elections that coincided with this period,
the ruling nationalist parties were toppled, for the first time giving the
CTP, which until then had always been in opposition, major gains.[20] The
three main towns of northern Cyprus (Lefkoşa, Mağusa, and Girne) were
to be administered by CTP municipalities. This was the movement's first
round of success, to be followed by gains in parliament and in the cabinet
of ministers under the prime ministry. The rallies that followed the CTP's
electoral victories were bombastic, with people celebrating the first-time
wins of the opposition in the northern Cypriot administration. One of
the common slogans chanted on such occasions was "Peace in Cyprus
cannot be prevented! (*Kıbrıs'ta barış engellenemez!*)."[21]

In April 2003, Denktaş, who was still president, announced that checkpoints along the border with the Greek side would be opened for crossing.
This declaration, and the opening of checkpoints for crossing to the
"other side," caught Turkish-Cypriots (as well as Greek-Cypriots) completely by surprise. It was as if the dream of the grassroots movement

amongst the Turkish-Cypriots had been realized. On the day after this announcement, thousands of Turkish and Greek-Cypriots lined up on both sides of the Green Line (the border) to cross to the other side.[22] The Green Line had been opened for access for the first time since 1974.

The research for this book was conducted in northern Cyprus between 1998 and 2003, while it was still shut. In the chapters that follow, I give an ethnographic account of aspects of Turkish-Cypriots' lives and experiences in and beyond northern Cyprus and derive from it conceptual terms. I do not study the period that followed the opening of the border, except for a brief commentary in the epilogue. But the analyses, frameworks, and concepts produced through this ethnographic study of a historic period have a bearing much beyond it.

Acknowledgments

THIS BOOK HAS BEEN a long time in the making. When I began the field-work for this project, I was a starting-level lecturer at the University of Edinburgh. I first thank colleagues in the Anthropology Department in Edinburgh who encouraged me in the very first stages of this project, especially Jeanne Cannizzo, Janet Carsten, Anthony Cohen, Anthony Good, Iris Jean-Klein, and Jonathan Spencer. The University of Edinburgh also provided the first fieldwork expense grants for the research, for which I remain grateful. They included the Faculty of Social Sciences Initiatives Fund, the Hayter Travel and Field Research Grant, the Munro Research Grant in Archaeology and Anthropology, and the Muray Endowment Fund (all received in 1998 and 1999).

This project followed me along to Cambridge and determined the research I was to conduct through more than a decade of teaching there. There are people in life who take a role of mentorship and support at a crucial early stage of one's career. I express my deep gratitude in this regard to three key people: Caroline Humphrey, Deniz Kandiyoti, and Marilyn Strathern. They will each know and remember turning points when they stood by my side. In Cambridge, I thank the late Sue Benson, Barbara Bodenhorn, Harri Englund, Stephen Hugh-Jones, Sian Lazar, Perveez Mody, David Sneath, and Nikolai Ssorin-Chaikov for their friendship and collegiality. The most enjoyable and rewarding part of being in Cambridge has been my work with PhD students. Eirini Avramopoulou, Zerrin Özlem Biner, Matthew Carey, Georgia Galati, Mantas Kvedaravicius, Juliana Ochs, Ross Porter, Marlene Schafers, Alice von Bieberstein, Fiona Wright, Hadas Yaron, and Umut Yıldırım have each traveled with me in the various stages of the intellectual journeys this book led me through. Undergraduate and masters students have heard me deliver lectures and run seminars on the theoretical and ethnographic themes

that make up this book. I thank them all for the immense joy that working with them has brought me.

I owe very special thanks to Jane Cowan, Ruth Mandel, and Valentina
Napolitano, who have been there as friends, colleagues, and interlocutors
throughout. They, as well as other friends and colleagues, have provided
valuable comments on draft chapters of this book. Here, I mention Alev
Adil, Athena Athanasiou, Andrew Barry, Georgina Born, Thomas Blom
Hansen, Rebecca Empson, Catia Galatariotou, Sarah Green, Peter Loizos,
Yiannis Papadakis, Geeta Patel, Maja Petrovic-Steger, Amiria Salmond,
Charles Stewart, and Kath Weston.

Earlier versions of chapters of this book were presented as seminars at
several universities, including Manchester, University College London,
Sussex, Cambridge, London School of Economics and Political Science,
the School of Oriental and African Studies, Edinburgh, King's College,
Birkbeck College, Oxford, Boğaziçi, Sabancı, Yale, Chicago, Oslo, and
Trinity College. I presented the key theoretical arguments of this book as
the Malinowski Memorial Lecture at the London School of Economics in
2007. Four of the book's chapters were presented as seminars to a small
group of scholars at the Écoles des Hautes Études en Sciences Sociales,
Paris, during a visiting professorship I held there in 2009. Chapters were
also presented as papers over the years in conferences at St. Peter's College (Oxford); the National Research Centre of Greece (Ermoupolis, Sy-
ros); the Zentrum Moderner Orient (Berlin); the Centre for Research in
the Arts, Humanities, and Social Sciences (Cambridge); the Pembroke
Center (Brown University); the University of Amsterdam; the University
of Cyprus; the Artos Foundation (Cyprus); the University of Nicosia; the
University of Sussex; Birkbeck College; and the University of Exeter, as
well as at the meetings of the American Anthropological Association
(Chicago), the European Association of Social Anthropologists (Vienna,
Bristol, Ljubljana), and the Association of Social Anthropologists of the
United Kingdom (Brighton). Comments I received during these seminars
and conferences shaped my work in progress.

Two long periods of research and writing were supported by grants I
received toward the project that made this book. I acknowledge the support of the John D. and Catherine T. MacArthur Foundation (United
States), the Arts and Humanities Research Council (United Kingdom),
and the Fortes Fund (Cambridge).

I feel lucky to publish this book with Duke University Press. I felt very privileged to work with Ken Wissoker through the editorial process. I thank the anonymous reviewers of the manuscript whose suggestions for revision turned this into a better book. Thanks, as well, to Toby Macklin, Tim Elfenbein, and Mark Mastromarino for their editorial work on the manuscript.

For their friendship and support through the years in Cyprus, I very warmly thank Fatma and Bekir Azgın, Olga Demetriou and Murat Erdal Ilıcan, Soulla Georgiou, Maria Hadjipavlou, Ruth Keshishian, Niyazi and Sylvaine Kızılyürek, Elli Mozora, Amber Onar and Johan Pillai, Şaziye Barış Yaşın, Zeki and Özcan Yaşın, and Şengül and Hakkı Yücel.

In the spirit of this book, which conceptually focuses on the affects discharged by spaces and materialities, I feel that I owe a big thank you to Cyprus as a space, as well as to its people. Being and living in Cyprus, as well as researching and writing there, has inspired me as has no other place to date. I also owe heartfelt thanks to our home in Cyprus and the spirits of my mother-in-law, Ayşe Süleyman İpçizade, and her sister, our great-aunt Süreyya Yaşın, who protect it. Though deceased, they have lived with us through the house and objects they left behind.

My parents, Leyla and Daniel Navaro, have always been there with boundless love and support. I embrace them with gratitude in return. My sister, Ilana Navaro, read an earlier version of the preface and gave me crucial comments and suggestions.

More than anything, it is the inspiration that came from being with Mehmet Yashin that led me to engage with the issues that make up this book. Here I thank him enormously, deeply, and very dearly. The most wonderful event of our life, our daughter Ayshe-Mira, was born in the period of writing this book, bringing us tremendous joy, light, and love of life. I dedicate this book to her and to her future.

A brief section of the introduction and most of chapter 1 were previously published as "The Materiality of Sovereignty: Geographical Expertise and Changing Place Names in Northern Cyprus," *Spatial Conceptions of the Nation: Modernizing Geographies in Greece and Turkey*, ed. P. Nikiforos Diamandouros, Thalia Dragonas, and Çağlar Keyder (London: I. B. Tauris, 2010), 127–43.

An earlier version of chapter 2 was previously published as "De-Ethnicizing the Ethnography of Cyprus: Political and Social Conflict Between Turkish-Cypriots and Settlers from Turkey," *Divided Cyprus: Modernity and an Island in Conflict*, ed. Yiannis Papadakis, Nicos Peristianis, and Gisela Welz (Bloomington: Indiana University Press, 2006), 84–99.

An earlier version of chapter 3 was previously published as "Confinement and the Imagination: Sovereignty and Subjectivity in a Quasi-State," *Sovereign Bodies: Citizens, Migrants, and States in the Postcolonial World*, ed. Thomas Blom Hansen and Finn Steputtat (Princeton: Princeton University Press, 2005), 103–19.

An earlier version of chapter 4 was previously published as "Affect in the Civil Service: A Study of a Modern State -System," *Postcolonial Studies* 9, no. 3 (2006), 281–94.

Earlier versions of sections of chapter 5 were published as "Make-Believe Papers, Legal Forms, and the Counterfeit: Affective Interactions between Documents and People in Britain and Cyprus," *Anthropological Theory* 7, no. 1 (2007), 79–96, and as "Legal/Illegal Counterpoints: Subjecthood and Subjectivity in an Unrecognized State," *Human Rights in Global Perspective: Anthropological Studies of Rights, Claims and Entitlements*, ed. Richard Ashby Wilson and Jon P. Mitchell (London: Routledge, 2003), 71–92.

An earlier version of chapter 7 was previously published as "Affective Spaces, Melancholic Objects: Ruination and the Production of Anthropological Knowledge," *Journal of the Royal Anthropological Institute* 15, no. 1 (2009), 1–18.

Introduction: The Make-Believe Space

I HOLD IN MY HANDS an object that is the product of a distinct administrative practice: a booklet produced by the Technical Expertise in Maps Department of the Ministry of Settlements of the "Turkish Republic of Northern Cyprus." The title is *K.K.T.C. Coğrafi İsimler Katalogu (Cilt-III)* (The catalogue of geographical names in the T.R.N.C. [volume 3]). The logo of the TRNC is printed on the cover, as is the name of the district, Girne (Kyrenia), to which the volume in hand pertains.[1] I turn the pages of the catalogue to find listings of names of districts, villages, neighborhoods, rivers, slopes, hilltops, mountains, and fields. These lists are subdivided into distinct classifications. On the left-hand side, I glance down through what the catalogue calls "the new names" of geographical units, all in Turkish. I read:

Anıt dere

Armutluk

Atabeyli

Ayhatun

Balıklı köy

Başpınar

Başeğmez deresi

The list continues. Across from each Turkish name, in the second column, are what the catalogue calls "the old names." Most of these so-called old names are in Greek. The old names that correspond to the newly assigned Turkish names listed are:

Kalamoullin River

Appidhies

Sterakoudhia

Mylonas

Ayios Andreas

Kephalovrysos

Mothides River

For these couplings of old with new geographical terms, the catalogue provides under a third column a rationale for the choice of the new name. This procedure of name allocation is called "the form of standardization." Certain geographical names in Turkish are assigned on the basis of "resemblance to the territory," as in the case of the village of Templos, which was renamed Zeytinlik, signifying "olive grove" in Turkish, because of its abundant olive trees. Elsewhere, the technical experts from the Maps Department have assigned a Turkish translation from the Greek. The third column across from Armutluk and Appidhies, for example, reads "its Turkish [version]." In other instances, administrators of the TRNC have invented completely new (Turkish) names for geographical units, therefore listing the "form of standardization" as "a new name." Sometimes, as indicated in the preface to the catalogue, local villagers were consulted about the name they would prefer for a given territory, field, or slice of land, and such choices were classified as "conventionally used names." If the old names for places were already Turkish, or if they sounded Turkish enough, they were accepted as the new standard and listed as "the same." When administrators were at a loss for new names, they introduced place names from Turkey to northern Cyprus. Finally, the administrators employed phonetic resemblance as a method of standardization, introducing Turkified or Turkish-sounding versions of old Greek names. For example, "Kalamoullin" was transformed into "Akmulla." For each name change, a map reference is provided in the fourth column, reading "XII.9.D2," for example, for Anıt dere in the village of Alsancak close to Girne. Finally, in the fifth column, the catalogue lists the coordinates for each geographical unit; for Anıt dere, this is "WE 21–11."

I turn to the end of the catalogue, where there is a listing of settlement units in the TRNC according to the names formally accepted by, and in procedure under, the administration. Across from each given name for a village, neighborhood, or district, the technical experts from the Maps Department have provided the old names for these places "according to Turks" and "according to Greeks." In most instances, the old Greek and Turkish names of villages and neighborhoods are the same, but the new name assigned by the administration is completely different. So, for example, the newly allocated name for a village reads "Aydınköy," while its old name, according to Turks, is "Prastyo," and according to Greeks, "Prastio." Likewise, the new "Aşağıtaşkent" was called "Sihari" by Turks and "Sykhari" by Greeks. It is clear that many geographical names were shared by Turkish- and Greek-Cypriots before the allocation of new names by the TRNC administration in northern Cyprus.[2]

Returning to the beginning of the booklet, I read, on the inside cover, that it was printed by the Defense Forces (the army) in the State Printing House in 1999. The preface, written by Halil Giray, the technical specialist in maps for the TRNC, reads:

> As is well known, every group of humans, whatever level of civilization they may have attained, defines the borders of its sovereignty in order to claim the land on which it has chosen to live and, taking due measures to protect this, gives names to the fields and geographical details which lie within these borders. It is natural that these names should be in the language spoken and understood by the group of people inhabiting this territory.
>
> Therefore, different groups and administrations that settled in Cyprus have instituted procedures along these lines.
>
> Following the island's passage to Turkish administration in 1571, it would have been normal and expected for them to have given Turkish names to the villages and neighborhoods left by the Venetians and settled by Turkish families.
>
> Likewise, Turkish villagers should not be judged for having given Turkish names to the fields they farmed and the geographical details that surrounded them. . . .
>
> With the transfer of the island's administration to the British in 1878, work along these lines took a different trajectory.
>
> Because the British saw the Turkish presence on the island as an impediment to their political goals, and in order to weaken the Turkish presence, they assumed the Sultan's properties and distributed them to Greek villagers. And in order to completely destroy Turkish traces in these regions, they replaced the existing Turkish names and assigned them Greek counterparts for everyday use.
>
> Likewise, with the procedure they instituted, following their takeover of administration on the island, they [the British] began to prepare a 1/63,360 scale map of Cyprus, to produce maps for title deeds, and to renew the registration of these deeds. With the assistance they received from the Greek title deed administrators, they changed thousands of Turkish names on the island, recording them in the Greek language on the maps.
>
> In the 8,000 or so title deed maps which were created by the British for the

entire island of Cyprus, of the 61,139 geographical names, only 1,731 of them are in Turkish, 795 are half in Turkish, half in Greek, and the remaining 58,613 names for places are in Greek.

In an island which was in Turkish hands for 307 years, where the Turkish population was higher than the Greek, for the names given to fields, slopes and rivers to be almost completely in Greek in the formal registers and maps is a concrete illustration of the future plans of the British and the Greeks.

However, the Turk of Cyprus, who has been conscious of this, has, against all odds, continued to use the Turkish names under the colonial administration as well as under the Republic of Cyprus which followed it, adding further new [Turkish] names up to this day.

The administrative work on the geographical names of Cyprus, especially on village names, was started in 1957 in Ankara under the Generalship for Maps, with the printing of topographical map series for Cyprus in the scales of 1/50,000 and 1/25,000 and physical maps in the scale of 1/250,000. The Turkish village names changed by the British and the Greeks were brought to the foreground again and all the villages that were settled by Turks, but which had Greek names, were assigned proper Turkish names.

The great majority of these names, after receiving the approval of the Cypriot Turkish Community Parliament and of the village folk, was used in maps and continues to be used.

The standardization procedures of geographical names in the territory under the sovereignty of the T.R.N.C. according to international rules and relevant laws and procedures was started by the Parliament of the Cypriot Turkish Federal State on 30 November 1978 under law number 28/1978. Along the lines of decision number C-289/79 taken by the Council of Ministers on 25 April 1979, the Permanent Committee for the Standardization of Geographical Names of the C.T.F.S. (later the T.R.N.C.) has continued its work for eighteen years and assigned Turkish names to every inch of land of the T.R.N.C. as a concrete illustration of our sovereignty and presence.

The project to standardize the geographical names of the T.R.N.C. involves the Turkification of all the geographical names in the area under the sovereignty of the T.R.N.C., which owns 35.04% of the island of Cyprus, consisting of 3,241.68 [square kilometers] of land and about 3,600 title deed maps.[3]

This ideological preface to the catalogue makes transparent its political motive. Giray argues that it is natural for those who claim sovereignty over a territory to want to assign names to geographical units on this land in their own language.

As the names were changed, Turkish-Cypriots recount, the old sign-posts signaling the entrance to villages (or exits from them) were removed. Any linguistic or symbolic reference to the Greek language was erased or uprooted in administrative practices on site that coincided with the activities of the Maps Department.[4] Only in a few places did shadowy marks of the Greek alphabet remain under paint that had washed off over the years. New signposts erected along an altered roadscape instructed the old and new inhabitants of northern Cyprus about their transformed space and assisted them in revising their orientation. The catalogue of name changes is available to the public today in bookshops and at supermarkets in northern Cyprus, alongside new maps of the island, so that Turkish-Cypriots can match the old and familiar places with the new names provided for them. As it has disoriented by altering names of places, the catalogue, in its printed form, aims to aid the inhabitants of the new territory in adjusting to the new phantasmatic space. "Beyler-beyi" now used to be "Bellapais." "Karşıyaka" now was once "Vasilya." "Karaoğlanoğlu" used to be "Ayyorgi."

The Make-Believe

This book is about a make-believe space. It is about the make-believe as a social form, referring not only to space and territory but also to modes of governance and administration and to material practices. The make-believe is an analytical category that emerged from my ethnographic work in the territory of the unrecognized state, the Turkish Republic of Northern Cyprus. As I construe it, the make-believe refers not singularly to the work of the imagination or simply to the materiality of crafting but to both at the same time. Much recent literature in anthropology and allied disciplines has problematically disassociated the phantasmatic from the material, as if they could be disentangled from each other. While scholars in the social-constructionist vein have emphasized the imaginative aspects of social formation,[5] the new materialists have upheld the agency of non-human objects in distinction from (and against) the work of the human imagination.[6] The concept of the make-believe that I introduce in this book challenges the opposition between these two approaches—the social constructionist and the new materialist—conceptualizing the phantasmatic and the tangible in unison by privileging neither one nor the other. The material crafting is in the making. The phantasmatic work is in the believing.

During my fieldwork in the late 1990s and early 2000s, Turkish-Cypriots who lived under the administration of the TRNC often referred to their polity by using the Turkish phrase *uyduruk devlet*, which can be translated literally as "the made-up state." The Turkish verb *uydurmak* refers to making something up, with connotations of falsehood, fakeness, or trickery. Good English renderings of uydurmak would include "to fabricate," "to dream up," "to concoct," "to cook up," "to mock up," "to manufacture," "to forge," "to fudge," "to improvise," and "to invent." The local northern Cypriot metaphor of the made-up state assumed all these meanings. Implicit in such representations of the administration on the part of its subjects was a reference to the lack of recognition of the TRNC, to its international status as an illegal state.

However, Turkish-Cypriots who chose to conceptualize their administration in this way were also referring to the actual labor that goes into making something up, a social practice, procedure, and process that they either were subjected to or were party to in the making. The make-believe as a driving analytical category in this book is a concept that I derived from the ethnographic (or local) northern Cypriot notion of making something up, by reference to administration as well as to territory, and therefore to the space of a distinct and historically specific polity. The imagination that goes into fabricating something is part and parcel here of the materiality of this manufacture, a process of making-and-believing, or believing-and-making, at one and the same time.

In this book, northern Cyprus figures both as real space to be described ethnographically and as an example of the make-believe that we shall conceptually explore. Northern Cyprus has been crafted in two senses of the term: through actual material practices on its land and territory and through the use of the political imagination. The catalogue, the form and contents of which I have described, is a solid illustration, as an object, of the sorts of material administrative practices and ideologies that have shaped this specific make-believe space. Arguably, all spaces, when aligned with state practices, have make-believe qualities.[7] In this regard, northern Cyprus is not an exception.

Space and Time

This book performs a conceptual incision into the space and time of northern Cyprus, which has been defined as a separate territory since the partition of the island in 1974. This means drawing attention to the spatial quality of temporality in this bordered territory whose inhabitants experienced time in a different and special way during the enclave period (between 1963 and 1974) and in the aftermath of the partition in 1974. Therefore, this ethnographic manuscript is as much about time as it is about space.[8] I argue that the aftermath of partition and the lack of international recognition created in the administrative zone of northern Cyprus, and among the people who inhabited it, a unique, territorially, and politically referenced feeling of stunted temporality. This was especially apparent in the period in which I conducted a large part of my fieldwork, between 1998 and 2003, up to the opening of checkpoints for access to the Greek side. Here I offer a historically situated account of spatially qualified time. The feeling of stunted temporality I refer to should be confused neither with "synchronicity" nor with a state of being out of time. I would rather interpret this, based on northern Cypriots' accounts of their experiences of time as the twentieth century ended and the twenty-first century began, as a historically referenced account of being spatially enclosed and temporally in a limbo status for an indefinite period. Turkish-Cypriots explained this special affect of halted temporality before 2003 in northern Cyprus by reference to the border with southern Cyprus and the confinement it imposed, the ongoing stalemate in negotiations with the Republic of Cyprus, as well as the unrecognized status of the TRNC and its inability to circulate in the international economy. This feeling of interrupted temporality was due to change after the checkpoints opened in 2003, something I attend to in the epilogue.

Cyprus was instituted as a bi-communal state in 1960 in the aftermath of decades of British colonialism. The administration of the independent and postcolonial Republic of Cyprus, which was to be shared according to constitutional prerogatives by the Greek-Cypriots and Turkish-Cypriots on the island, broke down into segregated components after critical events in 1963, when Turkish-Cypriots were attacked and killed by Greek-Cypriot gunmen or made to "disappear." For Turkish-Cypriots, 1963 constitutes the first landmark in the breakdown of coexistence with the Greek-Cypriots. It is therefore to be taken as a milestone of major significance for the subjects of this ethnography. The attacks by the Greek-Cypriots in 1963 pushed the Turkish-Cypriots to inhabit ghettoized enclaves until 1974, units of habitation separate from the Greek-Cypriots that were guarded by United Nations peacekeeping forces to prevent the recurrence of intercommunal conflict. In this interim period, Greek-Cypriots became the de facto owners of the

Republic of Cyprus, taking over all aspects of its administration, while Turkish-Cypriots began to develop their own administrative practice in the enclaves into which they were pushed to live.

In 1974, following a military coup in Greece, General Georgios Grivas of Cyprus attempted a parallel coup d'état against the Makarios regime in the Republic of Cyprus. This coup was brought down, almost immediately, with the invasion of northern Cyprus on 20 July by Turkey's military, which claimed to represent Turkish-Cypriots' interests. With the Turkish army's invasion of northern Cyprus, Greek-Cypriots who lived there were forced to flee southward from their ancestral homes, with many killed and missing. In turn, Turkish-Cypriots who lived in enclaves in the south of Cyprus were forced to flee to the north due to Greek-Cypriot attacks, as well as reprisals, against them, including killings and kidnappings. Since 1974, Cyprus has been partitioned, with Turkish-Cypriots living on one side of the island and Greek-Cypriots on the other, and a militarily guarded border (the Green Line) running roughly through the middle.[9]

The Republic of Cyprus, which has been claimed almost entirely by the Greek-Cypriots (against its bi-communal constitution of 1960, which included the Turkish-Cypriots), is a state recognized by the international community and has direct access to international trading circuits. Since 1974, it has administered areas south of the Green Line, although it claims to represent the entirety of Cyprus. In the north, Turkish-Cypriots have been governed by a series of administrations that led to the declaration in 1983 of a separate state, which has never been recognized by any member of the international community other than Turkey. Since 1983, the TRNC has claimed sovereignty over and representation of northern Cyprus, with backing by the Turkish army, which still maintains about 40,000 soldiers on the island. Economic embargoes have been imposed on the TRNC, making northern Cyprus almost completely dependent on Turkey. Political sanctions have been introduced, as well, so that the administrative practice of the TRNC and its representations in documentary forms are contestable outside northern Cyprus. As a result, Turkish-Cypriots have felt entrapped in a slice of territory, especially until the sudden opening in 2003 of checkpoints across the Green Line that allow access to the south.

The year 1974 is significant for Cypriots, both Turkish and Greek; it has affective properties, symbolizing a point at which things changed forever. Cypriots assign different meanings to this date and to the events that preceded and followed it, but it is memorable for everyone. In northern Cyprus, there are references to the pre- and post-1974 generations. There are discussions among Turkish and Greek-Cypriots about the relative importance of 1974 against 1963. Turkish-Cypriots will prioritize 1963 as the turning point on the island, both preceding and anticipating 1974—the reference is to attacks on Turkish-Cypriot community members by the Greek-Cypriot fighters of the Ethniki Organosis Kyprion Agoniston (National Organization of Cypriot Fighters; EOKA) under the umbrella of the Republic of Cyprus in that year and to the enclave period that followed.[10] In turn, Greek-Cypriots will most often refer to 1974 as the cutoff point or the brink in the recent history of the island, downplaying the importance of the period of intercommunal conflict between 1963 and 1974. But on both sides of the island, 1974 symbolizes a point at which the world turned upside down.

Since 1974, northern Cyprus has been designated a territory apart and distinct from the south of the island. Northern Cyprus did not exist as such before. To "make it up," the city of Nicosia (Lefkoşa, Lefkosia), the capital of Cyprus, was carved in half with the creation of a ceasefire line and a buffer zone through neighborhoods, marketplaces, streets, and even individual homes. Likewise, border marks and checkpoints were erected across the territory, dividing fields from the villages with which they were associated and rivers from the wells they fed, as well as cutting through the seashore. Numerous activities were geared to create northern Cyprus as a distinct entity with its own administrative structure and polity.

But 1974 was only a landmark. The partition of Cyprus had been imagined, as well as crafted, well before, not just by the Turkish army or by leaders of the Turkish-Cypriot community aligned with politicians in Turkey, but also by the British, at the time of colonial dissolution.[11] Partition—or, in Turkish, *taksim*—had been considered a countermeasure against Greek-Cypriot wishes and plans for *enosis*, or union with Greece.[12] With an eye to the future of the Turkish minority on the island in the event of union with Greece (which was the desire at the time of the majority of Greek-Cypriots), the partition of the island along ethnically segregated lines had been contemplated (and planned) as an alternative. So if northern Cyprus did not actually or materially exist as a distinct entity before 1974, it was present and vivid in the political imagination. In the 1950s and '60s, nationalists in Turkey walked in demonstrations in favor of the partition of Cyprus, chanting "Ya Taksim Ya Ölüm (Partition or Death)." Practices geared toward partition were well in place before 1974. Separate spheres of existence for Turkish and Greek-Cypriots, as well as ceasefire lines between them, had already been implemented when the island was under British sovereignty and administration (in the 1950s and until independence in 1960). When conflict emerged between Turkish and Greek-Cypriot fighters on the island between 1963 and 1974, some of the old ceasefire lines and separation barriers were re-erected and reactivated. Others were newly invented in this period of intercommunal conflict, segregating Turkish-Cypriots into ghetto-like enclaves, separate from the Greek-Cypriots.[13]

Partition in 1974, then, was the culmination or boiling point of earlier practices oriented toward the division of Cyprus along ethnically defined lines and has assumed a crucial role in the popular memory and imagination. But every feature of the imagination also has a concrete material counterpart. The year 1974 is not only a memory, a dream, an ideology, a nightmare, or a vision. It is inscribed all over the materiality, physicality, texture, surface, and territory of Cyprus. It has transformed the land (not just the landscape). It exists as a tangibility, in the solid and material form of barrels and barbed wire cutting through the city of Nicosia to the present day; of mines beneath village fields; of bodies in mass graves, identified and not; in bullets found in rocky cliffs full of thistles and thorns; at shooting points with a view to the sea hidden behind overgrown bushes; in bullet holes in buildings and rooftops; in the carved space that cuts through Nicosia. The make-believe is real. Therefore, every reference to the phantasmatic in this book is also a reference to the material or the tangible. The phantasmatic has an object quality, and vice versa. As argued by Begoña Aretxaga, the fictional and the real are not distinct; one does not precede, antecede, or determine the other.[14] Together they constitute a kernel.

How is a make-believe space made? What are its properties? What are the practices that constitute it? What does a make-believe space feel like? These are the key questions of this book. In flagging northern Cyprus's make-believe qualities, I do not isolate, corner, or carve it out as an anomaly or exception because it is an unrecognized state. The make-believe comes in the multiples, and although the ethnographic site or location for this research project is northern Cyprus, this territory and the administration that governs it are not unique or incomparable in their make-believe-ness. In the process of anthropologically thinking through the materiality of northern Cyprus, the make-believe, in this book, meta-morphoses from an ethnographically descriptive to a conceptual and theoretical category. Of course, knowledge production is another phantasm, another crafting. It is also another order of materiality. In this instance, and in proper anthropological fashion, the conceptual crafting emanates or emerges from the tangibilities of the field. It is a make-believe upon a make-believe, one thing upon another, like a palimpsest. When turned into a conceptual category, northern Cyprus, then, figures as a notion that could make us visualize or envision the make-believe qualities of other spaces and other social forms, not just the one that happens to exist in the north of Cyprus. In other words, the make-believe, and northern Cyprus in this instance, are good for thinking.

A Spectral Territory

Northern Cyprus is a space composed in the aftermath of a war that culminated in an unofficial exchange of populations along ethnically de-fined lines.[15] Before the association of place with ethnicity that developed in the enclave period (between 1963 and 1974), Cyprus was spotted with Turkish-Cypriots and Greek-Cypriots (as well as members of other com-munities, including Maronites, Armenians, and Britons) living across its territory. Many villages were mixed, with both Turkish and Greek-Cypriot inhabitants. Other Turkish-Cypriot and Greek-Cypriot villages were in close proximity to one another. In fact, until the rise of nationalism in Cyprus, with influence from mainland Turkey and Greece, Turkish and Greek-Cypriots did not necessarily conceive of each other as distinct com-munities in ethnic or national terms.[16] The difference in religion was acknowledged along the lines of the Ottoman *millet* system, which classi-fied communities on the basis of their religious affiliation. However, even these religious distinctions were ambiguous, as there were communities, famously the *linobambaki*, that switched their religious affiliation prag-matically, according to what was demanded of them by the Ottoman administration, or who practiced more than one religion.[17] Differences between Turkish and Greek-Cypriots were likewise unclear or complicated from the linguistic point of view, as a significant number of villages existed in which the inhabitants were Muslims who spoke Greek as their native language.[18] Such villagers were classified as "Turks" in the intercommunal conflicts that assigned them an ethnicity or nationality. This is not to paint a rosy picture of coexistence or cosmopolitanism prior to the rise of nationalism on the island; it is merely to state the facts of cohabitation or mixed dwelling prior to the segregation along ethnic lines that emerged with the enclave period from 1963 onward and with partition after 1974.

Prior to this period, Turkish and Greek-Cypriots did not live apart in total administrative distinction. All of the main towns and cities of Cyprus (Nicosia, Paphos, Larnaca, Limassol, Kyrenia, and Famagusta) had both Turkish-Cypriot and Greek-Cypriot inhabitants before partition. Each of these towns had Turkish quarters or streets with Turkish names specifically designating Turkish places of habitation or work. But living spaces in these towns were also mixed, and there were neighborhoods in all of these towns where Greek and Turkish-Cypriots lived side by side. Likewise, the marketplaces were shared, with shops and craftsmen from all of the communities on the island. Differences between the communities were acknowledged, recognized, or coded, and social practices on the island (including kinship and marriage) followed the knowledge of such difference. Yet distinctions had not yet been articulated in the form of separate ethnically or nationally defined, divided spaces for living.

The territory of northern Cyprus described in this book is a space carved out and composed after the fact of partition. Since 1963, Turkish-Cypriots had been living in segregated enclaves governed as well as protected by the armed Türk Mukavemet Teşkilatı (TMT), the Turkish-Cypriots' special fighting unit backed by Turkey.[19] In fact, for many Turkish-Cypriots, 1963 marks the date of their displacement from their ancestral villages or homes, when they moved to enclaves guarded by the TMT out of fear of being attacked by the unit's Greek-Cypriot counterpart, the EOKA. The separation lines between the Turkish-Cypriot enclaves and areas of Greek-Cypriot habitation were managed and guarded by the United Nations, but the Turkish-Cypriot enclaves were internally defended (as well as governed and administered) by the TMT.

With the advent of the war in 1974 and the invasion by the Turkish army of the northern part of Cyprus, Turkish-Cypriots who lived in the south, which was not occupied by the Turkish army, began to flee, via various mountainous routes, to the north in anticipation of Greek nationalists' reprisals. Many Turkish-Cypriot families, communities, and individuals were unable to reach the north quickly and describe their calamitous journeys, often hiding in caves or being rescued by the United Nations at the last minute before their villages were taken over by EOKA.

The consequences of 1974 for the Greek-Cypriot communities living in the northern parts of the island invaded by the Turkish army were drastic as well, as they had to find ways to escape and find refuge in the southern part of the island, which was left in Greek hands.[20] Many Greek and Turkish-Cypriots were killed or kidnapped in the conflicts, while others sought refuge on the side of Cyprus where they thought they would get protection.[21] Some personal belongings were taken along to the other side, but almost everything else—homes, fields, gardens, animals, house-hold furniture, dowry chests—were left behind. On all of these occasions, people were separated from their personal effects, from the materialities and environments with which they identified or with which they were associated. Although the people (villagers, town dwellers, farmers, house-wives, doctors, lawyers, teachers, traders, merchants, artists, writers, and others) were no longer there, having died during the conflicts or escaped to the south or north, their belongings, the things and spaces with which they were associated, remained behind. The people were cut off from their things.

In this sense, we might speak of northern Cyprus as a phantomic space (as distinct from phantasmatic, as I explain later), referring concretely to the presence of things that are perceived, by the contemporary Turkish-Cypriot inhabitants of the northern part of the island, as connected to the Greek-Cypriots who used to lived there. The "Greek side" of Cyprus could be studied as such as well, of course, with environments and spaces left behind by the Turkish-Cypriots. The objects left behind (homes, fields, trees, and personal belongings) continued to be associated with members of the community who had fled to the other side. The ascription *Rumdan kalma* (left from the Greeks), used to this day by Turkish-Cypriots in reference to objects, houses, or fields, is a recognition of the previous life of these materialities, as well as of the force or affect they maintain in their post-1974 afterlife. In other words, northern Cyprus is a space where the spectral is visible and tangible.[22]

The "phantom" in the attribution of the phantomic, then, has to be read for real, must be understood literally or concretely. The specter is not just a figment of the imagination, an illusion, or a superstition. In the ethnographic space and time in hand, phantoms or ghosts appear or linger in a slice of territory in the form of "non-human objects."[23] Al-though northern Cyprus was carved out as a territory for the separate habitation of "Turks,"[24] the Greek-Cypriots remained there, not phys-ically, but through their material objects, their dwellings, and their fields.

The Greek-Cypriots exert a phantomic presence in northern Cyprus. In spite of their bodily absence,[25] the Greek-Cypriots have had an enduring affective presence in the spaces where the Turkish-Cypriots have lived or settled since 1974 through the things they could not carry with them to the south and through the imaginations of the Turkish-Cypriots about them. Turkish-Cypriots have been living for decades now in (or in close proximity to) spaces evacuated by the Greek-Cypriots and with properties they left behind. These materialities have exerted a force over life (including politics, law, and the economy) in northern Cyprus through their very presence. I argue in this book that they carry an effect that can be studied and detected in all social, political, legal, and economic transactions in northern Cyprus.

A separate administration, distinct from the Republic of Cyprus, has existed among Turkish-Cypriots since the period of intercommunal conflicts between 1963 and 1974. From 1974, this administrative practice was geared to transforming northern Cyprus into a singularly Turkish space. The catalogue I described earlier is only an artifact, a concrete product, of this project to turn northern Cyprus into a new and distinguished space with its own administration and designated territory. A separate state under the name Turkish Republic of Northern Cyprus was declared by the Turkish-Cypriot administration under the leadership of Rauf Denktaş in 1983 but was not recognized as such by the United Nations. Although there has been an administrative practice akin to a state system in northern Cyprus, the polity is considered illegal under international law. Later in the book, I explore the meaning of administration and the law in a context of lack of recognition or illegality. For the moment, however, suffice it to say that the declaration of a separate state, as well as the prior organization of distinct administrative bodies for the Turkish-Cypriots, was part of the attempt to make out of northern Cyprus a new spatial-political entity, what I study through the concept of the make-believe.

Arguably, then, the phantasmatic (the make-believe state) was employed in this instance, bureaucratically and in practice, to gloss over the phantomic qualities of the new, carved-up territory. In other words, the phantasm of a new state that would provide protection to the Turkish-Cypriots from attacks by the Greek-Cypriots, as well as shelter, a livelihood, community, and conviviality, was supposed to gloss over the phantoms that remained in the territory of northern Cyprus in the shape of the materialities left behind by its former inhabitants. In my analysis, in northern Cyprus the phantasmatic has come into discursive and political

conflict with the phantomic as Turkish-Cypriots, depending on their political affiliations, either invoke the ideologies that support the separate
state in the north or remember the violations on which such a polity was
established.[26] Members of the political opposition in northern Cyprus,
represented by various organizations, parties, and trade unions, have
often invoked what I have called the phantomic, referring to the illegal
expropriation of Greek-Cypriot property, as well as to missing Greek-
Cypriot people to critique what I have called the phantasmatic practices
of the administration in northern Cyprus.[27] The phantomic is therefore
also a marker of political stances, affiliations, conflicts, and differences in
northern Cyprus.

In this instance, I propose that we understand the fantasy factor in the
phantasmatic not as a figment of the imagination, a construct, or a
discourse, but as a concrete manifestation of a social practice, as a tangibility, and as real. Here we do not employ fantasy as a constructionist
exercise in conceptualizing that which stands for and therefore influences
the real. Fantasy is not that which exceeds discourse.[28] I propose, rather,
that we construe fantasy, or the phantasm in the phantasmatic as a
materiality, an actual, tangible object. Here, there is no construct that
runs ahead of a material realization.[29] Rather, the fantasy element is in
the materiality itself, or the fantasy and the object are one and the same
entity. They cannot be disaggregated for conceptualization. They exist
and act in unity.

This book explores the phantomic as it "transmits an affect," in Teresa
Brennan's terms, through its material presence and endurance within a
phantasmatically crafted space and polity.[30] In that sense, it is a study of a
"haunting."[31] The ghosts that linger in a territory exert a force against the
grain of the make-believe. Or the phantoms, in the shape of built and
natural environments, survive and challenge the agencies geared to phantasmatically transform a territory.

Identifying *hauntology* as his project in *Specters of Marx*, Jacques Derrida has written:

> There has never been a scholar who really, and as scholar, deals with ghosts. A
> traditional scholar does not believe in ghosts—nor in all that could be called the
> virtual space of spectrality. There has never been a scholar who, as such, does
> not believe in the sharp distinction between the real and the unreal, the actual
> and the inactual, the living and the non-living, being and non-being ("to be or
> not to be," in the conventional reading), in the opposition between what is

present and what is not, for example in the form of objectivity. Beyond this opposition, there is, for the scholar, only the hypothesis of a school of thought, theatrical fiction, literature, and speculation. If we were to refer uniquely to this traditional figure of the "scholar," we would therefore have to be wary here of what we could define as the illusion, the mystification, or the *complex of Marcellus*. . . .

Inversely, Marcellus was perhaps anticipating the coming, one day, one night, several centuries later, of another "scholar." The latter would finally be capable, beyond the opposition between presence and non-presence, actuality and inactuality, life and non-life, of thinking the possibility of the specter, the specter as possibility. Better (or worse) he would know how to address himself to spirits. He would know that such an address is not only already possible, but that it will have at all times conditioned, as such, address in general. In any case, here is someone mad enough to hope to *unlock* the possibility of such an address.[32]

In addressing ghosts—specifically, the specters of communism that haunt Europe—Derrida asks, "*What* is a ghost? What is the *effectivity* or the *presence* of a specter, that is, of what seems to remain as ineffective, virtual, insubstantial as a simulacrum?"[33] I share with Derrida an interest in the specter, or in the force of the specter in the making of that which is contemporary. I agree with his observation that "hegemony still organizes the repression and thus the confirmation of a haunting," or that "Haunting belongs to the structure of every hegemony," which I consider a brilliant analysis of sovereignty.[34] In precisely this sense, the specters I study as exerting a force over the present of northern Cyprus should not be perceived as an anomaly, as examples for a localized ethnographic case unto itself, or as an incomparable space apart, one under a different unrecognized, illegal state. Quite to the contrary, and in keeping with Derrida's intentions in this instance, I mean for a reflection on "the haunting" in northern Cyprus to assist us in drawing a comparative conceptualization of the specters that underlie the making of nationalist modernity in more places than one—including, of course, the Republic of Cyprus south of the Green Line. (In that instance, the ghosts would be Turkish-Cypriot properties left behind in the south.)

Here I invite a comprehension of ghostliness that differs from Derrida's. He is a critic of positivism and, thereby, of any search for what he would call a "metaphysics of presence," or an objective truth.[35] Against the notion of presence, he privileges the simulacrum, that which is textual, constructed, or a second-order interpretation of the real. In his reading, the ghost is a simulacrum and should be taken seriously in that way.

Through the lenses of my ethnographic material from northern Cyprus, I propose another conceptualization of a ghost. Here, the ghost is material (if not physical or embodied). It exists in and through non-human objects, if not as an apparition in human form or shape.[36] Rather than standing as a representation of something or someone that disappeared or died—which would be a simulacrum—a ghost, as conceptualized out of my ethnographic material, is what is retained in material objects and the physical environment in the aftermath of the disappearance of the humans linked or associated with that thing or space. In other words, rather than being a representation of something or someone else, the ghost is a thing, the material object, in itself. It is the presence of such ghosts in the shape of material objects and environments in northern Cypriot social practices that I study in this book.

For something to have the effect of a haunting, an enduring force or afterlife despite physical absence, it is not necessary for those afflicted to have a metaphysical belief in ghosts. Here, my ethnographic material differs from that of Heonik Kwon, who studied narratives of apparitions (in embodied form) of the war dead in contemporary Vietnam.[37] In my research in northern Cyprus, I did not encounter local references to perceiving apparitions of the Greek-Cypriots (or of the Turkish-Cypriot dead). My employment of the notion of the haunting to understand social reality in northern Cyprus therefore is more conceptual. It is not that Turkish-Cypriots spoke of actual ghosts (or *djins*) appearing to them but that the objects and spaces left behind by the Greek-Cypriots exert an effect (and affect) of haunting through the ways in which they get tangled around the feet of northern Cypriots in their inhabitation of Greek-Cypriot properties, as well as their economic transactions in and through them.[38] This haunting, then, exerts a determinate force over politics in northern Cyprus.

An Animated Environment

This book is about the affect that is discharged by a postwar environment. In framing my project in this way, I invite a reconceptualization of the relation between human beings and space. In the social-constructionist imagination, space has meaning only insofar as it is embroiled in the interpretations projected onto it through human subjectivities. This would require a culturalist—or contextualizing—reading of the sorts of implications that its inhabitants graft onto a spatial environment. This is not completely wrong. I argue, rather, that this reading is limited in its possibilities of analysis. The assumption in human-centered frameworks in hermeneutics is that there is nothing that exceeds the human interpretation of spatial surroundings. No excess. No leftovers. No remains. Rather than negating the constructionist project outright, as do Amiria Henare and colleagues, Bruno Latour, Brian Massumi, and Nigel Thrift,[39] in this book I take a "both–and" approach, arguing that the human-centered perspective must be not eradicated but complemented with an object-centered one.[40] The argument is that the environment exerts a force on human beings in its own right, or that there is something in space, in material objects, or in the environment that exceeds, or goes further and beyond the human imagination, but that produces an affect that may be experienced by human beings, all the same. It is this excess, explored through the terms of affect, that I study ethnographically in this book. I argue that against the ideological, social, and political force of the phantasmatic, the phantomic makes itself present in an environment in the shape and form of affect.

"Is there anyone," writes Teresa Brennan, "who has not, at least once, walked into a room and 'felt the atmosphere'?"[41] Focusing on what she calls "the transmission of affect," Brennan studies affective energies that influence us from without, either from other people, externally, or from the outside, the outer environment. Writing in critique of psychoanalysis, Brennan argues that in the Western tradition, affect has been conceived to emerge solely, singularly, or primarily out of the interiority of a human subject.[42] Challenging the subject–object, subjective–objective divide that such framings entail, she proposes an approach that attunes to affective transmission between human subjects (in relation with one another) and between human beings and the environment.[43] Brennan takes seriously the affects emitted by what has been called "the objective," that which presumably lies outside the subjective or that which is supposedly distinct from it. She argues that "objective" (or outer, exterior) agencies may be interpreted as exerting affective forces or energies in their own right. She writes, "All this means, indeed the transmission of affect means, that we are not self-contained in terms of our energies. There is no secure distinction between the 'individual' and the 'environment.'"[44] This, I argue, radically challenges approaches to the realm of affect that would singularly center human subjectivity.[45]

Brennan studies not just intersubjectivity but also the relation between human beings and their environment as a locus for affective transmission. In this sense, she outlines a theory of relationality that moves beyond the distinction between people and things.[46] However, her work focuses primarily on intersubjective transmissions of affective energy: how, for example, one person can become a magnet for another's depression or inner tension.[47] She suggests that an exploration of the affective forces of an environment, in itself, on human beings falls outside the scope of her study.[48] This book picks up where Brennan, sadly because of her passing, left off. It also claims to study affect not just philosophically or theoretically but anthropologically, which means ethnographically.

Scholars other than Brennan have alerted us to the charges or resonance of spatial environments. Writing in critique of Weberian (or Kafkaesque) notions of a disenchanted modernity, the political theorist Jane Bennett has studied "the enchantment of modern life."[49] Against the monopoly over the notion of "enchantment" by theologians, or scholars of religion, where "some sort of divinity remains indispensable to enchantment," Bennett is interested in the animated properties or potentialities of secular modernity,[50] including its high-tech culture and bureaucratic practices.[51] She imagines "a contemporary world sprinkled with natural and cultural sites that have the power to 'enchant.' "[52] "To be enchanted," she writes, "is to be struck and shaken by the extraordinary that lives amid the familiar and the everyday. . . . [It is] to participate in a momentarily immobilizing encounter; it is to be transfixed, spellbound."[53] Through this attunement to the animated charges of secular life, Bennett would like to produce a philosophical ethics that takes affective resonance, rather than alienated distancing, as its raison d'être.[54]

Although I agree with Bennett's analysis of modern life as "enchanted," I differ from her in the positive attributes that she grants to this affective tuning in to the charge of the modern world. I detect a certain romanticizing celebration, an aestheticizing of affect in Bennett's work that can be observed in her attempt to extract an ethical philosophy out of it. For her, affect represents an openness to sensing the charges of secular modernity. In this intense connectedness, she envisions more progressive possibilities for ethical positioning. But this, I would argue, is a rather narrow reading of the propensities of affect—or, for that matter, of modernity. In line with her approach, Bennett is particularly interested in "joyful attachment" as an affect, representing a fashion of being in happy resonance with the outside world.[55] In studying a postwar environment, I explore "enchantment" not in the sense of positive ethical charging, but in the eeriness discharged by a territorial space and material objects left behind by a displaced community. Rather than "enchantment," then, in my study of this specifically postwar modernity I flag the notion of "irritability" as representative of the affects invoked by the environment of northern Cyprus. Of course, such interpretations can be made about south Cyprus, as well as other postwar environments.

"Irritability" is a term that I have produced in critical dialogue with the work of Gabriel Tarde.[56] I conceptualize irritability as a dis-resonating feeling produced by environments that harbor phantoms. This notion runs against the grain of Tarde's vision of "harmonious" inter-mental transmission, which Lisa Blackman has interpreted as a reference to contagions of suggestibility.[57] Reading Tarde as a theorist of affect (as Blackman does), I propose "irritability" as a reigning concept in this book against the grain of an imaginary harmonious attunement. Against the warm and cozy attributions of "enchantment," "irritability" gauges the uncanny qualities of environments and temporalities that might be glossed through ideological and material practices. The irritable quality of a postwar environment has a long-term afterlife; it persists.

Unlike in the work of Jane Bennett, then, in my ethnographic rendering, which reads an environment by being attuned to it, affect does not become a project in ethical self-formation. It is, rather, an analytical approach that allows sensing as a method to understand and conceptualize one's surroundings. I argue that affect is a charge that has a part to play in the sociality of the human beings who inhabit a space. Consequently, it must also play a part in the analysis produced by the anthropologist.[58] In fact, were the anthropologist to "cultivate detachment" or "distance" from her subject matter, in Amanda Anderson's sense,[59] such a reading or comprehension of an ethnographic environment would be impossible. I propose that anthropological practice requires a degree of affective attunement to one's surroundings (and to those of one's ethnographic subjects) as a component of the research experience.

"Ordinary affects," writes the anthropologist Kathleen Stewart, "are an animate circuit that conducts force and maps connections, routes, and disjunctures. . . . The ordinary registers intensities—regularly, intermittently, urgently, or as a slight shudder. . . . The ordinary is a circuit that's always tuned in to some little something somewhere. A mode of attending to the possible and the threatening, it amasses the resonance in things."[60] In studying the affects of a space that appears extraordinary—the realm of the unrecognized state in northern Cyprus and the postwar space carved out for it—I draw attention to the ordinariness, in Stewart's terms, of what seems unique.[61] The charges I describe as emanating from the natural and the built environment, as well as from material objects, in northern Cyprus are sensings of tension, disturbance, or jarring, which I study sometimes in terms of the uncanny and at others through the notions of eeriness or what I have called irritability. As a methodology, a sensing of the affects discharged by the environment requires an openness to the possibility of dis-resonance or non-harmony. The chapters that follow can be read as different entry points into this jarring sensation that a contemporary postwar environment produces.

Affect beyond Subjectivity

I propose that affect can be explored beyond the realms of subjectivity but not in complete opposition to or negation of it. Conventionally, the affective realm has been associated with human subjectivity or with the inner world of human beings, their interiority.[62] Significantly, the discipline of psychoanalysis has elevated the notion of "the psyche" (or "the unconscious," as studied by Freud) to a status where it has been taken to represent the heart or core of affective possibility or potentiality.[63] In this tradition, the notion of "the psyche" matches specifically with an imagination of a human subjectivity with an "inside." Non-human (or, at least, non-organic) beings are never argued to have psyches (or unconsciouses).

Variant streams and currents of psychoanalysis have to be acknowledged, of course, and the subtleties of psychoanalytic notions of subjectivity must be duly granted. For example, in the British Kleinian school of psychoanalysis, object relations has been prized as a method through which it is possible to study people's (especially children's) inner worlds. Famously, Melanie Klein studied children's play with toys and wooden objects, as well as their paintings, prioritizing relations between people and objects in her analytic approach.[64] However, this relation between subject and object in Kleinian psychoanalysis could be argued to have reduced the object to the status of a reflector or mirror of the subject's psyche. In this reading, the object is no more than a tool for the analyst into the unconscious of her patient. Therefore, human subjectivity, envisioned as an interiority (or an "inside"), still reigns supreme.

In the French Lacanian tradition, other subtleties in the approach to subjectivity must be acknowledged. For Lacan, subjectivity is never a ready-made product or a bare and given reality. Lacan's notion of the "mirror phase" articulates the manner in which an infant only develops his identity as a separate being or subject through the ways in which this is reflected onto him in his intersubjective relations with his parents or caregivers.[65] So in Lacan, subjectivity is a product of relational construction. The psychoanalytic notion of transference also describes the intersubjective relation that influences a person's psychical mechanism, how one revisits one's childhood experiences with one's primary caregivers by way of projecting them onto others in adult life, including the analyst.

Therefore, no one could argue that in psychoanalysis there is a stand-alone or independent notion of the "human being" or "human subjectivity" (let alone of "the individual"). Rather, intrinsic to psychoanalysis, including its various schools and strands, is an emphasis on the making of subjectivity in relation to other subjects. Yet I would argue, with all of these qualifications, that psychoanalysis to this day prioritizes the human self or subjectivity as the primary locus for affective charge or energy.[66] I challenge this assumption, which we could call the psychologizing of affect. I argue that affect is to be studied or detected not only in the interiority or inner worlds of human beings. However, my argument also differs from that of Nikolas Rose, who has suggested that the psyche does not exist other than as a product of the discourses (in the Foucauldian sense) of the psychological disciplines and professions.[67] By relegating it to the status of a discursive construction or truth effect, Rose radically attacks the notion of a human interiority ("the soul" or "the inner world"). The conceptual path of this book is different.

Let us first consider the inside–outside distinction. How has an "inside" been conceived in Western philosophical traditions? And what is the "inside" an inside of? As I suggested in reference to the psychoanalytic traditions, an imagination of a human interiority has dominated approaches to the origins and trajectories of the affective realm. Or, until recently, affect was regarded as coinciding with a notion of an embodied and psychical inside, imagined as the inside of a human being.[68] The psychoanalytic idea of the unconscious is the product of such an imagination of human subjective interiority.[69] Now, let us see if we can muddy the water a bit and mess with the distinction between the inside and the outside, what Brennan has called "the subjective and the objective."[70]

Why assume a separation between interiority and exteriority? Why conceive of human beings as distinct from the environments, spaces, and objects with which they coexist, correlate, or cohabit? Likewise, why presume that interiority (conceptualized as a separate entity) will always reign supreme, that it will, through its projections onto the "outer" world, determine everything? This would be a limited approach.

More recently, scholars have given due attention to the outside—to the environmental, spatial, and tangible material world. Famously, Michel Foucault has argued that the inside is an effect of the outside and that the two cannot be disaggregated or analyzed apart.[71] If we were to take Foucault's notion of "subjectivation" seriously, subjectivity would be read as existing only as a product of governmentalizing practices (Foucault's notion of the outside) that bring a "subject" into being.[72] According to Foucault, the subject does not exist sui generis or merely as such, in and of itself. In fact, through Foucault's work we could go even further, to argue more radically that subjectivity does not exist at all, that it is only an effect of truth, the reflection of governmentality.[73]

Bruno Latour takes his cue from Foucault's privileging of the outside. In a vast attack on the human sciences and their imaginaries, à la Foucault, Latour proposes an "object-centered" approach, one that particularly attends to the embroilment of human beings in relations with what he calls "non-human actants."[74] Material things, tangible objects of various sorts, are considered effective in this approach, to have agencies in their own right, outside and beyond what may be projected onto them by human beings.[75] Latour can be read as having enhanced Foucault's critique of humanism in Western philosophy, where "man" or the "human being" was taken as the singular or primary being, the ultimate entity. In seeing so-called human potentialities in the outside world, Latour has proposed that we must "distribute subjective quality outside."[76]

In this book, I take my cue from such positionings and look, with them, "outside." In place of the agoraphobia of the humanist disciplines, including psychoanalysis, which would primarily look inward, I explore what exteriorities, outer spaces, environments, and objects, may offer for interpretation. But in following this trajectory, there is another danger, a counterpart to agoraphobia—that is, what we might call the claustrophobia of the recent theoretical orientations to open "out." If the exterior was left unattended in the humanistic disciplines and approaches, in recent calls for an "object-centered philosophy," there is an equal danger of losing touch, through theoretical negation or distancing, with anything that might be associated with human subjectivity or interiority.[77]

Instead of tilting the seesaw singularly in one or the other direction, I propose to maintain it in a position of balance. In this book, I propose an approach that merges the inside and the outside, making them indistinguishable.[78] The ethnographic material in hand pushes us to question any distinction between interiority and exteriority, the subjective and the objective, or the human and the object. Approaches that would favor the outside (or the objective), as in Actor-Network Theory, are as vulnerable to impoverishment (by way of outright negation of the inside) as those, like psychoanalysis, that have conventionally privileged the inside (the subjective). In what follows, I propose an anthropological approach that would study affect and subjectivity in tandem. The purpose is not to privilege a new theory of affect against previous constructions of subjectivity but to develop a perspective that could be called the affect-subjectivity continuum, one that attends to the embroilment of inner and outer worlds, to their codependence and co-determination. "Affective geography," in the subtitle of this book—a key thematic and concept for the whole manuscript—precisely captures this factor of being inside–outside or outside–inside. It claims to draw a cartography, at one and the same time, of the affects of an outer environment and those of interior human selves, as they are interrelated.

To date, most anthropological work on the emotive domain has focused on culture and the self.[79] Anthropologists until very recently have not studied affect; rather, they have considered the emotions or feelings from a cross-cultural or cultural-relativist perspective. In such works, emerging from the culture and personality school carried into the psychological anthropology of the 1980s and 1990s, the project was to study the cultural constructedness of the emotions against Western renderings of them as biological or psychological.[80] In the culturalist–poststructuralist trajectory of such works in the anthropology of the emotions, language was highlighted as the primary site for the interpretation of emotions.[81] Emotive worlds were understood to be shaped by and expressible through words that coincided with specific culturally determined ways of feeling.[82] The contribution of these works was to divorce the emotions from their primarily psychological attribution, or to kidnap the emotions from the psychological disciplines, turning them into anthropological objects of study. This was certainly a turn to the outside. And "culture" was understood to be that outside.[83] So the emotions were to be no longer psychologized but, rather, interpreted in terms of the different cultural contexts through which they were put into discourse. This turn appeared to suggest a move beyond Eurocentric notions of the "self"; instead, it was proposing to couple the notion of culture with the self, studying notions of the self as culturally variable or multiple. The main limitation of this approach, I would argue, was its singular association of the emotions with human beings, "culture" being construed as a context, base, domain, or background produced by humans.

Anthropologists have shown a similar tendency in studies of "culture and depression," "social suffering," and "subjectivity."[84] Here we find a meeting point between cultural, political, medical, and psychological anthropology; the project is to explore how subjectivity is formed within a fraught and conflicted political field and in distinct cultural contexts. In *Violence and Subjectivity*, Veena Das and Arthur Kleinman write, "It becomes necessary to consider how subjectivity—the felt interior experience of the person that includes his or her positions in a field of relational power—is produced through the experience of violence."[85] The anthropologists who contribute to this collection and who conceptualize in this vein are interested in studying the interiorization of violence, how people in their inner worlds experience drastic political events or cataclysms through the moral repertoires provided by their specific cultural milieus. In this vein, and in reference to their first edited volume, *Social Suffering*, Das and Kleinman have written: "It gave illustrations of how transformations in cultural representations and collective experiences of suffering reshape interpersonal responses to catastrophe and terror."[86] The question is how subjectivities, understood as human interiorities or as "the lived and imaginary experience of the subject," are produced in engagement with or subjection to violence.[87] From one vantage point, the project of Das and Kleinman may appear close to mine. There is, however, a difference. There certainly is an attempt to bridge the gap between an inside and an outside in these works on subjectivity in a political field, where the inside is understood as the emotional world of a subject (their subjectivity) and the outside, as his or her moral, discursive, and cultural references in a broader arena of violent politics.[88] Yet I would argue that in the manner in which subjectivity has been conceptualized (as referring to human interiority) and the fashion in which the exterior (in this case, the cultural and political) world is considered as made singularly by human hands, these works on "social suffering" and "violence and subjectivity" remain within the humanist philosophical tradition. I suggest that there is a way to build on the contribution of these studies while moving further.

If affect does not refer to subjectivity, if it is something that simply cannot be reduced to human interiority, then what is it? And if affect is different from the emotions or feelings, how are we to conceptualize it? Furthermore, if we were to take the notion of affect on board, how would we have to alter our notions of subjectivity without losing the possibility of analyzing human emotionality altogether? And finally, one of the core questions of this book: Is it possible to imagine affect and subjectivity as embroiled in one another, as cohabiting, or as being mutually implicated? For such a conceptualization, what sorts of new terminologies or categories of analysis would we need to invent?

On "affect," I suggest that we return to the sources. I refer to Spinoza's *Ethics*, in which man is regarded as being part of nature, not as standing apart from it, commanding over it, or superior to it. Man and nature are not distinct in Spinoza's philosophy; they are inextricable, or one and the same. Human nature is not different from or separate from nature. Spinoza construes his notion of "affect (*affectus*)" in this light:

> Most of those who have written about the affects, and men's way of living, seem to treat, not of natural things, which follow the common laws of Nature, but of things which are outside Nature. Indeed they seem to conceive man in Nature as a dominion within a dominion. For they believe that man disturbs, rather than follows, the order of Nature, that he has absolute power over his actions, and that he is determined only by himself. And they attribute the cause of human impotence and inconstancy, not to the common power of Nature, but to I know not what vice of human nature, which they therefore bewail, or laugh at, or disdain, or (as usually happens) curse.[89]

In line with his encapsulation of man within the broader category of nature ("for Nature is always the same"), Spinoza crafts his notion of affect as a category that applies to human beings and the natural world alike, or at one and the same time:

> The affects, therefore, of hate, anger, envy, and the like, considered in themselves, follow with the same necessity and force of Nature as the other singular things. And therefore they acknowledge certain causes, through which they are understood, and have certain properties of any other thing, by the mere con-

templation of which we are pleased. Therefore, I shall treat the nature and powers of the affects, and the power of the mind over them, by the same method by which, in the preceding parts, I treated God and the mind, and I shall consider human actions and appetites just as if it were a question of lines, planes, and bodies.[90]

According to Spinoza, a proposition that nature and human nature should have different properties, forces, or potentialities would be laughable, because man and nature are made of the same properties, the same materials: they were co-created. Were we to follow this trajectory of thinking, we would no longer be able to consider human emotionality a genre apart from the affects of the natural environment. Spinoza's notion of affectus applies to both man and nature, radically challenging the binarism in Cartesian philosophy. In affectus, affect and subjectivity coincide; they do not refer to different orders of phenomena or species.

It is in this merging of the forces, energies, and affective potentialities of human beings, with their natural, built, and material environment, that I locate the core theoretical framework for this book. Out of this unison, which we could call a co-charging or co-inhabitation of nature in man and man in nature, we derive a conceptual apparatus for studying what I call the affect-subjectivity continuum in a postwar environment, a meaning captured in the notion "affective geography" in the subtitle of this book.

A Make-Believe State

I return to the field, to the space of northern Cyprus, and I pick another object up from it: the *North Cyprus Almanack*, which was published as a "national handbook" in 1987, soon after the declaration of the TRNC as a separate state. The publisher and chief editor is Kemal Rüstem, the owner of a famous bookshop in Nicosia, and the almanac has been endorsed by Rauf Denktaş, the former president of the TRNC, as the official manual on every aspect of administration in northern Cyprus. I describe this handbook in some detail as an illustration of the element of the phantasmatic in state practices, which I am studying under the rubric of the make-believe.

The *North Cyprus Almanack* was produced as a tangible object to render concrete an unrecognized state by describing its administration. As we have seen, an administrative practice akin to a state system has existed amongst the Turkish-Cypriots since the period of enclaves. Before the declaration of the TRNC as a separate state in 1983, the Turkish-Cypriot administration in the enclaves and in northern Cyprus was given other names: the General Committee (from 1963), the Provisional Turkish Cypriot Administration (from 1967), the Turkish Cypriot Administration (from 1971), and the Turkish Federated State of Cyprus (from 1975). These series of administrations in practice among the Turkish-Cypriots have had only de facto statuses. The Republic of Cyprus, of which the Turkish-Cypriot administration is an offshoot (or breakaway), considers the TRNC illegal. Officially, Greek-Cypriots construe the difference between the Republic of Cyprus and the TRNC as that between law and the outlaw. Legalistic discourses and practices, then, imbue relations between northern and southern Cyprus.

In this book, I study what existence is like under a de facto state. The make-believe can be read as a play on the notion of the de facto: something that exists, but not really; an entity that has been crafted and erected phantasmatically, that has been believed through the making or materialized in the imagining. What, then, does it mean to be a "citizen" of a de facto state whose documents are not properly recognized anywhere in the world outside northern Cyprus? I explore how the make-believe seeps into the everyday, how the phantasmatic is rendered ordinary, how it is normalized. In focusing on such an entity, I do not intend to encourage comparisons with other offshoot states in different parts of the world, such as Kosovo, the most recent example, or Abkhazia, in the Republic of Georgia, currently fighting for its independence. Such comparisons would be a narrow reading of what an ethnographic lens onto a de facto administration can offer, though they should not, of course, be ignored. A more interesting comparative viewing, I propose, would be through a consideration of the phantasmatic elements in the making of the TRNC as a separate state. These, I suggest, are not at all unique to northern Cyprus but promise to bring to the fore aspects that have not been analyzed under other, legally recognized states—by which I mean all of those states that are officially recognized by the United Nations and that count as member states of the international system. There is a phantasmatic element to all state practices. The *North Cyprus Almanack* makes this practice in the make-believe only more visible. I would like readers to consider the extent to which the practice of delineating a space with a territory and a population resembles conventional ethnographic practices of circumventing place, the phantasmatic element in the writing of ethnography.[91]

Under the heading "Basic Facts on the TRNC," the *Almanack* lists the following:

Founded on: 15 November 1983

President: Rauf R. Denktaş

President of the National Assembly: Hakkı Atun

Prime Minister: Dr. Derviş Eroğlu

Number of Seats in the National Assembly: 50 . . .

Area: 3,355 square kilometres (1,295 square miles)

Population: 160,287

Per capita income: 1,300 U.S. Dollars

Yearly economic growth: 7%

Density per square kilometre: 47.78% (average)

    In towns: 51%

    In villages: 44%

Principal Towns (with estimated populations)

    Lefkoşa (Nicosia): 37,400

    Gazi Mağusa (Famagusta): 19, 428

    Girne (Kyrenia): 6,902

Güzelyurt: 11,179 . . .

Exports

    1984: 38.8 (million U.S. dollars)

    1985: 44.1 (million U.S. dollars)

Imports

    1984: 136.3 (million U.S. dollars)

    1985: 145.6 (million U.S. dollars) . . .

Finance

    Turkish currency (q.v.) is in use[92]

Numbers are employed in the *Almanack* to render the de facto concrete. Numbers have a phantasmatic quality; they give a semblance of solidity. They make the tentative appear symbolically more tangible or true. I would argue that they are therefore real, because statistics actually and concretely generate (and not only reflect) social practices. The administration in northern Cyprus has mimicked state practices elsewhere, circumscribing its territory with figures quoted in square kilometers, providing counts for its population and averages in calculated percentage for indices of economic growth.[93] These are the figures a state practice needs to be recognized as real.

A separate state must also have its distinct history. For this, the *Almanack* provides what it calls a "Chronological History," beginning in 4000 B.C., identified as the "New Stone Age," and ending on 15 November 1983 with the "Proclamation of the Turkish Republic of Northern Cyprus." Cyprus's history, with its roots in ancient times, now culminates in the foundation of the TRNC. Hence, the TRNC is inscribed in stone, is rendered akin to archaeological ruins, is turned into a fossil, a solid carving on a rock. This could be studied as mimicking the practices and discourses of the Republic of Cyprus, now on the "Greek side," which claims roots in the ancient Hellenic past of Cyprus.

The *Almanack* next provides a genealogical history of administration among the Turkish-Cypriots. This section describes how all areas of Turkish-Cypriot habitation were assumed under the new governmental practices. In reference to the Provisional Turkish Cypriot Administration, the *Almanack* provides the following description: "The Basic Law of this Administration consisted of nineteen sections. Section 1 thereof provided that until all the provisions of the 1960 Constitution were implemented, all Turks living in Turkish-Cypriot areas of Cyprus were to be attached to this Administration, and Section 2 thereof provided for the establishment of a Legislature to enact all necessary legislation for the Turkish zones."[94] Implicit in this description is the inventiveness that was built into the making of administration. A Legislative Assembly was introduced; regulations were put in place to define the powers of the Executive Council.[95] When the Turkish Federated State of Cyprus was formed, a Constituent Assembly was founded to draft a constitution, which was then voted in for approval and published in the *Official Gazette* in 1975.[96] The *Almanack* provides detailed accounts of government in northern Cyprus, including the constitution, the presidency, the National Assembly and its functions, the party system, the prime minister, the cabinet, ministerial responsibilities, the national anthem, defense, the police force, the judiciary (including the Supreme Court, subordinate courts, and the Supreme Council of Judicature), the legislature (including political parties), the functions of government departments (including ministries, the Public Information Office, the State Planning Bureau, and the Office of Population Censuses), the bar association, the district administration (including local authorities and municipalities), and town and country planning (including the Department of Land and Surveys).[97] And in a classification of functions akin to recognized states in the international system, the official handbook lists further facts on health, economy and finance, agriculture, other natural resources, flora and fauna, the cooperative movement, trade and marketing, industrial relations, education, religion, art and culture, transport and communications, geography and climate, and tourism.[98]

The booklet, with the logo of the TRNC printed on its cover, is an attempt to render solid (in the form of its own object quality) the stateness of the administration in northern Cyprus by way of illustrating, concretely through description, each and every element of its form of governance. The implication is that no aspect of administration is missing from this state practice, that its system of governance and its span lack nothing in comparison with recognized states.

As a phantasmatic object, the *Almanack* illustrates the agencies and creativity involved in the making of a stand-alone administrative practice akin to a state system. Nowhere in the *Almanack* is there any reference to the illegal status of the TRNC under international law, only that the TRNC "is not yet a member of the United Nations."[99] Here, I would like to follow in the lead of the inventiveness of this administrative practice to argue that it can assist us in reconsidering legal, theoretical, and analytical distinctions between law and the outlaw.

Affect in Law and Administration

This book charts affect in unlikely sites. An interest in affect in itself requires an openness to the possibilities of sensing in multiple realms, beyond projections out of human subjectivities. This widening of the scope for the study of affect has led me to observe institutions and administrations, modes of governance, and legal practices as capable of inducing, and being charged with, affect. Here, I do not consider administration solely as a product of human agency (and therefore only as an entity charged with affectivity). Although administrations are certainly "manmade," I would argue that they also have the potential to generate and exert affective forces in their own right. The tools of administration, such as official handbooks, gazettes, legal forms and documents, filing cabinets, office furniture, buildings, as well as institutional practices such as surveys, audits, censuses, legal practices, and procedures in national assemblies and in court-hearings, have ways of producing affect.[100] This institutional (or legal and administrative) affect is not just a reflection of the human agencies that practice in and through it. My argument is that institutions have a life (or liveliness) of their own that goes further than, and beyond, human life. Institutions exceed, and are excessive of, human potential. They are animated (alive) in their own right. To borrow Bennett's term, institutions are "enchanted." They are not simply "disenchanted," as Max Weber influentially called them.[101] In this book, I ethnographically explore the liveliness of (the charge within) a specific set of institutions, those under (what the Greek-Cypriots call) a "pseudo-state." However, I would emphasize that it is not the pseudo-factor in the TRNC that makes it more prone to inducing affect. A focus on this particular set of administrative practices in northern Cyprus only makes it necessary for us to qualify the genre in which affect makes itself sensed, or apparent, in this specific case. Institutionally induced affect, then, comes in variegated forms and fashions and must be qualified.

Studying an institution anthropologically, through attention to administrative practices, is a project of this book, and here I follow the works of anthropologists who have studied audit cultures, organizations, documentary practices, and industry.[102] An ethnographic interest in administration, it must be stressed, is different from one in the state,[103] even if the administrative practice in question is representative of, and aligned with, a state practice. Rather than picking out states as phenomena supposedly of a different order for anthropological analysis, a focus on administration renders the difference between state and non-state practices of governance and modes of institutionality more banal. The intention is explicit. I am trying to bring state practices down to earth, to reduce the potency they exert by way of comparing them, by implication, with other institutional practices. When studied at the scale of the everyday, in the minute practices of lower-level civil servants, social workers, and border guards, a state practice (its administration) appears much more ordinary. Having brought it down to ground level, I then extract the extraordinariness implicit in administrations more broadly.

The counter-Weberian framework is well known. If Weber argued that bureaucracies in the formation of capitalism would lead themselves to produce forms of disenchantment and alienation (made iconic in his famous image of the iron cage), others have suggested that institutions cannot be studied solely through the terms of rationalization.[104] Reading Foucault's interest in discipline and the rationalities of government in a similar light, attention has been drawn, instead, to the psychical manifestations of power, or power as fantasy. In this book, in line with Ann Laura Stoler's work, I develop this argument, further exploring the "non-rational" potentialities and inclinations of institutions. This requires that we conceptualize governance (here, administration) in a fashion that moves beyond Foucault's notion of "governmentality." Implicit to governmentality is the concept of "political reason," and many have studied neoliberal institutions in this guise.[105] In the notion of governance I explore, administrations are read not singularly as exemplars for governmentality (or cool and distant, rationalized disciplinary practice) but as working through exuding affect and potency. Another portrait of institutions come to light, then, in this study, akin to Karl Deutsch's notion of "the nerves government."[106]

I am trying to work against the grain of the sterilization and desensitization induced by bureaucracies and argued academically to be representative of them. Rather than mimicking the rationalizing postures of institutions in my writing style and ethnographic description, then, I explore the affects that are generated by this sterilization as a practice and process, which I study as *the senses of governance*, or *governance as sensorial*. Desensitization (what some have called "detachment") is an affect of sorts, with a certain quality.[107] So is what Michael Herzfeld has called "indifference."[108] I study the affects discharged by institutions, their objects, and practices. We can conceive of institutions as having nerves or tempers or, alternatively, as having calming and quieting effects. We can study documents as charged with affect: documents that induce fear; others that inflict confidence; and likewise those that transmit apathy among those who use them.[109] Here I study administration as animated, as having its own charge.[110] We explore, therefore, what could be called, following Stoler's notion of "affective states," an *affective administration*.

Part I Spatial Transformation

1. The Materiality of Sovereignty

I SIT IN THE SMALL OFFICE of the Maps Department of the TRNC, in Lefkoşa, the neighborhood of Yenişehir quite close to the local police station. The Maps Department, linked directly to the Turkish armed forces in northern Cyprus, is considered one of the most important units of the TRNC administration. Civil servants who work in the department conduct regular cartographic surveys of the territory of northern Cyprus; the maps they produce are used officially not just by the army, but also by the Office of Title Deeds for property allocation, by schools for geography lessons, by town and city councils for local administration, by the police for criminal investigation, and by the Office of Identity Cards and Passports for registration and verification purposes. In this chapter, I begin my account not through the maps (as the products of representational abstraction), but through the work (the practices) that went into their making.

An officer working for the Maps Department, Kemal Bey, a Turkish-Cypriot originally from a village in southern Cyprus, described elements of this work:

> In villages, there were land maps (*arazi haritaları*) held by the elected heads of villages (*muhtars*). We started with these maps, as well as others that we found in the villages, here and there. We produced new maps for the villages left behind by the Greek-Cypriots. For example, it was us who produced a map from scratch for the village of Demirhan. Then, suddenly, a villager appeared and said that he had found the old map for the village. We compared the old map with the new one we had produced. In the new map, we had parceled land up in a different way.

Kemal Bey opened a drawer and took out an example of an old village map to illustrate what he was describing:

Look, for example, this is the old map for the village of Yenağra. This map was originally produced in 1911 by the [British] Department of Land Surveys and was copied in 1970. On the map, you can see that parcels of land and portions for title deeds have been enumerated. These numbers have been the same since earlier than 1911, and they are still used in title deeds of the TRNC. Now, in this old map, you find the previous name of the field (*arazi*) in the middle of this village. We adapted this old name to Turkish and changed it.

Kemal Bey opened another drawer and took out a map of Cyprus, which he said the Maps Department had produced in 1987. "There are some small mistakes in this map," he said:

For example, there is no reference to Güzelyurt [Omorfo for Turkish-Cypriots; Morphou for Greek-Cypriots] on it; you see, that space is blank. This is because Güzelyurt was not registered as a separate district in the period when we were conducting the name-changing project; it was connected to Lefkoşa. Only afterward did Güzelyurt acquire a distinct administrative identity. Similarly, we had united the three villages where there were martyrs [people killed by Greek-Cypriots]: Murataĝa, Sandallar, and Atlılar, and renamed them Şehitler [Martyrs] as a single administrative unit. On this map, there is only a reference to Şehitler; the other village names do not appear. Now, this map can be considered old by today's standards, but you may have a look at it.

Kemal Bey gave me a copy of the map from 1987 as a present. He then continued to recount the work that went into the project to change place names in northern Cyprus:

We had founded a committee to change the names of villages. But it was primarily me and Halil Bey [the head of the Maps Department] who worked on this. This work took twenty-two years. We created charts, matching old village names with the new ones we had assigned, and against each such pairing we provided a description of the rationale for the change. In some instances, we used to put a question mark for a specific village or location. We would send an officer to that village and have him interview the local muhtar or the elderly men of the village to ask what they used to call a specific parcel of land, a field, or a hill. We would then, if appropriate, name this place accordingly.

I asked Kemal Bey, "What if the villagers there were refugees from the south or migrants from Turkey and they didn't know the old names for these places?" "Well," he replied, "if they had been living in that specific location for some time, then we would ask them 'What name do you give to this field?' Or, we would ask, 'Is there any martyr from your village?' and if there was, we would name that field after the martyr. Or we would give a name that recalled, for the villagers, the village they left behind in the south" (see map 1). A genre of fieldwork, then, was part of the work of the Maps Department, akin to (and referencing) what were called "survey methods" in the cartographic practices of the British. What is significant in the account of Kemal Bey—the senior officer of the Maps Department and an agent in the territorial reconstitution of northern Cyprus—was the extent to which mapmaking and the renaming of places, in this instance, was done by encouraging a degree of collaboration on the part of Turkish-Cypriots who inhabited these spaces to achieve some degree of agreement or acquiescence.

However, if the surveying work itself involved some relationality between the administrators and the villagers, at the end of the project (and of the long-term process) the new place names were formalized through an official procedure. "After assigning new names, we submitted them to the Council of Ministers (Bakanlar Kurulu)," Kemal Bey explained. "The

Map 1. Extract from a map prepared by the Maps Department of the TRNC showing the divided Lefkoşa, with Turkish names for places in the north and Greek names in the south.

council approved them; they were published in the *Official Gazette* and went into procedure. We did a lot of work standardizing place names in this way." In the middle of describing the administrative procedure for toponymic changes, Kemal Bey said, "Most of our maps are kept secret, because they are military."

Another officer in the Maps Department said he was originally from Sıvas, Turkey, but had been living in northern Cyprus for seventeen years. He explained that the Maps Department of the TRNC is linked with the General Commandership for Maps (Harita Genel Komutanlığı) in Turkey. "We are a small unit under them," he said. "This office is also under the Commandership of the Defense Forces (Güvenlik Kuvvetleri Komutanlığı; GKK). Even the construction of our building was sponsored by the GKK. The Turkish army gives a lot of importance to this office, but in my opinion, people who work here do not have the character to understand its significance." The administrator thus was claiming a certain know-how vis-à-vis Turkey and the Turkish army that he thought the Turkish-Cypriot civil servants lacked.

Kemal Bey went on to describe a new and modernized cartographic practice that had been introduced by Turkey to northern Cyprus: "These old systems will be changed. We are bringing a new cartographic system from Turkey. From now on, the surface area on title deeds will be measured not in *dönüms*[1] but in square meters. We have selected the village of Değirmenlik as the pilot area. The parceling method will be altered." As Kemal Bey described it, the work of the Maps Department was linked directly not only with the Turkish army, but also with the Office of Title Deeds, which distributed Greek-Cypriot land and property to Turkish-Cypriots on the basis of what was called the "property of equal value system (*eşdeğer puan sistemi*)." Kemal Bey described the procedure for obtaining a "title deed" under the TRNC: "To obtain a deed (*koçan*) from the Office of Title Deeds, first one has to get an equal point document from the Settlements Office, which checks out the applicant's property dossier. This dossier number is then registered on the title deed, as well." Kemal Bey also described the procedure for measuring and enumerating the proportion and value of landed property. Showing me an example of a title deed for immovable property produced by the Office of Title Deeds bearing the logo of the TRNC, he described how such a document is to be read and interpreted:

You see, first you write the name of the town or village and the neighborhood for the property. Then you inscribe its location (*mevki*) and its surface area (*yüzölçümü*). According to the new system we have imported from Turkey, from now on the surface area will be calculated not in *dönüms*, but in square meters. Some of the villages have been sub-divided into "blocs" since the old days. If the property has a bloc, then this is registered in the deed. The map and section (*pafta*) number of the property is also put in and the scale (*ölçek*) is quoted. Underneath that, we define the boundaries (*hudud*) of the property and provide an exact description for it (whether it be a house or a parcel of land). The old registration number of the property is provided, as well. Below that, we write the name of the person whose name is registered against the property in the title deed volumes, and we define his rights, or portion of rights, over it. If the land or property was acquired through the equal-point system, then we write the number of the dossier for equal points in the Settlements Office. For people who left property behind in the south, the numbers for their title deeds registered in the south are available through the Office of Title Deeds.

Working a Territory

A significant body of anthropological work on space and place has framed its object of analysis as a culturally contextualized and differentiated study of landscape.[2] Against Western as well as geographical reifications of landscape through representational (visual or literary/textual) means, anthropologists have researched non-Western ways to engage with and define land.[3] Following Tim Ingold, Eric Hirsch has proposed a framework for the conceptualization of landscape as a "cultural process," studying the practices of everyday social life on a landscape in a fashion that is culturally contextualized and differentiated.[4] Studies such as these have developed ethnographic tools and methodologies for exploring variegated and processual engagements with landscape.

At the root of such anthropological re-framings of landscape is a disquiet with human-centered (humanist) Western approaches to space and place that privilege the study of memory, discourse, the imagination, and representations. In the social-constructionist tradition, spatiality has been interpreted as a projection of the human imagination onto the broader physical environment. Accordingly, studies of memory as configured in space have interpreted the workings of landscape within human selves or subjectivities.

Against the grain of this established (humanist/constructionist) approach to space, scholars such as Kevin Hetherington have urged a move toward a "post-humanist" appreciation of the entanglement of (non-human) materialities and (human) subjectivities in the making of place.[5] Contesting the abstractionism of geometry and the representationalism of hermeneutics in relation to space, and employing Actor-Network Theory (ANT) methodologies, Hetherington proposes that we give due attention to "the materiality of place," an approach that attends to the agency of objects vis-à-vis human actors.[6] In the "complex topology" he addresses, Hetherington writes:

> If we stop thinking of places just in terms of human subjectivity and the way it narrates identities such as the identities of spaces, then we no longer have to look at place as fixed by subjectivity. Place is the effect of similitude, a non-representation that is mobilized through the placing of things in complex relation to one another and the agency-power effects that are performed by those arrangements. Places circulate through material placings, through the folding together of spaces and things and the relations of difference established by those folds. They are brought into being through the significations that emanate from those material arrangements and foldings.[7]

My northern Cypriot material calls on me to develop a theoretical approach that builds on, while differing from, these frameworks. Anthropological studies that have emphasized cultural difference and delineated the force of cultural context on interpretations of landscape (through humanist or post-humanist frameworks) have often shied away from studying what we could call political process. In the northern Cypriot case I have begun to account for, place is a product of political work upon the land. The administrators from the Maps Department, who form the centerpiece of the project to change place names in northern Cyprus in the aftermath of war and partition, openly declared their work as "political." The remapping of place names was received as a political act, and was therefore assumed or critiqued by both Turkish and Greek-Cypriots as well as by immigrants from Turkey. In this chapter, I therefore analyze the political work (as hands-on practice) that goes into the making (or recrafting) of a territory.

In their studies of the political, theorists of sovereignty such as Giorgio Agamben, have granted agency only or mainly to the "will of the sovereign." Following Carl Schmitt's notion of the political as the right of the ruler of a polity to decide on a "state of exception," Agamben's famous theory of sovereignty, in my interpretation, reinserts a humanist trajectory into the study of politics in associating agency singularly with human beings (in this case, the one with ultimate power).[8]

In turn, and building on my ethnographic material, I would suggest a theory of politics that would allow for distributed agency between human beings and materialities in a broader terrain.[9] Here, my approach builds on that of Actor-Network theorists, such as Kevin Hetherington, who would study the mutual entanglement of human and non-human agencies. Yet I would differ from ANT frameworks that would assign synchronicity— what I would interpret as a nonpolitical symmetry—to the networks of people and things they study. In the transformed territory I have studied in northern Cyprus, human and non-human assemblages are political workings in progress. Another way to put this is to suggest that sovereignty is worked on through a network of people engaged with, and engaged on, through materialities (e.g., tools of cartographic measurement, instruments for aerial military photography, calculation devices for geographical maps, documents of title deed, the office building of a Maps Department, methodologies for assigning value to distinct properties). This practiced network between humans and instruments, then, is what makes sovereignty. Or, sovereignty is only actually realized through an enactment of agency (back and forth) between people and things in and on a given territory. Further than ascribing political agency to the singular authoritarian will of a ruler, then—which in the case we are studying would be the Turkish state and army—in this closer ethnographic reading, sovereignty appears as a field that is worked on through an agency distributed between human beings and material devices. More significantly, my material, emerging until now through the account of the geographical administrator Kemal Bey under the TRNC, suggests that sovereignty is a field of practice (not a momentary declaration of a state of emergency). Sovereignty is worked on in a given territory through time and is a long-term process of negotiation, contestation, and mediation between various actors within a terrain of materialities and physical properties. This is therefore an ethnographic and grounded (rather than top-down) account of sovereignty.

Cataloguing New Place Names

Let us return to "The Catalogue of Geographical Names in the T.R.N.C. Volume—III." The catalogue was the product, in published and tangible form, of the very cartographic practices that Kemal Bey described to me. Halil Giray, the head of the Maps Department where Kemal Bey worked, wrote a preface to the catalogue (quoted in the introduction) rationalizing the procedure of Turkey-fying place names in northern Cyprus as part of the act of assuming political sovereignty in a given territory.[10] Giray argued that this is what all sovereign states do when they acquire new land, referring especially to the colonial practices of the British in Cyprus. He thus made the political intentions of mapping practices transparent in the preface to the very document that testifies to it.

In this instance, this specific human relationality with the physical environment has to be analyzed as a political practice. The territory of northern Cyprus is a product of such political work. The catalogue itself makes the practices that went into its making quite transparent. The old names for places have not been simply glossed over in the hope that they would be lost to oblivion. Rather, it explicitly refers to the old place names, reminding its users of their orientation across the northern part of the island. Old names for places in Greek, Latin, and the Turkish-Cypriot dialect of Turkish are registered against newly allocated Turkish names.

This is the product of a political practice: sovereignty in its making. This sovereignty is not a singularly human and top-down act of political will or event (as in the Agambenian version). It is, rather, a worked-on terrain of relationality between human actors, material land and property, and tools or devices of measurement, numeration, and allocation. This is a description of a practice of settlement and appropriation, a claiming of territory, land, and property for one (Turkish) community against another (Greek), a description of an emergent state practice in the process of its making. Sovereignty could not be enacted other than through a working relation between human actors and material properties and devices, including the catalogue, which is a political object in its own right. Likewise, the network of practices between people and materialities, in this instance, is the work of sovereignty in itself.

A Militarized Terrain

The territory of northern Cyprus, comprising mountains, plateaus, hills, and valleys, has been decorated with inscriptions and symbols signifying Turkey's military sovereignty and its claims over northern Cyprus. Writings have been materially placed by soldiers on slopes overlooking roads or passageways, using whitewashed stones that read, for example, "Motherland First" (referring to Turkey), "Loyalty to the Army Is Our Honor" (referring to the Turkish army), "How Happy Is the One Who Calls Him-self a Turk," or "Shoot, Kill, and Take Pride." On the Beşparmak (Penta-daktilos) mountains facing the Greek side (and visible from the streets of both sides of Lefkoşa/Lefkosia and the village roads leading into it), a TRNC flag has been painted by soldiers in red and white, the symbolic colors of Turkish national identity (see figure 1). This gigantic flag shape painted on the mountain is lit up at night, making an uncanny sight of a flickering flag in the midst of a dark landscape. On a hill overlooking a common road in the area of Kormacit (Kormakitis), a portrait of Mustafa Kemal Atatürk, Turkey's founding and national leader, has been painted by soldiers alongside flags of Turkey and the TRNC. Likewise, on the Girne (Kyrenia) range of the Beşparmak (Pentadaktilos) mountains over-looking the road to Güzelyurt (Omorfo, Morphou), a metallic profile of Atatürk symbolically climbing up to Samsun to start the "Turkish War of Liberation" (referring to 1919) has been erected. A similar object has been planted on a hill overlooking the turn around the mountain from Girne (Kyrenia) to Lefkoşa (Nicosia). A lot of practical work and effort has been geared to Turkey-fying the geography and the material and physical sur-roundings in northern Cyprus. The star and crescent, symbolizing Turk-ish national identity, have been drawn or painted on slopes overlooking plains and fields in numerous locations, turning the colors red and white into a material component of the natural environment. Forestation areas have been named after Atatürk, with inscriptions over the land reading "Atatürk Forest" even before the new trees have fully grown. These mate-rial as well as symbolic inscriptions are noticeable to Turkish-Cypriots who live in northern Cyprus, and glaringly so to those who return after a long stay abroad, as marks that have transformed the appearance of physical properties and the environment in northern Cyprus.

This symbolic and material Turkey-fication of place and territory is evident and visible in every town and village in northern Cyprus, as well. At the center of all administrative districts and units, often near the old Greek-Cypriot church and the local marketplace or circle of shops and the school, a standard bust of Atatürk can be found beside two flagpoles, one for the Turkish flag and the other for that of the TRNC. The busts of Atatürk, and the material podium around them, are often better main-tained than the village dwellings that surround them. In some towns and villages, the army has sponsored the building of new mosques with tall minarets.[11]

1. Flag of the Turkish Republic of Northern Cyprus on the Beşparmak
(Pentadaktilos) Mountains, with ruins of Greek-Cypriots' homes nearby.

Turkish-Cypriot civilians often mention that 95 percent of the territory
of the TRNC is owned by and under the command of the Turkish military.
Space is filled with military sites: barracks, no-access zones, and training
areas. Entrance to such places is "strictly forbidden," as announced by
military signs posted along barbed wire. For Turkish-Cypriots, terminol-
ogy such as "first degree military area (*birinci derecede askeri bölge*)" is
commonly understood. Residential areas are often surrounded by army
zones. According to official statistics, there are 40,000 Turkish soldiers in
northern Cyprus. If we include the soldiers' families, the number rises to
70,000.

In the center of Lefke (Lefka), facing residential homes, is a shooting
field, an open-air space for military practice. Again, right beside domestic
dwellings is a cemetery for soldiers who fell during the war, along with a
monument in their honor. Numerous villages and properties owned by
Greek-Cypriots, including the town of Varosha (Maraş), have been appropriated by the army. Entire villages, evacuated by their previous owners in
the aftermath of war, have been blocked off with barbed wire and turned

into barracks. Dwellings in such villages have been transformed into military accommodation sites. Particular natural features of the land, forests, and slopes have been built on or destroyed to make space for military practice zones.

Turkish-Cypriots are fully aware of the militarization of their surroundings and frequently comment on it, even if such practices by now have been normalized. An elderly man said, "The ill luck of Cyprus is its strategic position. For centuries, political powers have battled for control over Cyprus." He was lamenting the transformation of his physical surroundings for political interests.

The Tangibility of Sovereignty

Several scholars have studied how sovereignty is practiced through a reworking of materialities in the space of a territory. Significantly, Paul Hirst has written: "Spaces interact with and are constructed by forms of political power, armed conflict and social control. Space is a resource for power, and the spaces of power are complex and qualitatively distinctive."[12] Scholars working on Israel/Palestine have led the study of the material practices (architectural, archaeological, cartographic) that make up territorial sovereignty. Eyal Weizman has studied Israeli settlements as "politics in matter,"[13] as architecture that tangibly and concretely sustains an occupation. Likewise, Rafi Segal and others have studied the role of construction technologies in the shaping of the Israeli state.[14] Meron Benvenisti's *Sacred Landscape* (2000) gives a full ethnographic account of the cartographic methods used to change the old Arabic Palestinian names for places in Palestine as it was turned into Israel. And Nadia Abou El-Haj's *Facts on the Ground* (2001) is an account of the embroilment of Israeli archaeological and geographical techniques in the project of state building. All of these works refer to cartographic surveying and name-changing methodologies as a central component of territorial sovereignty. Benvenisti and Abou El-Haj trace the project of changing place names in Palestine/Israel back to the British Mandate and colonial techniques in cartography. The historical link and analogy with Cyprus, which was contemporaneously under British sovereignty, is quite clear. In fact, Lord Kitchener was the first full-scale cartographer of Palestine, as he was of Cyprus, appointed for both projects by the British colonial government.[15]

The specific project of changing place names and the material reinscription of a territory along nationally redefined lines has a colonial past with a comparative outlook (the references and analogies with Palestine are striking), as well as a postcolonial trajectory. The experts in the Maps Department of the TRNC learned their trade by reference to a number of state practices and traditions. Halil Giray makes direct references to the British in Cyprus and their surveying methodologies as a precedent for the TRNC's practices over the territory of northern Cyprus. Kemal Bey, working under Giray, also acknowledged the direct influence of Turkey through its military presence in northern Cyprus and its new cartographic systems and techniques.

By engaging my material from northern Cyprus with studies of the materiality of sovereignty in Israel, I aim to address a gap in the anthropological literature on place and space, which has emphasized the cultural and the symbolic, bracketing away the material and the political. Here, I study the tangible reworking of a territory with political intention through the application of geographical expertise and technologies over land.

Contested Sovereignty

But how, we must ask, was this political transformation of the land received by the Turkish-Cypriots who were to inhabit it? Were the new place names assigned by the civil servants from the Maps Department assimilated for use in everyday life? Were the old names for places forgotten or buried away?

As I found out, the distinction between the old and new names for places was a line the Turkish-Cypriots used in defining the political. Knowledge of the old names for places was considered "local knowledge," and Turkish-Cypriots differentiated themselves from settlers from Turkey on the grounds of that knowledge. The old names for villages aroused a sense of intimacy and familiarity, while the new names were associated with procedure, officialdom, and administration.[16] Villagers of the official "Serdarlı" referred to one another as fellows or kin on the basis of belonging to "Çatoz," the village's old name. All Turkish-Cypriots referred to the traditional "Bellapais" (or "Balabayıs," in the local Turkish-Cypriot dialect) and found the new name, "Beylerbeyi," completely inappropriate for the village overlooking Girne (Kyrenia), famous for its beauty.

I also found some confusion in the association between old places and new names, where Turkish-Cypriots (especially the elderly) expressed a sense of disorientation in northern Cyprus. One Turkish-Cypriot woman described to me how she had called directory services to find the phone number of a friend who lived, as she thought, in the village of Ayyorgi. The person on the other end of the line told her, in a Turkish (of Turkey) accent, "There is no such place as Ayyorgi." The Turkish-Cypriot woman expressed bewilderment: "Ayyorgi doesn't exist? What happened to it?" She remembered later that Ayyorgi had been renamed Karaoğlanoğlu, after a Turkish general who was instrumental in conquering it in 1974. The story of her confusion with place names was recounted among her friends and relatives with humor.

Similarly, an old man running a *taverna* with his children in the town of Girne (Kyrenia) was confused when he was asked for directions to the village of Vasilya. His son informed him that the village had been re-named Karşıyaka to honor a general who was from a district of that name in Izmir, Turkey. "Do you mean it says 'Karşıyaka' on road signs leading to Vasilya?," asked the old man with astonishment.

In the coffeehouse of Gönendere, elderly men described how new place names were invented for their village. This village had not changed hands from Greek to Turkish-Cypriots; it had always been inhabited by Turkish-Cypriots, even before 1974. "Our village used to be called Konetra," said an old man, "before it was re-named Gönendere. . . . They didn't find the sound of "Konetra" Turkish enough, so they changed it." He added: "We never got used to these new names."

Another old man said that even the names of village fields had been changed. The owner of the coffeehouse explained that, among villagers, each village field is referred to by a given name: "Different parts of the plateaus surrounding the village are known as distinct areas among the folk, and each of these areas used to have a different name. For example, this field across from us is called Broz; after that is the field of Akuntu; then come others all the way to the field of Maludya." The old man showed me the way to the village fields with a motion of his hand. "They came and changed the names of each of these fields one by one. Can you imagine?," he said. "But the new names do not stick in our minds." Another old man intervened to say, "We inherited those old names for fields from our ancestors; our grandfathers taught them to us. Others are left from the time of the Ottomans or the time of the British." One of the old men in the coffeehouse said, "This name-changing business didn't start in 1974. It goes back to the 1955–58 period, when the troubles [with the Greek-Cypriots] began. A general from Turkey arrived at the time to begin to change the names of places."

I encountered, then, a certain disaffection among the Turkish-Cypriots vis-à-vis the new names for places, even among those who considered themselves politically close to the ideology of the TRNC regime. The new names were not easily assumed; they were mainly used for official, procedural, bureaucratic, or administrative purposes. As thorough as the experts from the Maps Department had attempted to be in their assigning and application of new place names for the territory of northern Cyprus, this declaration of sovereignty was not unproblematically accepted by the people for whom it was intended. The Turkish-Cypriots critiqued, contested, and subverted the renaming of their geography through the practices of the TRNC administration under the guidance of the Turkish army. This must therefore be studied as a problematic and partial, rather than thorough and complete, sovereignty.

2. Repopulating a Territory

IN MUCH WRITING on "the Cyprus question," the problem has been construed as a conflict between two ethnic groups, labeled "Turks" and "Greeks."[1] The concept and framing of ethnic conflict has been all too central and determinative in scholarship on Cyprus.[2] Here I wish to do something different. Rather than researching conflict in the conventionally studied fault line between Turks and Greeks or between Turkish-Cypriot and Greek-Cypriot national discourses and ideologies, I will study conflicts internal to northern Cyprus, the territory marked apart and repopulated after Turkey's military invasion in 1974 and predominantly reserved for the habitation of people categorized as "Turks." This chapter focuses on the social and political configurations and dynamics that developed in northern Cyprus in the aftermath of repopulation. I focus specifically on conflict between people officially registered as "Turks" in the census books of the TRNC: Turkish-Cypriots who are autochthonous to the island, on the one hand, and immigrants from Turkey who were invited to settle in northern Cyprus by the TRNC regime in the aftermath of 1974, on the other. I study repopulation practices as a significant aspect of the material transformation of northern Cyprus, a distinctive dimension of the remaking and reconfiguration of a territory.

In Turkish nationalist discourses (or officially produced ideology), Turkish-Cypriots and citizens of Turkey are represented as sharing a nationality and an ethnicity. In public discourses in Turkey, Turkish-Cypriots have been referred to as "our kinsmen (soydaşlarımız)," a term that signifies common blood and lineage. Turkey has presented its military intervention in northern Cyprus as an act undertaken to rescue its kinsmen, the Turks of Cyprus, from the threat of being exterminated by the Greeks. Members of this community have been named "Kıbrıs Türkü" or "Kıbrıs Türkleri" (Turks of Cyprus, Cyprus Turks, Cypriot Turks) in official Turkish discourses, all phrases that emphasize Turkishness. In this book, I employ the term "Turkish-Cypriot" to refer to indigenous Cypriots of Turkish contemporary identity. The identities of Cypriots have changed and switched historically in complicated ways, and "Turkish-Cypriot (Kıbrıslı Türk, Kıbrıslıtürk)" is a relatively new and contingent term for the designation of identity.[3] This term is commonly used by autochthonous Turkish-Cypriots at present for self-identification. The term "Cypriot (Kıbrıslı)," without the ethnic or national label or reference point, is used even more widely.[4] Identity constructs are used situationally. In the contemporary period, "Cypriots" signifies distinction from "people of Turkey (Türkiyeliler)," as settlers in northern Cyprus are called by Turkish-Cypriots. Here I intend to display the tentativeness, historicity, complexity, and social construction of identities in Cyprus. Therefore, all of my references to identity are contingent and situated.

In official Turkish discourses, Turkish-Cypriots are considered an extension of the people of Turkey, left outside the Republic of Turkey after the consolidation of national borders at the collapse of the Ottoman Empire. In Turkish nationalist discourse, Turkish-Cypriots and citizens of Turkey are all "Turks" or "Turkish," seen as part of the same national or ethnic group, and Turkish-Cypriot culture is constructed as a continuation of Anatolia (Anadolu), which is taken to represent the heart or cradle of Turkish culture.[5] The long-term political leader of the Turkish-Cypriot community, Rauf Denktaş, used to describe himself as "a Turk coincidentally born on Cyprus (hasbelkader Kıbrıs'ta doğmuş bir Türk)," emphasizing and highlighting his Turkishness and rendering his Cypriotness epiphenomenal or accidental. Denktaş has said:

> I am a child of Anatolia. I am Turkish in every way, and my roots go back to Central Asia. I am Turkish with my culture, my language, my history, and my whole being. I have a state as well as a motherland. The notions of Cypriot culture, Turkish-Cypriot, Greek-Cypriot, [and] a shared Republic are all nonsense. If they [the Greeks of Cyprus] have their Greece and we have our Turkey, why should we live under the roof of the same Republic? . . . Some individuals are producing fiction about the existence of Cypriots, Turkish-Cypriots, Greek-Cypriots. There is no such thing as a Turkish-Cypriot. Don't dare to ask us whether we are Cypriots. We could take this as an insult. Why? Because there is only one thing that is Cypriot in Cyprus, and that is the Cypriot donkey.[6]

Denktaş spoke these words in public in 1995, reflecting on Turkish-Cypriot folk-dancing performances that emphasized figures shared with Greek-

Cypriots. Many Turkish-Cypriots said they were angry, insulted, and humiliated by his words, and his donkey metaphor is remembered and widely criticized in popular accounts of this public declaration. On another occasion, Denktaş said: "There isn't a nationality called the TRNC. We are Turks of the TRNC. We are proud of being Turks. The motherland [Turkey] is also our motherland, our nation. We are part of that [Turkish] nation that has formed a state in Cyprus."[7] As long as he represented the political regime in northern Cyprus, Denktaş's words about his identity constituted the official policy of the TRNC. Under this guise, administrative sources were channeled toward eliminating Cypriot and bringing out Turkish cultural elements in northern Cyprus. And claiming national and ethnic affinity with Turkey (as Turks tout court) served the Denktaş regime's desire to go further than partition (*taksim*) and integrate with Turkey.

In publications of the administration in northern Cyprus, the geographical position of the island of Cyprus, about forty miles from Turkey's southern shores (in contrast to four hundred miles away from Greece), is interpreted as proof of the connection of Cyprus to Turkey. Official publications of the TRNC, such as history books for children in northern Cyprus, claim that Cyprus was once geographically attached to Anatolia, but geological transformations caused it to break away to become an island.

Turkish-Cypriots and People from Turkey

In northern Cyprus in the period that I conducted this research, one of the subjects that most preoccupied Turkish-Cypriots was their experience of living side by side with immigrants from Turkey who had settled in northern Cyprus through the population policies of the TRNC regime. Paramount were expressions of feelings of having been disturbed by settlers from Anatolia.[8]

Before checkpoints at the borders were opened in April 2003, conflict with Greek-Cypriots did not preoccupy or worry Turkish-Cypriots as much as their everyday experience of living with immigrants from Turkey, who had been granted housing (Greek-Cypriot property), jobs, and citizenship privileges by the regime in return for settling in northern Cyprus. Unless older members of indigenous families were specifically asked to recount their memories of the intercommunal conflicts and the war in Cyprus, everyday conversation before the opening of checkpoints did not consist of references to "Greek-Cypriots" as much as it was filled with critical references to "people from Turkey." Turkish-Cypriots use the term "people of Turkey (*Türkiyeliler*)" to refer to settlers from Turkey, or citizens of Turkey in general, differentiating themselves as "Cypriots (*Kıbrıslılar*)."[9] Turkish-Cypriots on the left of the political spectrum who were critical of Turkey's ongoing military and political presence in Cyprus were not the only ones, during my research, to express discomfort with the presence of settlers from Turkey. Turkish-Cypriots of all political convictions expressed similar sentiments.

When speaking about the settlers, Turkish-Cypriots made references to space. They associated the arrival of the settlers, and their continuing presence, with the radical spatial and material transformation of the places most familiar to them. In reference to Girne (Kyrenia), for example, Hatice Hanım, a fifty-year-old Turkish-Cypriot woman, said, "It's not Cyprus; it doesn't feel like Cyprus anymore—neither the look of it, with the presence of people from Turkey, nor the feel of it is Cyprus." Many Turkish-Cypriots who had moved house said that they had done so as a consequence of the settlement of people from Turkey in the walled-city (*surlar içi*) neighborhoods of the major towns of northern Cyprus. Hasan Bey, a sixty-year-old locksmith who supported one of the right-wing Turkish nationalist parties (the UBP) at the time of my fieldwork, said, "They threw us out of here," referring to people from Turkey who lived within the city walls of the northern part of Lefkoşa. Hasan Bey had been born and brought up in Lefkoşa, but a few years earlier he had moved his family out of the inner city to the outskirts. "We are afraid," he said. "If you try and walk around here at night these days, you are sure to get mugged or knifed." He said he was afraid of what he experienced as the rough and violent ways of some of the settlers. He recounted that when he asked a man from Turkey not to park his car in a spot that would block the window of his locksmith shop, the settler brusquely turned around, as if getting ready to hit him, and said, "Do you know who governs this place?" The settler was symbolically associating himself with Turkey's military regime in the TRNC. The paradox was that Hasan Bey, too, was a supporter of Turkish authority in northern Cyprus and in favor of Turkey's ongoing political, economic, and military presence there. He had been a member of the TMT, the Turkish resistance organization that had fought EOKA during the intercommunal conflicts between 1963 and 1974. For the settler who argued with Hasan Bey, however, there was a difference between them to be pronounced; he expressed a consciousness of having (or wanting to have) more political power than the native Hasan Bey, and even power over him because of his origins in Turkey and in association with Turkey's sovereignty over northern Cyprus. The settler identified with the Republic of Turkey as a subject. He wore his identification with the Turkish state as a garment in his interactions with Turkish-Cypriots to claim power in his everyday relations with them. That is why what Hasan Bey, a supporter of the right-wing UBP who told me this story, is significant. In private, Turkish-Cypriots of all political affiliations expressed discontent with the presence of people from Turkey in Cyprus.

Turkish-Cypriots often conflated or confused the settlers with soldiers from Turkey, failing to differentiate between these social groups. In relation to soldiers from Turkey, Yılmaz, a Turkish-Cypriot and an enthusiastic reader of the opposition newspaper *Avrupa* (later *Afrika*), said, "We are terrified." His wife, Emel, added, "I am afraid especially of the soldiers. I warn my children not to open the door to soldiers when they're alone at home." There are so many soldiers from Turkey in northern Cyprus, Turkish-Cypriots would often tell me, that the economy addresses their needs. The marketplace (*arasta*) in northern Lefkoşa had been transformed, at the time of my fieldwork, into a shopping place for off-duty soldiers.[10] "This place is finished," said the owner of a shoe shop. He recounted how the inner city of Lefkoşa had been taken over by shops that operate phone booths for soldiers calling home, as well as soldiers' coffee shops, tea houses, casinos, and brothels.[11]

Rasime Hanım, a sixty-year-old Cypriot shop owner who sold second-hand bags, books, and odds and ends in the Lefkoşa marketplace, recounted, "One day, a Turkish soldier came and asked me why we don't like them."[12] She continued, "I replied [by] telling him that I had fed the Turkish soldiers for years during the war." Turkish-Cypriots remember being relieved and joyful in 1974 when Turkish soldiers landed in Cyprus with planes and parachutes, because they thought they would be saved from attacks by Greek-Cypriot nationalists. However, their relations with the soldiers turned out to be longer lasting and more complicated than they had anticipated. Although Turkish-Cypriots did not necessarily express fear, they indicated a degree of unease about the Turkish soldiers. Tamer, an eight-year-old boy, wanted to draw my attention to "what the Turkish soldier does" and said, "One day, two Turkish soldiers were passing by our garden. They stopped under our orange trees and started to fill their bags with oranges. My father came and asked them why they were picking the fruit without permission. And the soldier said: 'Who saved you [*Seni kim kurtardı*]?" The little boy was aware of Turkish soldiers' discourse about the presence of the Turkish army in Cyprus. Accordingly, soldiers had arrived in Cyprus in 1974 to rescue their kinsmen from being exterminated by the Greek-Cypriots. Yet Tamer was also conscious of the irony of this soldier's brusquely claiming entitlement to his family's orange grove. Tamer's mother, Emel, said that after the incident in the orange grove, she had warned her husband against arguing with people from Turkey, whether they were soldiers or settlers. "If you argue with them, they can bring you trouble," she said. "You can't know what they are capable of doing." There is a representational gloss here, again, between the settlers and the soldiers from Turkey. Yılmaz, Tamer's father, stated that he was careful with people from Turkey in general. He said he did not defend himself when harassed. "This place belongs to the soldiers and to people from Turkey," he said. "Everything else exists only by chance. There is an extraordinary situation here, a state of emergency. If you were to worry every day about what happens here, you would lose the endurance to live here. If you live here, you have no choice but to accept the situation as it is. We, for example, have submitted ourselves. We have let ourselves be abased [under the presence of settlers and soldiers]. Otherwise they would not let us survive." This was a description of a survival strategy with a consciousness of relations of power under what, at the time, were military laws, an enforced and unwillingly assumed condition of submission. Yılmaz bowed to the authorities, he explained, because he knew that he was the subject of a repressive political regime. He sensed the repression in the no-access zones that surrounded his everyday itinerary, in his relatives' and colleagues' cautious demeanor around him when he dared to be critical of the Denktaş administration, in the convoys of military trucks passing by. But he had nowhere else to go. He had to live in northern Cyprus, so he felt he had to acquiesce to a degree.

Turkish-Cypriots specifically complained about the settlers. Pembe Hanım, an elderly woman, said. "The infidels were infidels [*gâvur*, referring to Greek-Cypriots in common language], but things were never as bad living with them as neighbors as they are now living with the *fellahs* [a term used by Turkish-Cypriots to refer to people from Turkey]. When we had financial difficulties, the infidel used to lend us money. If we were sick, he would help; he would call a doctor. Now, the fellahs would not give you anything. On the contrary, they take, they steal from you."[13] Pembe Hanım's pitting of "Greeks" against "Turks" in her comparison was retrospective and contingent. She reflected on her past experience of neighboring Greek-Cypriots compared with her present experience of living beside people from Turkey. She distinguished herself markedly from both Greek-Cypriots and people from Turkey, using "othering" terms (*gâvur* and *fellah*, respectively) to refer to each. However, she said that despite the difference in religion (note her use of the term "infidel"), life was better living side by side with Greek-Cypriots than it was living with people from Turkey who are co-religionists. Of course, some of this talk was rhetorical in that Pembe Hanım was trying to emphasize her discomfort in living alongside the settlers by portraying her past experiences of coexistence with Greek-Cypriots lightly.

Settler communities from Turkey are heterogeneous. Most settlers are in Cyprus because they experienced difficulties—some social, some economic, some political—back in Turkey. When they received promises of jobs, land, and free housing in northern Cyprus after 1974 under the TRNC's population policies, they arrived with hopes of better prospects. Although they were all categorized as "Turks" by policymakers, settlers have diverse backgrounds—Laz (from Turkey's Black Sea region), Kurdish, Arab, Alevi, and Turkish. However, many settlers identify as Turkish (at least officially) and speak in favor of Turkey's military presence in Cyprus because it is as a consequence of being categorized as Turks that they obtained benefits in the TRNC. Generally, until the late 1990s, settlers from Turkey (including Kurds, Alevis, and members of other communities who would have identified as left-wing in Turkey) cast their votes for the right-wing Turkish nationalist parties in northern Cyprus (the DP or the UBP). The DP and the UBP were known to distribute citizenship, as well as other favors and benefits, to settlers from Turkey in return for votes. Settlers therefore perceived these parties as serving their interests. In addition to the official settlers who were brought into Cyprus through the population policies of Turkey and the northern Cypriot administration in the aftermath of 1974 and granted property and citizenship rights, many other categories of immigrants from Turkey exist in northern Cyprus. Some arrived for temporary work; others work "under the table" and are considered illegal immigrants by the TRNC regime. However, in Turkish-Cypriot representations, all immigrants from Turkey are lumped together, as if there is no internal social or cultural differentiation among people arriving in northern Cyprus from Turkey.[14]

Turkish-Cypriots express and analyze their distinction from settlers using terms that signify cultural difference and social class.[15] The demarcations of distinction refer particularly to lifestyle. Turkish-Cypriots tell Cypriots (*Kıbrıslılar*) apart from people of Turkey (*Türkiyeliler*) on the basis of certain symbolic markers they have come to associate with the culture of Turkey. Veiling or the multiple styles of wearing a headscarf out of habit or faith (unless done in the traditional Cypriot village style, with the corners of the scarf tied on top of one's head), for example, is commonly associated with the culture of Turkey. "Cypriot women generally do not tie their heads," said a young Turkish-Cypriot woman, using a common idiom in Turkish for veiling.[16]

"You can tell someone from Turkey through the way she keeps her house," said a Turkish-Cypriot woman, articulating a commonly made distinction. "For example, a Cypriot would never put a fake or plastic carpet on the floor. Anyway, in summer we don't have a habit of using carpets." Turkish-Cypriots also told people from Turkey apart by observing their gardens. İbrahim Bey, an eighty-year-old gardener who had lived in Lefkoşa for the later part of his life, was annoyed by the way he thought the settlers treated trees. "They do not know about trees," he said. "We were born in the midst of trees; we grew up with trees. Where people from Turkey come from, there are mountains, there are forests. . . . They know how to hoe, but they cannot tell a flower and a weed apart." İbrahim Bey frequently told stories about settlers' leaving trees to dry or burning flowers and bushes to create fields, wanting to imply that the settlers lacked certain local knowledge.

The power relationship between Turkish-Cypriots and people from Turkey is a complex one that cannot be explained solely by recourse to social-class analysis. It ought not be confused, for example, with the relationship between Germans and worker immigrants from Turkey or that between Istanbul's upper middle classes and immigrants to the city from rural parts of Anatolia. The relationship between people from Turkey and Turkish-Cypriots, rather, has to be evaluated in the context of Turkey's sovereignty in northern Cyprus. Turkish-Cypriots' attitudes toward the settlers cannot be analyzed in a vacuum, by applying universalist frameworks for the study of class or migration. They must be analyzed within the particularities of the political situation in northern Cyprus and the related sociopolitical spectrum. In most domains of social, economic, and political life in northern Cyprus, Turkish-Cypriots maintain a standing, holding, for example, privileged access to jobs as civil servants in most departments of the administration. With their social ties and kinship networks (*torpil*), Turkish-Cypriots are able to manipulate the administration to serve their needs or those of their families. However, although Turkish-Cypriots are able to play the card of sociocultural capital against the settlers, some settler individuals or communities attempt to assume affinity with (or patronage from) the Turkish state and army in Cyprus to claim another kind of power over the Turkish-Cypriots.[17] At the time of my fieldwork, Turkish-Cypriots expressed qualms about political subordination under Turkey's sovereignty by projecting symbolically charged commentaries onto the settlers from Turkey. At the same time, they assumed power over the settlers through their positions in the civil service or as their employers in numerous sectors of the economy (especially on construction sites). Turkish-Cypriots employed their status, lifestyles, income levels, and claims to autochthony in their differentiation tactics vis-à-vis the settlers. In turn, some settlers (those who could) attempted to overcome their sociocultural marginalization in Cyprus by declaring their alliance with Turkey as its citizens, assuming a Turkish nationalist discourse, or voting for the right-wing parties of the TRNC regime.

Since 1974, Turkey has followed a policy of increasing the "Turkish" population of Cyprus vis-à-vis the "Greeks." Extensive institutional efforts have also been made to assimilate Turkish-Cypriots into what is called the "Turkish culture" of Anatolia, policies implemented through schools, the media, the army, and other bodies. One dimension of the context for Turkish-Cypriots' othering of the settlers is the minute and enforced Turkey-fication policies of the Denktaş administration.[18] Turkish-Cypriots expressed a poignant sense of being culturally overtaken, annulled, or assumed through the feeling of being outnumbered by the settlers from Turkey. Indeed, numerous Turkish-Cypriots have migrated out of northern Cyprus over the years, creating sizeable communities in Turkey, Britain, and Australia. This out-migration of the Cypriots was lamented by those who remained behind in the context of the increasing population of immigrants from Turkey in northern Cyprus.[19] In response to inquiries about the migration of Turkish-Cypriots out of northern Cyprus, Turkish-

Cypriots frequently quoted Denktaş disapprovingly for having said, "One Turk leaves, and another one arrives." This was interpreted as indifference to the out-migration of Turkish-Cypriots, as though they, like the settlers, were simple strategic indices in a politics of population in relation to the Greek-Cypriots on the island. The Turkish-Cypriots expressed feelings, at the time, that Denktaş's TRNC administration favored the settlers as loyal subjects of the regime over them, the indigenous inhabitants of the island. Articulating a sense of being physically and culturally annihilated through the population policies of the administration, Emin, a thirty-year-old Turkish-Cypriot whose close friends had left Cyprus for Britain and Canada, said, "We are 'the Last of the Mohicans.' They turned us into Indians. They got rid of a whole culture. At least there are people who still remember the Indians. But who will remember us?" It was very common, at the time of my fieldwork, for Turkish-Cypriots to express qualms about what they perceived as their "extinction" (*yokoluş*) as a community vis-à-vis the increasing and vast number of settlers from Turkey in northern Cyprus. "*Yok oluyoruk* (we are disappearing)" was an ordinary way of putting words into this feeling.

Other Differences, Other Conflicts

In the discourses of international organizations, as well as in much academic scholarship, the conflict in Cyprus has two sides: the "Turkish" side and the "Greek" side. Official discourses in Turkey, Greece, the Republic of Cyprus, and the TRNC would have it as so, as well. The language of ethnic conflict is still central to politics in Cyprus. But since partition and the implementation of specific administrative policies in the north (as well as in the south), social and political dynamics in Cyprus have changed in fundamental ways. Through the population policies of the TRNC, Turkish-Cypriots and immigrants from Turkey have created contingent, complex, and specific relations of power with one another. If Turkish-Cypriots take higher ground vis-à-vis the settlers in claiming local knowledge and socio-cultural capital (as well as through their positions in the civil service and as employers in the private sector), distinct settler communities have, in turn, tried to mobilize Turkey as their patron state against marginalization by the Turkish-Cypriots. Although they are classified as "kinsmen (*soydaş*)" or as members of the same ethnic, national, or even cultural group, in the prevalent political discourses, Turkish-Cypriots and settlers from Turkey construe difference vis-à-vis each other. Although international discourses construe a Turkish side to what is conventionally called ethnic conflict in Cyprus, such an essential side does not exist. Those who have been discursively classified as members of the same ethnic or national group (i.e., Turkish) do not perceive or experience themselves as such in the specific relations of power they have developed among themselves under the existing regime in northern Cyprus. They have their own theory of difference.

3. The Affects of Spatial Confinement

"KLERIDES [THE GREEK-CYPRIOT LEADER] can see our flag from his window," said Cevat Bey, a man closely aligned with the TRNC administration and active in several of its propaganda bodies. When I met with him, he and his associates had founded what they called the Organization to Light up the Flag on the Beşparmak (Pentadaktilos) Mountains, aiming to raise a fund of up to 1 million British pounds to project light onto the flag so it would be visible even at night. "First the star and crescent in the middle will light up in red, to symbolize the flag of Turkey," said Cevat Bey, who owns a small shop in the Lefkoşa marketplace. "Then, after five seconds, suddenly the two stripes at the top and the bottom will light up, to symbolize the flag of the TRNC. . . . This flag is the symbol of our sovereignty. It is visible even from Larnaca, the very south of the island, the Greek side." He continued: "Even if we go totally bankrupt and hit rock bottom, we are sovereign here. Nobody can touch our sovereignty. We have power. The Greek-Cypriots have understood this!"

Northern Cyprus had gone bankrupt in the period when I was interviewing Cevat Bey, hit with repercussions from Turkey's vast economic crisis. The offshore banks that kept the accounts of Turkish-Cypriots had collapsed in the year 2000, swallowing their customers' savings. There was significant unemployment and deep-running discontent. It was in this climate that Cevat Bey made his remarks about Turkey's enduring sovereignty in northern Cyprus. The more the TRNC regime was losing its legitimacy among its subjects, the more its defenders were resorting to ideology and political symbolism.

But such flamboyant expressions of sovereignty were rarely made by Turkish-Cypriots in this period. On the contrary, many at the time were quite openly critical of their regime and its ideological excesses. A major grassroots movement under the name Bu Memleket Bizim Platformu

2. Celebrations on 20 July, with military ceremony by Girne (Kyrenia)
gate in northern Lefkoşa.

(This Country Is Ours Platform) had sprung up in the aftermath of the
collapse of local banks, criticizing both the TRNC administration and
Turkey's presence in northern Cyprus. Supporters of the administration
(then under the leadership of Rauf Denktaş) had been marginalized in
popular discourse. Only a minority loyal to the administration would have
been moved at the time by declarations of uncompromising sovereignty
for its own sake. Members of This Country Is Ours were producing tren-
chant critiques of the Denktaş regime, at times describing Turkey's sovereignty over northern Cyprus as an "occupation (işgal)," a view that was
considered blasphemous in the official circles of the TRNC, as well as in
Turkey.[1] Those who participated in the movement did so with trepidation,
as well as courage, knowing that they could face punishment.

The most important national holiday in northern Cyprus, celebrating
the arrival of troops from Turkey in 1974, is called the 20 Temmuz Barış ve
Özgürlük Bayramı (20 July Peace and Freedom Holiday) (see figure 2). On
this and other occasions, Turkish-Cypriots are reminded that the arrival
of the Turkish army and the subsequent partition of Cyprus brought them
"peace and freedom." In the late 1990s and early 2000s, the regime in
northern Cyprus still attempted to maintain its legitimacy on the grounds
of having saved the Turkish-Cypriots from attacks by the Greek-Cypriots

in the decade preceding 1974. But the ideological rhetoric of peace and freedom stood in direct contrast to Turkish-Cypriots' experiences of living in northern Cyprus and their expressions of confinement. Turkish-Cypriots were not deluded by the regime's ideological apparatus. The systematic propaganda defining the northern side of the border as a zone of freedom for them did not have the Orwellian effect of having subjects of the TRNC believe that confinement is freedom or that war is peace.[2] Instead, people sat in their homes and backyards, in spaces of utmost intimacy and familiarity, with television sets tuned to nationalist programs and propaganda but confiding with one another in the most counter-ideological modes. The criticism of ideology was ordinary and widespread. The nationalist rhetoric bombastically spread through schools, the media, the army, and the civil service did not move Turkish-Cypriots to flock to the streets and join in celebrating the numerous national holidays.

The Spirit of Terror

In 2000 and 2001, when there was rampant discontent, as well as public mobilization, against the Denktaş regime, Turkish-Cypriots would say that "the spirit of the TMT [Türk Mukavemet Teşkilatı]" haunted the contemporary in northern Cyprus as the residue of an old political ethos. The TMT, the Turkish resistance organization, was a fighter group founded underground in 1958 by Turkish-Cypriot community leaders in collaboration with Turkey's Special War Unit.[3] It took its inspiration from the Greek-Cypriot Ethniki Organosis Kyprion Agoniston (EOKA), which was fighting the British for independence and for *enosis*. The mimicry and mirroring between these two underground organizations and the administrative practices they engendered is significant. As they generated or escalated the intercommunal conflict between Turkish-Cypriots and Greek-Cypriots, the members of EOKA and the TMT also became representatives of their respective communities in the administrative body of the Republic of Cyprus when it declared independence from Britain in 1960. When members of EOKA attacked Turkish-Cypriot communities in 1963, the whole island was parceled into ethnically segregated enclaves with complicated borders guarded by the United Nations. Turkish-Cypriot administrators defected from the bi-communal Republic of Cyprus and, under the initiative of the TMT, began to form their own, separate administrative system in the enclaves. This was the beginning of a distinct state practice among the Turkish-Cypriots. The structure of the TMT and its political spirit informed the organization of the successive administrative entities under which the Turkish-Cypriots became both civil servants and subjects. A Turkish-Cypriot lawyer explained, "The TMT was protecting the Turkish-Cypriots from attacks by EOKA, and the Turkish-Cypriots had to recognize this force that was protecting them."

The old fighters, including Denktaş, were still leaders and members of the administration at the time of my fieldwork, more than forty years after the formation of the TMT. There was a taboo around discussing the culture of terror inflicted on the Turkish-Cypriots by the TMT. In official representations (in the administration's newspapers and in propaganda speeches delivered in national ceremonies, school textbooks, and television programs), TMT fighters were presented as heroes who had saved Turkish-Cypriots from extermination at the hands of the Greek-Cypriots. Although this interpretation was partially accepted by the Turkish-Cypriots, it was also criticized and complicated by most who were not directly associated with the Denktaş regime, in spaces where people felt that they could speak their minds. In the most intimate encounters, among close friends and family, people would recount stories of Turkish-Cypriots murdered by the TMT or speculate that their officially "martyred" relatives had in fact been assassinated by the TMT and not, as officially claimed, by EOKA or by Greek-Cypriots. Numerous stories circulated in private quarters about TMT atrocities against Turkish-Cypriot individuals. Turkish-Cypriots would provide evidence for, and examples of, how Denktaş and other members of the TMT plotted to sabotage Turkish-Cypriot heritage sites, such as mosques, blaming the Greek-Cypriots for the attacks to create the rationale for a counterattack by Turkey. The assassination of the well-known public intellectual Ayhan Hikmet, who favored the endurance of a bi-communal Republic of Cyprus, was also blamed on the TMT.

Cemil, who was born around the time the TMT was created, said:

> The system that to this day has continued to govern this country is the TMT system. The TMT was founded in 1958 and started to administer the Turkish-Cypriots. Even the postal service was in TMT hands in the period of enclaves between 1963 and '74. Now we have the continuation of that administration, only under a different name, the "Turkish Republic of Northern Cyprus."
>
> The spirit of 1958 still haunts us. People who have grown up under this system have learned to be discreet, to watch their words and speech. I never learned to be this way. This is why they sacked me from a number of jobs.

Somebody heard that I was saying something critical about the administration to somebody else, and that was the end of that.

With the old fighters still in power, though wearing civilian or administrative garb, and offshoots of the old organizational forms springing up under new guises, people claimed that the TMT was still alive in northern Cyprus not only as a culture of politics,[4] but also as an actual and implemented political organization. When Turkish-Cypriots referred to the "TMT spirit," they remembered the culture of terror and enforced secrecy that, they recounted, was the order of the day between 1963 and 1974.

Savalaş Bey, a former fighter (*mücahit*), gave an account of the culture of politics spread through the TMT:

I joined the organization at the age of eighteen. During the day, I used to work in the village cooperative. But at night, I used to leave home and go underground. There was secrecy then. You couldn't tell anything even to your mother or father. My old man was a bit slow. One time, two times, he didn't understand what I was up to. But one night, he once again saw me returning home very late. He asked me: "What are you up to?" "I was tying the donkey to the tree," I told him. When he saw that I kept returning late, he got mad. I was married then. I realized this wouldn't work. I spoke with my wife; I said to her, "Look, I am in the organization; that's why I am always going out at night. But don't tell anybody or they will have me killed." My wife went to my parents and told them I needed to work in the cooperative at night, and everyone locked their mouths. They never asked me anything again. Anyway, our language was coded then; we spoke with passwords so nobody would understand.

Some Turkish-Cypriots almost viscerally remembered the fear instigated by the TMT. Pembe Hanım, in her sixties, said:

The TMT came to our village and made a fighter out of every thief and idle man. These men became the leaders of the TMT in our village. We were afraid of both Greek-Cypriots and Turkish-Cypriots. The TMT spread fear among us; that fear remains. They killed many Turkish-Cypriots, you know. For example, they killed the husband of our neighbor Behice Hanım, who was a policeman in the British bases. One night, the TMT came to his house and said he should leave the gate to the bases open for them to go in and smuggle guns. But if he hid this from his British employers, he would be left without a job, so of course he told the British. The following day, the TMT called him up to the village square. They beat him viciously. His bones were broken. He was practically lynched. He died soon after.

3. Posters of the National Peoples' Movement (UHH)
on billboards in northern Lefkoşa.

In 2001, an organization was founded under the name Ulusal Halk Hare-keti (National Peoples' Movement), commonly referred to as the UHH. An offshoot of Mücahitler Derneği, the society of retired TMT fighters, the UHH was founded in reaction to the This Country Is Ours Platform. In 2000 and 2001, thousands of members of This Country Is Ours Platform walked to the border in a number of public demonstrations, demanding that it be opened. In response, the UHH declared itself a "civil society organization," claiming to represent "the voice of the Turkish-Cypriot people."

The activities of the TMT veterans were received with a mixture of worry and irony on the part of Turkish-Cypriots. It was regarded as general knowledge that the UHH had been created by Denktaş as an underground organization that would work as a supplementary secret service for the administration (see figure 3). But Mustafa, in his forties, said, "I am not afraid of the UHH. It's obvious who they are—the same group of men who are everywhere. Denktaş's men, members of the Na-tionalist Justice Party, and the UHH are one and the same thing. Has anything changed with the foundation of the UHH? No."

Ahmet Bey, an eighty-seven-year-old member of the TMT who was once a guerrilla, was frank in his account of the culture of politics in which he had lived: "During the troubles [the height of intercommunal conflict between 1963 and '74], there was fear of the organization [the TMT]. The TMT had spread fear so that everyone would obey them. The TMT threatened people, killed many. Often the TMT didn't even hide that they were behind the murder of Turkish-Cypriots. Had they not spread this terror, they wouldn't have been able to make people submit to their authority." I asked Ahmet Bey whether he felt there was more of a culture of fear in the past than in the present. "Of course, in the past," he said. "Now they have sprung up under a different name, the UHH, and they try to scare people. But nobody is scared; everyone laughs at the UHH." The UHH was met with bitter humor and nonchalance by Turkish-Cypriots because it seemed to them an old, familiar story involving well-known characters. Pembe Hanım reflected, "Anyway, we have always only talked in our backyards. We lock our mouths in other places. Now, with the UHH, what is going to change? We will continue to manage the way we have done."

Mental Borders

The border demarcating a zone separate from the south is probably the single most important mechanism and symbol of sovereignty in northern Cyprus. The idea of partition (*taksim*) had been at the centre of the TMT's vision for Cyprus, countering EOKA's quest for union with Greece (*enosis*). A border dividing the island between its so-called Turks and Greeks was a crucial component of the political imagination of Turkish-Cypriot administrators from the days when they were fighters under the TMT. "Ya Taksim Ya Ölüm (Partition or Death)" was the slogan of Turkish-Cypriot and Turkish nationalists in the 1950s and '60s. Borders erected by the United Nations in 1963 as demarcation lines between community enclaves and units were revised in 1974 with the Turkish army's invasion, this time dissecting the island with a complicated line right down the middle, passing through towns, neighborhoods, and villages. The TMT's dream of partition was realized and implemented. The border, guarded by the Turkish army since 1974 (and by Greek-Cypriot soldiers on the other side), would mark, physically as well as symbolically, the dividing line between the south of the island, in the hands of Greek-Cypriots, and the north, where activities ensued for the further creation of a separate political reality under a new polity.

Some old residents of Lefkoşa remember the day a wall was built in the

4. House bisected by the border that divides northern and southern Lefkoşa,
with military sign forbidding access.

middle of their street, at times separating the entrances from the balconies of their houses (see figure 4). They sit outside, in front of their homes, with backs turned to the wall. The market area, which, according to elderly craftsmen and shop owners, bustled with life between 1963 and 1974, was marked in 2000 and 2001 by military no-go areas at the end of every street leading to the south of the city. The space on the other side of the border was a "dead zone," partitioned between the Turkish army, the United Nations, and the Republic of Cyprus.[5] However, the immediate northern side of the border in Lefkoşa was perceived by its inhabitants as dead, as well. Most of the workshops, stores, and warehouses on the streets bisected by the border had remained shut for decades. Rusty iron gates covered the windows of old shops leading to the border with the Greek side, which was closed to access. "Life is dead here (*Hayat ölüdür burda*)," said a man who worked at a restaurant next to the ruins of a house in this area.

This border, marking a separation in lives and life histories, was defended by the administration in northern Cyprus as the symbol and

materiality of sovereignty. The army had erected monuments to designate no-entry and no-access zones. In several places along the barricades,
walls were painted with nationalist slogans, inscribing the border with its
official symbolic meaning. From the point of view of the TRNC administration, the border was there to protect Turkish-Cypriots from Greek-
Cypriot attacks of the sort that took place between 1963 and '74. So the
slogan "Hey, Turk, Don't Forget the Massacres" highlighted the end of a
street blocked by barricades in the border area of northern Lefkoşa,
inscribing in stone how the border should be interpreted (see figure 5).
Rauf Denktaş was commonly quoted as saying in his refusal to negotiate
with Greek-Cypriots, "We will not return with a pen [a peace agreement]
what we obtained with blood." In his numerous public speeches, he associated the line across Cyprus with the blood of Turkish and Turkish-
Cypriot "martyrs (şehitler)" spilled on the ground.[6]

The actual border between north and south, highly loaded symbolically,
was not the only means of preventing access to subjects of the regime in
northern Cyprus. Many parts of divided Nicosia, as well as villages and

5. Border wall in northern Lefkoşa that reads,
"Hey, Turk: Don't Forget the Massacres."

areas in the countryside, had been designated "first-degree military zones" and were off-limits to civilians. Fences and barbed wire all over the territory separated areas allocated to civilians from those exclusively accessible to soldiers. So anyone living in northern Cyprus as a categorized civilian had to operate within an area of limitations.

But a border is no border in and of itself, even if enforced through military means and emblematized as the central motif of sovereignty. What interests me is the mark of the material border (or the border as a tangibility) in the subjectivities and imagination of Turkish-Cypriots who were subjects of the TRNC—the side, covert, or unseen effects of a specific kind of sovereignty.

Spatial metaphors were at the center of Turkish-Cypriots' ways to express their experience of living as subjects of the polity in northern Cyprus. "This is an open-air prison," was one of the most common expressions used in 2000 and 2001. The open-air prison (açık hava hapishanesi) metaphor is heavy with implication and contains an intrinsic paradox. Turkish-Cypriots at the time experienced the "outside" (outdoors, the air, the mountains, the sea, the sky, the landscape) as an "indoors," an enclosed and framed space. One of the gravest offences at the time, in northern Cyprus, was to cross the border to the south. Many people had been brought to military court for crossing the border, intentionally or accidentally, and punished with prison sentences. Expressing, again, the experience of confinement, Turkish-Cypriots also described northern Cyprus as a "camp for prisoners of war (esir kampı)," referring to themselves as the prisoners kept "inside" by administrators of the regime and by soldiers.

The metaphors were multiple and creative, but they all communicated an experience of enclosure. "It's as if they locked us in a cage," said Atiye, a woman in her fifties. "From my neighborhood, I look one way, toward the Greek side, and see the barricades; I look the other way and see the dry [Beşparmak, Pentadaktilos] mountains; in the middle, we live in cement constructions. It's as if they have taken us and put us in here, inside a prison." Selen, in her twenties, said, "It's as though they took us and put us in a zoo like an endangered species." "This place feels like an asylum," likewise said Kemal, in his forties. In Lefkoşa, sitting out in his garden in the quiet of a summer evening, eighty-year-old İbrahim Bey complained: "No goodness has been left in this place. You can't pass here; you can't pass there. Here, soldier; there, police. On this side [referring to the

Turkish side of Cyprus] they strangle people. They fear that if the borders open, people on this side will rejoice. If the borders open, let me tell you, no one would remain on this side. Everyone would go to the other side [the Greek side]."

Until 2003, when the Denktaş regime suddenly decided to allow crossings through the border, Turkish-Cypriots were mostly banned from access to the Greek side and from contact with Greek-Cypriots unless they obtained special permission.[7] Turkish-Cypriots therefore expressed a sense of feeling northern Cyprus as a zone of spatial and temporal surreality. Estranged from places formerly known to them in a different way and disoriented by the changing of place names, by the material transformation of the physical and built environment, and by the population shifts in northern Cyprus, Turkish-Cypriots expressed a sense of alienation vis-à-vis the place in which they lived. Many said, "We feel like we're being strangled by our throats," expressing a feeling of suffocation and entrapment in a slice of territory. One man described his brief visit out of northern Cyprus as "the permitted stroll of the prisoner in the courtyard to take in some air." I frequently visited a public park called Zafer Burcu, which the Turkish-Cypriot municipality of Lefkoşa had built over a hidden ammunition store right beside the barrels and barbed wire that divide the city. Every time I went, Turkish-Cypriots, settlers from Turkey, and off-duty soldiers were holding on to the fence and looking curiously at life on the Greek side.[8]

The border held a central place in the Turkish-Cypriot political imagination because it symbolized the limits and limitations of their polity. It was regarded as the precipice. We could analyze "the border" as the self-fashioned fault line of the northern Cypriot regime. Between 2000 and 2002, many Turkish-Cypriots, having arrived at breaking points in their lives in northern Cyprus, tried to break through the border, to cross to the Greek side.

The story of Ömer Bey, who had attempted several times to cross the border to the south, is instructive. The following excerpt is from my field notes dated 11 March 2002:

Ömer Bey has been at breaking point for some time. He used to sell clothes piecemeal, but with the economic crisis, he was left unemployed. His wife, Sevgül Hanım, does house cleaning in Lefkoşa six days of the week, and the family (with three children) barely manage to maintain a living on her income. Ömer Bey has been looking for a job for more than two years, without results.

Meanwhile, he has been searching for a way to get out of northern Cyprus to work abroad. He tried to get a British visa on his TRNC passport, but he was refused three times by the British High Commission in Lefkoşa. His intention was to find access to the UK and therefore to some form of work. In order to travel to Europe, he then tried to obtain a Republic of Cyprus passport. He applied through a middleman operating from Pile [Pyla], the mixed village on the border, but he is still waiting. Last week, he heard that he might not be able to obtain his Republic of Cyprus papers, which was his only hope for an exit from northern Cyprus. He reached his limit. He could take it no longer. He had been feeling terrible over the long term, jobless, deeply in debt, and not able to maintain his family. He went to his wife's workplace and told her: "If I return home tonight, I return; if not, I will be on the Greek side." He said he would try to cross the border to the other side and find a job in the south. And he left.

Sevgül Hanim, his wife, was in despair. "If he crosses to the other side, it's finished. He won't be able to return. If he returns, they [will] bring him to military court," she said. In the end, Ömer Bey wasn't able to cross the border; he worried that he would be spotted by a soldier. Having reached his breaking point, he tried, but seeing the dangers, with soldiers on duty by the barricades, he returned.

The border with the Greek side was perceived as the limit, and when one reaches the limit, one hits the limit. It is as if Ömer Bey, having hit a limit in his life, wanted to put his chest against the border as the symbol of his entrapment, the ultimate limitation. He knew he could be killed or arrested while attempting to cross the border and that he might not be able to see his family again, even if he crossed successfully. Crossing that threshold, he thought, would have been a turning point. But unlike Ömer Bey, most Turkish-Cypriots did not dare or attempt to cross because of the dangers of being caught.

Borders on the Imagination

What marks does a material border leave in the subjective experiences of those who live within its confines? Spatial confinement was the centermost fashion in which social control was implemented in the TRNC before the opening of checkpoints in 2003. Through physical borders and their rationalization through propaganda, the TRNC was able to constrain not only the lives, but also the imaginations, of its subjects.

The reflections and comments of Turkish-Cypriots in the period preceding 2003 are instructive. Taylan spent his childhood in Mağusa (Ammochostos, Famagusta), which had been carved up into enclaves before 1974:

> We lived right on the Green Line in Mağusa. Between 1963 and 1974, this line divides the Greek and Turkish sides of the city. In my childhood, my mother would always warn me against crossing to the other side, saying, "There are Greeks there." There wasn't a fence or barricades on the Green Line. We just knew that the other side of our street was "the Greek side," and we didn't cross. After 1974, when the other [Greek] side of the Green Line was attached to this side, too, for many years I was unable to visit the coffeehouse that used to be Greek. I couldn't walk to the other side.

Serhat, who was listening to this conversation, said, "We imprisoned ourselves. And now we are unable to get out of our self-made prison." Taylan continued to recount his experience: "People who have lived within borders for thirty years are unable to imagine that these borders will be lifted if Cyprus becomes a member of the European Union. Our vision is so narrow and limited. People are still asking whether the Lokmacı barricade in Lefkoşa [the main and most central one] will be opened for crossing. They can't imagine a borderless world."[9] "Inside this place (*bunun çinde* in Cypriot Turkish)" is an idiomatic way to express the experience of living in northern Cyprus. Those who lived their everyday lives within the confines of the areas that were permissible and accessible, without breaching the boundaries, experienced the entire space of northern Cyprus as an inside, an enclosure. Taylan reflected on the lives of his relatives and other Turkish-Cypriots who had emigrated to England: "Cypriots who have lived in London for many years never go to the center of the city; they don't learn English. . . . They live between two streets as if they were still in Cyprus between '63 and '74, or in northern Cyprus after 1974." One might think that for people who so fundamentally experience their subjectivity through the materiality of spatial boundaries, who so consciously articulate their everyday experience as a form of confinement, and whose citizenship rights and economic livelihood have been constrained, a crossing or removal of the border would be desirable (see figure 6). But borders leave contradictory and complicated marks on the subjective worlds of people who have experienced spatial segregation for such a long time.

Consider the words of Olgun, a young man born in 1978, four years

6. Rusty barrels and dumped furniture by the border in Lefkoşa.

after the demarcation of Lefkoşa's present border. "What can we do, we young people," he complained, "locked between walls and barrels? We have had enough; we have reached our boiling point, our point of explosion." I reflected on his frustration, saying, "It would be great, wouldn't it, if there were an agreement and you could cross to the other side of your own city?" Olgun replied:

> Look, my map ends where the border begins. . . . I once got permission to cross to the other side, to attend a number of bi-communal activities for young people. But when I cross the border, I don't feel like I'm in my own city. When I'm on the Greek side, I feel like I'm in another country. When people look at me, I think they're looking at me because I'm Turkish, even though they're just looking at a human being. When I cross to the Greek side, I feel scared. I get very anxious. Once I was in a car with a few Greek-Cypriot friends. We stopped at the traffic lights, and I felt a rush of panic, as if something was going to happen to me. I felt unsafe. When I return to the border and see the flag of the TRNC, I relax. When I cross the border back to this side, I feel back at ease. I feel like I have returned to my country. I grew up here.

"Here," for Olgun, is the northern side as a spatial as well as administrative zone. Olgun felt relief not only because he had returned to his space of familiarity, but also because he had returned to his proper polity, the

TRNC, with its flag as symbol. Commenting on refugees' feelings of long-ing for villages and houses left on the other side in 1963 and 1974, Olgun said, "There is nothing that I miss on the other side, because I was born on this side. My family has a house and a field in a village in the south, and I don't feel like we should reclaim our property. Why should I? What do I have to do there?" Olgun was a citizen of the TRNC, a status that gave him no right to international recognition. Like many Turkish-Cypriots, he had obtained a Republic of Cyprus passport so he could travel out of Cyprus more easily. But Olgun's feeling about the passport was interest-ing. "I have a Greek-Cypriot passport, but I don't like having it," he said. "I don't feel like it's my own passport. I feel like I'm taking advantage by having a passport like this." Olgun was uneasy about being outside the designated area of the polity in which he had grown up. Although he complained, along with his friends, about feeling confined, about feeling bored and lacking energy, he also felt at ease within the political reality in which he was brought up. The border and the idea of crossing it to the mythicized "other side" was so dominant in his imagination that the actual experience was scary. He felt relief once he stepped back into the zone of the very regime that had determined the subjection and confine-ment he so complained about.

I spoke with many young people like Olgun who have known no political reality other than the successive administrations of northern Cyprus.[10] Such youth for whom northern Cyprus was a domain of intimacy and familiarity were named the "'74 generation" by older Turkish-Cypriots who could remember Cyprus at another time and as another kind of space. To the children of people who longed to see their villages and towns on the other side, the borders were not disturbing. I asked Deniz, born in 1987, what he thought about the border. "It doesn't affect me," he said, "because I don't know. I haven't seen the Greek side." The symbolic weight loaded into "the border"—standing, in ideological Turkish-Cypriot representa-tions, for peace and freedom—have taken a toll on the subjectivities of subjects of the TRNC, and especially on young people who have experi-enced nothing else firsthand.

Twelve-year-old Seçil said, "I don't want there to be a peace agreement with the Greek-Cypriots." "Why?," I asked. "What would happen if there were an agreement?" She answered, "The Greek-Cypriots would come to attack us again. I feel scared of that. They would do to us what they did between 1963 and 1974. If there were an agreement, the Greek-Cypriots would start coming to this side. I fear this, I wouldn't want it." "Should it remain like this?" I asked. "Yes," she said. "I'd like this place to remain as it is. . . . A friend of mine was saying, 'I want peace; I want peace.' I told her, 'What are you going to do with peace? Should the Greek-Cypriots come and attack you again?' She stopped and thought and said, 'You're right. Let there be no peace then.'"

Seçil's parents and other family members were supporters of peace and critics of the Denktaş regime then prevalent in the north, but Seçil went to school where the main component of the curriculum was a standard account of the massacre of Turkish-Cypriots by Greek-Cypriots between 1963 and 1974. I asked Seçil whether she was curious to see the other side of Cyprus. She firmly said no. The ideas of partition and separate sovereignty and the project of creating a new political reality have been partially successful, one could argue, given the subjective worlds they have created among subjects of the regime.

Spatial confinement and a phantasmatic and material reconfiguration of territory have been fundamental aspects of practices of Turkish sovereignty in northern Cyprus. In this chapter, I have studied how the radical reshaping of an inhabited geography through sovereign means, including the cultivation by its fighters and administrators of a spirit of terror among its subjects, induces specific kinds of affect and distinct forms of interior experience within a population. Transformations in the outer (spatial, physical, built, material) environment through political means provoke qualified forms of inside (interior, inner, subjective) experience that are expressed in embodied and metaphorical forms.

In the late 1990s and early 2000s, before the opening of checkpoints for access to the south in 2003 and when I lived and conducted fieldwork in northern Cyprus, Turkish-Cypriots understood the political as a form of power over the management of space. The bans on movement across the border and the difficulty of traveling out of northern Cyprus with TRNC papers made Turkish-Cypriots reflect on their interiorities with references to a politically circumscribed exteriority. The inside and the outside blended, then, in this situated experience of sovereignty. The experience of confinement, expressed by Turkish-Cypriots in this period as a form of suffocation in a slice of land, can be interpreted as a "hidden injury" of sovereignty.[11] Here, we have studied what we could call the *insides of sovereignty*.

Part II   Administration

4. Administration and Affect

"I SEE THE SIGNS of a good deed (*kısmet*) for you," said Zühre Hanım, who was reading fortunes in the coffee cup. "A door will open for you in a state office (*devlet dairesi*)." She continued, "I see two men with hats," interpreting them as "men from government (*hükümet adamları*)." "Look, over here there is a bird on one of their hats, this means luck. They are going to offer you a job." And then, "Here I see you at the gate of government." Ayten, who was having her fortune read, seemed pleased. In northern Cyprus, such a prophecy is highly valued. "Health to your mouth," Ayten said to the fortuneteller, as if she were thanking her for wishing her well.

In this chapter, I study Turkish-Cypriots' desires for jobs in state offices and reverence for administrative positions, alongside their despising of civil servants and ironic view of the state.[1] The anecdote I just recounted reveals a dominant sentiment in relation to the civil service (*devlet memurluğu*) in contemporary Turkish-Cypriot society. As one of my informants put it, "Turkish-Cypriots strongly desire to be appointed as state officers." Parents exploit their social networks (*torpil*) to arrange such positions for their children. Families of brides-to-be search for civil servant grooms. To the extent that the laxity of civil servants and the inefficacy of the "state" are parodied, such positions and the people who retain or obtain them are highly regarded.

Why is this so? Although the TRNC is considered illegal under international law, and many transactions carried out in the state offices of the TRNC are not recognized anywhere outside northern Cyprus, Turkish-Cypriots nevertheless compete with one another for positions in the administration. Why does a community governed by an unrecognized state have such an attachment to the civil service? How can this desire for jobs in the state administration, mixed with feelings of apathy toward the state, be analyzed? Turkish-Cypriots are fully aware of the limitations of their polity, referring to its lack of recognition and its dependence on Turkey. They joke about it among themselves, calling the TRNC a "pirate state" or, at times, a "make-believe state." Yet they aspire to state positions.

The central concern of this chapter is the affect engendered by the civil service under an unrecognized state. Recent scholarship on modern bureaucracies has tended to portray administration as a realm of emotive neutrality. Bureaucracy has been studied as a rationalizing apparatus, instigating discipline and organizing audit procedures, with no room for affect.[2] My material on the civil service highlights another dimension of institutions and organizations. Administration, I argue, evokes a complex spectrum of affect.[3] In northern Cyprus, this is experienced through seemingly opposed emotions: Turkish-Cypriots feel desire for and apathy toward their state administration at the same time. Based on this material, I propose that bureaucracy be studied not as a practice that counters or extinguishes affect but as one that produces and incites specific modes of affect in its own right.[4] This is a study of affective civil service or of bureaucracy as an emotive domain.

In other studies of administration, focusing on totalitarian regimes, bureaucracy has indeed been studied as emotively charged. Hannah Arendt and Zygmunt Bauman, in their own specific ways, have studied bureaucracy as provoking destructive and violent emotions.[5] Where Arendt, envisioning democracy as a rationalized practice, argued that this propensity for rousing affect was a feature of totalitarian regimes, Bauman suggested, more radically, that a potential for excessive emotion was built into the bureaucratic structure of modern political systems themselves. I follow these scholars' lead in centering affect in my study of bureaucracy.

The unrecognized state in northern Cyprus is a peculiar amalgam of biopolitics and sovereignty, akin to the affinity of discipline and might that Giorgio Agamben studies in modern states.[6] In this sense, I do not study the TRNC as an anomaly or as an administrative practice that entirely counters the valid procedures of modern and legal states. Turkish-Cypriots modeled their state administrations on the bureaucratic practices of legal and recognized states—Britain, the Republic of Cyprus, and Turkey. In other words, the TRNC is not a culturally "other" state structure; it has similarities to other modern administrative systems. Yet because it is illegal and dependent on the sovereignty of another country and its military, the civil service under this "state" evokes a peculiar mix of affect. The complexity of the emotions induced by the civil service under a modern yet unrecognized and dependent state and the reasons for this are what I explore in this chapter.

The Affect of the Civil Service

In an office of the state administration in the TRNC, two civil servants discuss their professions. "The civil service has a lot of status here," says one of them, called Hakan. "Everyone wants to be a civil servant. Those in particular who do not hold positions in the state administration do just everything to be appointed. They exploit their social networks; they ask their relatives and friends to find jobs for their children in the state office." "Yes," says the other, called Gülşen, "but civil servants are not respected. We have social status, but we are also ridiculed for our idleness, for having no work to do or for not doing it, or for the salaries we get." Laughing, Hakan and Gülşen point at their colleague in the office next door, who is visible through a glass barrier and who is asleep. "You know, there is a saying appropriate to this in Turkish-Cypriot society," says Hakan: "The civil service is idleness." "Indeed," says Gülşen, "don't we also say, 'The end of the month is behind the door' to imply that we will soon get our paychecks? . . . There are civil servants who sleep in the office; others who arrive late. Indeed, there are many who receive a salary from the state without having a real function." Jokingly they refer to the driver who brings the minister to work in the morning and rests all day, then drives him home in the evening. Hakan mentions the position of the "messenger (odacı)," whose role is to carry papers from room to room in the state administration. "In other countries, the civil servants would take the documents themselves," says Gülşen. "Yes!," says Hakan. "And do you know how much these messengers protest when we ask them to do some extra work?"

Gülşen talks about civil servants who are allowed to take on extra working hours for more pay. Using a Turkish idiom, transformed by Turkish-Cypriots in reference to their relation with the state, she says, "Such employees become tied to the state by their belly (devlete belden bağlanırlar)." This is an expression of an embodied relation with the state. Such attachments involve at least partial loyalty.

Hakan recounted a joke about the civil service that was popular among Turkish-Cypriots:

> The state's breeding farm was looking for a good ram. Everybody recom-
> mended Uncle Ali's ram, saying it would charm all of the farm's sheep. The
> officers of the state farm went to Uncle Ali and asked, "Would you give us your
> ram?" Uncle Ali replied, "Yes, but under one condition: only if you give my

daughter a job in the state administration." "No problem," said the officers, and Uncle Ali gave them his ram. But several weeks went by and there was no action in the state farm. The ram had pulled himself under a tree and was sleeping all day in the shade. The sheep were trying to charm him, but he was not even giving them a glance. The farm officers went back to Uncle Ali and said, "You cheated us; your ram is not doing his job." Uncle Ali came to the farm and stood beside the ram. "My ram," he asked, "what has happened to you?" The ram replied: "*Meeee–mur* [civil servant]."

As in this joke, the Turkish word for civil servant, "*memur,*" was used by Turkish-Cypriots as a metaphor for comfort and idleness, especially after having attained a position in a state office.

In characterizing their civil service, Turkish-Cypriots (including those in civil service positions) referred to the economy of plunder. One Turkish-Cypriot lawyer who later obtained a position in the civil service said, "People here got used to earning money without too much work. You know, after 1974, there was loot. People obtained loot. And in a similar manner, they work as civil servants and get a monthly salary without working too much." Such analogies between work in the civil service and looting existed among Turkish-Cypriots in the nature of criticism and cynicism about their administration. A "looter," in Turkish-Cypriot representations, is somebody who gets rich without working for it. Civil service was likewise associated with benefit without labor.

Most dominant in Turkish-Cypriot narratives about the civil service were references to "*torpil,*" or patronage networks and connections through which state jobs were distributed and work in state offices got done. People in northern Cyprus noted that positions in the state administration were awarded for loyalty, especially to political parties that ran the government. Political parties employed relatives, friends, or clients of their members. Parties close to the regime were known to distribute jobs before elections in return for the promise of votes. Until the turnover of government to the previous opposition (the CTP) in 2002, numerous Turkish-Cypriots had complained that appointments and promotions in state offices were made on the basis of loyalty to parties of the regime (the UBP and the DP) and their nationalist ideologies. Once the CTP was in government, similar complaints were made against its abuse of *torpil* networks on behalf of its allies.

"There is no such thing as merit in the civil service," said Dervişe, a Turkish-Cypriot civil servant. "No one gets to a position in the civil service because he has merits. He is promoted because he has *torpil*, through relations between partners and friends (*eş-dost ilişkisi*)." Young people complained that they could not get jobs in the state administration because they did not have *torpil*. Mustafa Bey, a middle-age Turkish-Cypriot gardener, said, "If you don't have *torpil*, there is no way that you will have your work done or a transaction accomplished in a state office. For example, once when I was ill, they gave me an appointment for four months later at the state hospital. Then my sister-in-law, who works at the hospital, intervened, and I was immediately called for a doctor's appointment. You see, even our health is dependent on *torpil*. In this country, you can't get anything done if you don't have relatives, friends, or partisans who hold social influence or have connections." *Torpil* is the way Turkish-Cypriots manipulate their administrative system. Hüseyin Bey, an elderly Turkish-Cypriot man, said, "If they took *torpil* from our hands, too, we would not be able to survive here at all. We hold no power other than this in this country. I needed to correct a mistake in my son's identity card, so I went to the state office. They said they couldn't fix it; they created a lot of problems. Then one of my relatives said, 'Why didn't you go with Arif?' And, really, I went along with Arif, and our job at the state office was done. They all know Arif at the state office. He has connections."

In these reflections about state offices, Turkish-Cypriots are pointing at a paradox. The high esteem associated with positions in the state administration is mixed with disrespect for civil servants and the state system. "Those who do not hold positions in a state office always put us down," said Hakan. "They have a saying about the civil service: 'Let the month pass; let the money come.' But at the same time they envy us. The person who says this would also die to be appointed as a civil servant."

"There is apathy (*isteksizlik*) in me," said Nurcan, who had held a position in the civil service since her graduation from university. "I feel indifferent. It's as if I have automated myself. I do my work without thinking. I finish what I have to do in an hour or so, and often nobody asks if I am not in the office after that." She continued, "In fact, those who are in the best situation in this society are us, the civil servants. We have a regular, guaranteed salary. We eat and drink well. On the surface, we lack nothing. But everyone in the office is depressed (*hepimiz bunalımdayız*)." Other civil servants said that they experienced a breakdown in both morals and morale in the state offices.

As I conducted the major part of my fieldwork in 2001–2002, civil servants also expressed feelings of caution and reserve toward colleagues who supported the regime (at the time, under Denktaş). "I have never been promoted," said Burhan, "because they know I support the opposition party." "We don't discuss politics in the state office," said Turgay, "for fear of being identified as critics of the regime."[7]

One of the greatest objects of desire of a society, a post in a state office, should provide elation and satisfaction when attained, but it actually leads to feelings of depression, caution, cynicism, and lack of motivation. Desire and reverence for the state administration, on the one hand, coexist with resentment, irony, apathy, and dissatisfaction, on the other. How can this be explained?

The Making of a State Administration

To analyze this attachment to the civil service and the affects it engenders properly, we need to flash back to the period in the 1960s when Turkish-Cypriots were estranged from the Republic of Cyprus and began to form their own, separate state administration; when the structure for this specific unrecognized state administration was first established. The Republic of Cyprus, which became independent from Britain in 1960, was a bi-communal entity in which employment in the civil service was organized by proportional communal representation. According to the London-Zurich Agreements of 1959 on which the Republican constitution was based, Turkish-Cypriots would hold 30 percent of civil service positions, higher than their 18 percent representation in the population of Cyprus.[8] Soon after the foundation of the republic, Greek-Cypriots began to object. They also criticized the constitutional idea of ethnically divided municipal services in towns other than Nicosia.[9] Turkish-Cypriots defended themselves on the basis of the constitution. But trouble soon broke out, leading to civil war, and the bi-communal structure of the republic broke down.[10]

The creation of Turkish-Cypriot enclaves between 1963 and 1974 had repercussions in the civil service. Richard Patrick writes, "Many Turkish-Cypriot employees were turned out by their Greek-Cypriot employers; some left on their own initiative. However, most Turkish-Cypriots simply found it too dangerous to attempt to go to work in Greek-Cypriot areas. As a result, the Cyprus police, the government and the civil service became de facto Greek-Cypriot organizations."[11] In his memoirs, Fazıl Plümer, a Turkish-Cypriot lawyer who was a parliamentarian under the Republic of Cyprus, describes the period following the Greek-Cypriot attacks on Turkish-Cypriot communities and the first formation of a separate Turkish-Cypriot administration: "In the days that followed the Bloody Christmas of 21 December 1963, we did not have the possibility of going to the Ministries or state offices in the Greek neighborhood [of Lefkoşa]. The Turks who were working in state offices had been isolated from their duties in the government mechanism. . . . Under these conditions, in order to protect the Turkish community and to administer it well, a General Committee was founded."[12] The researcher Metin Münir Hakkı recounts that, having been deprived of their authority and functions under the Republic of Cyprus, the Turkish-Cypriot vice president of the republic, ministers, and parliamentarians began to form a separate administrative system in areas of Cyprus, the Turkish-Cypriot enclaves, that were not controlled by the Greek-Cypriots. Moreover, Turkish-Cypriots who preferred to work with the Greek-Cypriots under the roof of the republic were threatened by the Turkish-Cypriot fighters of the TMT and forced to join the Turkish-Cypriot administrative body. In 1967, this parallel Turkish-Cypriot administration was given a name: the Transitional Cyprus Turkish Administration.[13]

Here we observe the birth of a separate administrative system under the threat of extermination by Greek-Cypriot fighters and under pressure from their Turkish-Cypriot counterparts. In ethnically segregated enclaves formed between 1963 and 1974, Turkish-Cypriots were subjected to and took part in the creation and implementation of a state administration. Subjection to this state system in a time of conflict, to the violence between the two communities, and to confinement in the enclaves created a dependence on the administrative system that was being forged among the Turkish-Cypriots.[14] This dependence on the administration that now claimed to represent them was exacerbated by an economic embargo introduced by the government of Cyprus (now wholly in Greek-Cypriot hands) on the Turkish-Cypriot enclaves, blocking trade routes between the communities.[15] With restrictions on freedom to travel across the enclaves, few Turkish-Cypriots were able to continue working in their previous jobs. Moreover, refugees had been isolated from their old livelihoods.

Significant aid from Turkey began to arrive in this period. Patrick notes, "By 1968 the Turkish government was injecting £8,000,000 per annum into the Turkish-Cypriot economy. Apart from the welfare programs,

Turkish-Cypriot leaders, civil servants and the entire Fighter organization were also paid from these funds."[16] Through the pressures of the enclave period, then, an entire population was rendered largely dependent on a makeshift state administration supported by another country. Reflecting on the period of enclaves, one of my informants, a Turkish-Cypriot doctor, recounted what happened this way: "The TMT fighters said to us: 'Leave your job, settle in the enclave, join the resistance. Here is flour; here is a salary for you.' Then came the subsequent state administrations, all of which said: 'Here is the civil service for you; here is a salary.' As a result, Turkish-Cypriots are very attached to their positions in the state administration."

Although Turkish-Cypriots considered this de facto welfare system beneficial, and received it with some gratitude, it also provoked resentment (as well as fear) because of the pressures that the TMT fighters and administrative leaders were putting on their community. In return for supporting Turkish-Cypriots by distributing jobs and salaries, the newly formed state administration, and its successors, demanded strict obedience and allegiance. In his memoirs, Hikmet Afif Mapolar recalls the fear created among Turkish-Cypriots by their leaders and by the TMT. He writes that the state administration established in the period of intercommunal fighting was in effect a surfacing of the previously underground TMT organization.[17] Richard Patrick substantiates this: "In many cases, the *de facto* leadership at the level of the village and quarter, of the district, and of the community as a whole, was assumed by the Fighters. Therefore, the community's government structure was in fact a civilmilitary synthesis."[18] Mapolar writes that the administration generated an atmosphere of surveillance, much in the nature of a military force:

> The "administration" that was built was a dictatorial regime; it was carrying things back and forth, but it was impossible to question its might. . . . Perhaps in wartime, according to organization rules, "dictatorship" could be considered "freedom," but the system and weight of our "administration" was something else. Our "administration" felt much like the gallows. Our "administration," with its regime and rules, was a force that held both rope and soap in its hands.
>
> The "administration" was completely a regime of force. Its rules and procedures were as holy as the Qur'an, as rulebound as the orders of the Qur'an. . . . In this situation, people were caught in a nightmare. Nobody had a tongue; everybody had been silenced out of worry of being threaded with needles of fear. . . .

Most people didn't know how they could exist; how they could survive under such a regime.[19]

Many of my informants recalled the acute fear that was inflicted on them by the TMT fighters and the administration it created in the enclaves.[20]

The grounds and structure for the present state administration in northern Cyprus, now called the TRNC, were established in the enclaves in this manner in the period of civil war. Structural and affective residues of this early administrative formation can be observed in the contemporary Turkish-Cypriot regime and society. The political and economic dependence on Turkey, the unrecognized status, the civil-military complex, and the tendency toward "big government" (a broad civil service) were all established in that period. The Turkish-Cypriots' leaning toward civil service positions, the core question of this chapter, was enhanced by the period of enclaves through their dependence on the state administration that was distributing jobs, food, and salaries.[21] The roots of Turkish-Cypriots' attachment to civil service jobs, mixed with feelings of apathy, caution, and resentment, therefore lie in that period of initial de facto state formation.

A Series of Administrations

The TRNC came into being through several stages and constructions of statehood. During and in the aftermath of British colonialism and through the times of conflict with Greek-Cypriots, Turkish-Cypriots administered themselves under such constructions as the Cyprus Turkish Minority's Association (after 1943); the TMT (after 1957); the Cyprus Turkish Associations Federation (formed in 1958); separate Turkish councils in big towns , such as the Nicosia Turkish Council (after 1958), the Republic of Cyprus, recognized as a bi-communal state by the United Nations (1960); the Turkish Cypriot General Committee, announced when Turkish-Cypriots were living in the enclaves (between 1963 and 1974); the Provisional Turkish Cypriot Administration (declared in 1964 and dropping its provisional status in 1967); and the Turkish Federated State of Cyprus (announced in 1975 after the Turkish army's invasion in 1974 and imagined as a component of the proposed Federal Republic of Cyprus). State practices in northern Cyprus were managed through this series of administrative constructions until the TRNC was declared as a separate state in 1983.[22]

Most of these administrations have been recognized by no member of the international community other than Turkey.[23] According to the United Nations Security Council, the TRNC is "legally invalid." Greece and the Republic of Cyprus refer to the TRNC as a "pseudo-state."[24] Since 1983, Turkish-Cypriot officials have been involved in all sorts of lobbying, soliciting, and propaganda activities to gain international status as a "state" for the TRNC. When Rauf Denktaş was the president of the TRNC, he was at the forefront of activities geared toward recognition.[25]

Here, I would like to draw attention to the great interest in the subject of the "state" and international recognition among officials and supporters of the TRNC. The vocabulary of statehood and its numerous constructions (federal, confederate, sovereign) imbues public discourses in northern Cyprus. The topic of statehood predominates in international meetings and conferences abroad about Cyprus, as well. In northern Cyprus, an official discourse of Turkish-Cypriot independence glosses over political and economic dependence on Turkey and the lack of international recognition. This ambiguous situation has produced an indeterminate and complicated language of statehood among Turkish-Cypriots. An "ethnography of the state" in such a context, betwixt and between the absence and presence of statehood, deserves particular analysis of the everyday imaginary of the "state."[26]

In textbooks and lessons about northern Cyprus, children are presented with contradictory references to their "state." On the one hand, they are taught to revere the independence of the TRNC, while on the other, they encounter references to Turkey as their state. For instance, I saw the statement, "Our state was founded on 29 October, 1923," written on the blackboard at an elementary school in Lefke. The teacher had not thought it necessary to distinguish between the foundation of the Republic of Turkey and that of the TRNC. "It is confusing," one mother said. "Sometimes they teach the Republic of Turkey as our state and sometimes the TRNC. But in time, children grasp the situation." In schools today, Turkish-Cypriot children, as well as children of immigrants from Turkey, are taught two separate history classes, one named "National History (İnkılap Tarihi)," using standard textbooks produced by the Ministry of Education in Turkey, and the other named "History of Cyprus (Kıbrıs Tarihi)." Such lessons serve to reify Turkish statehood.[27] Children are taught to identify with a vague "idea of state" and to see themselves as descendants of generations of state makers over the centuries.[28] "History" is constructed as a succession of state entities. Often referred to as the "History of

Turkish States," it includes what are called "the first Turkish states in Central Asia" (the Hun and Göktürk empires), and continues through the Selçuks, the lordships in Anatolia, the making of the Ottoman state, the foundation of the Republic of Turkey, and, finally, the declaration of the TRNC. Identity is constructed in close association with the presence of statehood, despite (or perhaps because of) its legal absence. With the official term "infant-land (*yavruvatan*)" that is used for the TRNC in relation to Turkey, the "motherland (*anavatan*)," Turkish-Cypriots are taught to identify their statehood with that of Turkey. Strongly militaristic in content and imagery, narratives of history recount Turkish conquests of territory, and northern Cyprus figures as the last such achievement. A subtext of identification with Turkey, then, underlay official discourses and administrative policies in northern Cyprus in the late 1990s and early 2000s; at the same time, any identification with the Republic of Cyprus was banned and subject to punishment.[29]

However, paradoxically, despite such bombastic and triumphalist references to "Turkish statehood," Turkish-Cypriots showed little pride in their "state" (the TRNC) or in Turkey in the period that I conducted research. Instead, there was pervasive irony, cynicism, and critique. What Turkish-Cypriots often complained about were the constraints imposed by the lack of recognition of their administration as a state. The TRNC papers they held did not allow them easy travel out of northern Cyprus to countries other than Turkey.

The stigma of non-recognition, as experienced by the Turkish-Cypriots, can be likened to the situation of a character in *Yaşar Ne Yaşar Ne Yaşamaz*, a novel by the Turkish author Aziz Nesin:[30] Yaşar Yaşamaz (whose name can be translated as "Lives and Doesn't") discovers that he is registered as dead in the census books and reflects, "One must be alive in government notebooks to be living. Unless government officials say that you are alive, you may go on forever screaming that you are alive, only to console yourself. . . . [But] just because the notebook writes "dead,' can someone be counted 'dead'?" In practices of the international system, existence is linked with the appearance of membership in a reified, recognized state. The lack of adequate representations—papers, symbols, and practices of statecraft—prevents international access, connection, and privilege. Many Turkish-Cypriots did not identify with the TRNC that purported to represent their ethnically defined interests, yet they were dependent on its administrative practices.

Civil Service under an Unrecognized State

According to figures released in 2002 by the Cyprus Turkish Civil Servants' Union (KTAMS), there are about 12,500 civil servants in the TRNC. They include teachers, state workers, and police. Ali Seylani, the president of KTAMS, whom I interviewed at the time, gave me an account of the Turkish-Cypriots' recent history in the civil service. "The significant rise in levels of civil servants among the Turkish-Cypriots begins with 1974," he said. "If we include the public sector initiatives, the teachers, the municipal workers, and the police, 18 percent are public sector workers in northern Cyprus." Seylani explained the reasons for this: "In 1974, when the northern part of the island was taken over by Turkish administration, state offices were opened for employment. First, there was a real necessity; second, the politicians distributed jobs in state offices in return for favors, and therefore there was over-employment; and third, because industry wasn't developed, there weren't too many other job opportunities. The public sector was loaded up with civil servants." Funding for Turkish-Cypriot salaries comes from Turkey. "In order to sustain the administration here, Turkey created employment in northern Cyprus under the cloak of 'public sector work,'" said Seylani.

Civil servants in northern Cyprus know that their salaries are dependent on aid from Turkey. "If aid isn't received from Turkey, public sector salaries cannot be paid," said a former high-level civil servant. "That's why, when we were in government, we had to regularly send our ministers to Turkey to beg for money." A lower-level civil servant said that "the government would be proud here one day if they were able to pay their civil servants' salaries from their own budget." Employing an idiom used by Turkish-Cypriots to describe the functioning of their system, Hakan said: "This mill turns with water that comes from Turkey."

However, Çetin Uğural, an economist, explained that talk about "aid from Turkey" is exaggerated for political reasons. Indeed, such attributions of Turkish-Cypriots' survival to Turkey's assistance were supported daily by politicians making public promises about the next aid package that was due to reach the island from Turkey. "Civil servants are kept under the illusion that dependence on Turkey is necessary for their job security," said Uğural when I interviewed him. This is sustained "under an economy of gratitude (şükran ekonomisi). Civil servants are attached to the politics of the administration as they are made to think that they should be grateful to Turkey." Uğural had published studies to dispel this idea, showing that Turkey gains more economically from northern Cyprus than the aid that it donates.[31] But these facts do not overcome civil servants' belief that their livelihood depends on Turkey's support. An affect of thanksgiving to Turkey, as well as one of dependence, has been encouraged as a policy by the successive administrations of northern Cyprus. Civil servants have internalized this policy to some degree. However, the dependence on Turkey was expressed as gratitude only in formal, public, or official circumstances. In fact, both resentment and opposition also existed among Turkish-Cypriot civil servants. They reflected on the futility of their jobs and their lack of motivation, relating this to the state administration's lack of sovereignty in northern Cyprus, where the real sovereign is Turkey.

To explain that administrative work under a dependent and unrecognized state does not produce its intended results, one civil servant, Artun Bey, used a Turkish idiom to describe his work:

> It's as if we're pounding water in a mortar (*havanda su dövmek gibi*). Our work in the state office is in vain. For example, one of the duties of our office is to detect illegal workers. For this, we have regulations. There is a plan, a program, a law . . . and we follow these. We follow all the procedures; we open files about the illegal workers, write warning letters to the employers, and send the files to the police. But the police do nothing. There is a policy that supports illegal workers from Turkey under this regime, and the police are attached not to the Ministry of Interior Affairs, as they should be, but to the Turkish army. In other words, the police have to follow not the state administration's but the Turkish army's regulations. And there we have a conflict. The police don't follow our procedure and carry out their task. Therefore, our work is in vain. For this reason, inspectors from our office no longer go out on duty very often to detect illegal workers.

The TRNC can be studied as a two-tiered system in which there are administrative procedures, laws, and regulations on a par with those of legally recognized states, but the functions of the administration are limited to the extent that they depend on Turkey's military sovereignty in northern Cyprus. Recognition of this can help us avoid simplistic analyses of, and projections onto, an illegal state. The TRNC, although unrecognized under international law, is nevertheless a state that implements the practices and procedures of modern legal states. It has modes of governmentality, in the Foucauldian sense akin—at least, in theory and style—to practices in state offices and administrations in other modern states.[32] Promotions are based on social influence and political alliance, and yet appointments and salaries are not completely arbitrary. The salaries of state officials are regulated by law and have a classification and advancement system (*barem*). Civil servants often told me their level on this scale. Likewise, as an example of calculated regulation and "audit," in Marilyn Strathern's sense,[33] civil servants in northern Cyprus are subject to review by higher-level appointees. This system, which produces registers of the service of each state employee (*sicil*), is riddled with corruption, yet a regulating system is in place. In other words, this illegal state is not without legality in its practices and modes of governmentality.

The modes of regulation and practice implemented by Turkish-Cypriot civil servants are interrupted at crucial stages by another mode of power: Turkey's sovereignty in northern Cyprus and aspects of the TRNC regime that support it. Here a Foucauldian analysis that would privilege governmental modes of power in the study of modernity has to be matched with an Agambenian view of the coexistence of governmental and sovereign modalities of power. The TRNC, although illegal and under the sovereignty of another state, is not an administrative system ruled simply or solely by military might. In fact, much like other modern states and legal systems, the TRNC is a two-tiered entity in which governmental and calculable functions are in constant and ongoing tension with modes of sovereign power.

Having said this, the significance of the TRNC's lack of recognition and its dependence on Turkey in the sentiments produced in the public sector cannot be underestimated. In annual ceremonies celebrating the TRNC's independence, posters were hung in state offices that read, "Our Republic Is the Symbol of Our Sovereignty." But while these props of statecraft abounded, civil servants did not have faith in their state's legitimacy or a belief in its "sovereignty." Criticism of the state was common in state offices and, more generally, in social circles in northern Cyprus as I conducted my research. When the electricity went off one day in an office of the state administration, as happened frequently, a civil servant ironically said, "You see what kind of state this is?" A civil servant sitting by his desk also commented, using a self-deprecating idiom that is common among Turkish-Cypriots: "What do you expect from the work of the Muslim (*Ne beklen Müslümanın işinden*)?"[34]

The dependent sovereignty of the TRNC, as well as its unrecognized status, have a role to play in the affect generated by the civil service. Administration is a mode of raison d'être among Turkish-Cypriots; civil service positions are highly sought after. And yet civil service incites bad faith, lack of motivation, caution, and apathy. These mixed feelings about and within the administration must have something to do with the TRNC's complex status as both sovereign and dependent, both independent and unrecognized, both present and absent. "Pounding water in a mortar," the idiom used by one civil servant, expresses well the affect generated by civil service under such a complex arrangement of governmentality, on the one hand, and sovereignty, on the other. The work of the civil servant makes a lot of noise, but lacking results, it often seems fruitless. And at every stage, the procedural work of the civil servant is seemingly interrupted by another modality of power: the military sovereignty of another country. Does the high status associated with the civil service, then, feel like "much ado about nothing"?

The affect engendered by the civil service appears to be contradictory, expressing both want and its lack. But this apparent contrariety in affect in relation to a state administration is also connected more generally with the nature of subjection. "As a form of power," writes Judith Butler, "subjection is paradoxical." Power works through incitement by way of evoking desire in the subject. In desiring to survive, the subject enlists— unknowingly, of course—in the very condition of his or her own subordination.[35] Under the unrecognized and dependent state administration of the TRNC, this intrinsically contrary nature of subjection is evident. The civil service induces desire and apathy simultaneously because that which one wants, and glosses as the condition for one's survival, is an effect of one's dependence and subordination. The coexistence of want and its lack, then, as the affect of civil service here is not contradictory. This is the color, in affective form, of power and subjection.

Affect in the Civil Service

I began this chapter by pointing to a gap in the anthropological literature on bureaucracy. Most recent works on organizations and institutions, following a Foucauldian paradigm, have focused on the rationalizing, regulating, measuring, calculating, and governing aspects of bureaucracies. I have suggested that the civil service under the TRNC does not lack these qualities. However, the focus on governmental rationality and calculability in recent work on organizations gives the impression that bureaucracies work against the grain of affect, to manage, control, pacify, or extinguish it. The ethnographic material I have presented on the civil service in northern Cyprus suggests otherwise. Administrative practices incite a range of affect. But there is no aspect of modern bureaucracy, I would argue, that could be studied as non-affective.

Although recent anthropological work on modern bureaucracies has tended to concentrate on administrations' rationalizing and governmentalizing qualities, students of bureaucracy under totalitarian regimes, such as Arendt and Bauman, focused on the propensity of these bureaucracies to incite excessive and violent emotion. In this chapter, I have studied the administration in northern Cyprus as a "modern" entity through and through. Taking Agamben's lead, I have argued that the TRNC shows a mix of governmental and sovereign political modalities and thus is not an anomaly to modern state systems. Like other modern states, including "legal" ones, the TRNC was established through an act of originary violence—the Turkish army's invasion of northern Cyprus, violence against the Greek-Cypriots, and the appropriation of their properties and belongings. Walter Benjamin has studied such violence at the foundation of modern law.[36] In this sense, the TRNC is not an exotic other as a state structure or "legal" entity. However, while attempting to familiarize the mode of administration of the TRNC by illustrating its modern (i.e., governmental, as well as "legalistic") aspects, in this chapter I have also drawn attention to its particularities by referring to its unrecognized and dependent quality. The specificity of the TRNC bureaucracy expresses itself in the peculiar mix of want and apathy I studied in the civil service. However, this peculiarity should be read not to throw light on a seeming anomaly, an illegal state, but to bring another dimension to thinking on modern forms of administration. In my analysis, affect is to be centered in studies of modern bureaucracy.

5. The Affective Life of Documents

IN RECENT ANTHROPOLOGICAL writing on the state, it has become quite common to conceptualize the entity, polity, or existence of "the state" in quotation marks. The implication, to use the words of Michael Taussig, is that "the state" is "a fetish," an abstraction imagined to be "a thing" in both public-political and scholarly discourse.[1] This emergent literature suggests that the anthropologist might write ethnographies that deconstruct the notion of the state, focusing instead on the everyday social relations that make it up. In this chapter, I focus on the quotation mark not simply as a theoretical tool for deconstruction, but as an anthropological object in its own right, as a device employed in international legal transactions. The reference here is to a state practice that has literally been placed in quotation marks in international documents. An illegal, pirate, or pseudo-state, as it is variously called, the "Turkish Republic of Northern Cyprus" is always placed in quotation marks in references outside northern Cyprus and Turkey to highlight its questionable legal status.

In the legal profession, Costas Douzinas and Ronnie Warrington observe, "disputes about the placing of humble punctuation marks can still make all the difference between the success and failure of cases."[2] Indeed, quotation marks generate specific policy effects in international law.[3] In official documents, as well as in semi- or non-official publications coming out of the Republic of Cyprus, Greece, and the United Nations, all direct and implicit references to the existence of a state in northern Cyprus are qualified by the use of quotes. The use of quotation marks writes and erases the reference to statehood in one motion, mentioning "the thing" without recognizing it. By contrast, references to the Republic of Cyprus are straightforward in international documents.[4]

What interests me is the experience of subjects of this unrecognized state that has been kept on hold (and in question) within quotes. The sorts of transactions that subjects of this state practice have had to undertake to be recognized on paper invite reflections on the problematic boundary between "the legal" and "the illegal" in international law. My objective in this chapter, is to draw attention to what I call the dialectical relation between the legal and the illegal.

International Relations from Below

It would be difficult to write anthropology on Cyprus without a reference to international relations, and, indeed, much ethnographic work on both Greek-Cypriots and Turkish-Cypriots is prefaced with some account of this.[5] However, anthropologists have generally taken international relations for granted, positing it as a background or context for their own micro-analyses. My intention here is to turn international law itself into an object of anthropological analysis.[6] Here, I propose not only a Foucauldian-type discursive analysis of the language of the international system and its truth effects or of policy documents and the production of new forms of selfhood.[7] The hall of mirrors in which legal and illegal papers reflect on one another, the so-called boundaries between the legal and the illegal that people "trespass" in their transactions, and the experiences of being caught in between demand reflections that move further than discourse analysis.

Among young Turkish-Cypriots, international relations and political science have been favorite topics in higher education for decades. Indeed, the language of international relations imbues everyday conversations in Cyprus. One informant reflected, "You see, if Cyprus wasn't considered strategic, we wouldn't have any of these problems." There is enormous public awareness about the positioning of Cyprus on the axis of international interests. Ordinary everyday conversations refer to the recent attempts to hold bi-communal meetings between the Greek-Cypriot and Turkish-Cypriot officials, the last pronouncements of British, American, United Nations, European Union (EU), Turkish, and Greek political leaders, and the various proposed solutions to "the Cyprus problem"—"federation," "confederation," "joining the EU," "integration with Turkey," "union with Greece." The issue of the recognition of the TRNC is a subject of discussion in homes and offices and at coffeehouses. Therefore, a focus on the experience of the subjects of the unrecognized state and their precarious positions in bureaucratic paperwork has much to relate back to the language and practice of international law.

Quotation Marks

Resolution 541 was adopted by the United Nations Security Council on 18 November 1983, three days after the unilateral declaration of independence by Turkish-Cypriot officials in northern Cyprus. Notice how the document constructs a "state" that falls outside the bounds of "the law":

> *Concerned* at the declaration by the Turkish Cypriot authorities issued on 15 November 1983 which purports to create an independent state in northern Cyprus,
>
> *Considering* that this declaration is incompatible with the 1960 Treaty concerning the establishment of the Republic of Cyprus and the 1960 Treaty of Guarantee,
>
> *Considering* therefore that the attempt to create a "Turkish Republic of Northern Cyprus" is invalid, and will contribute to a worsening of the situation in Cyprus, [the Security Council] . . .
>
> *Calls upon* all States to respect the sovereignty, independence, territorial integrity and non-alignment of the Republic of Cyprus;
>
> *Calls upon* all States not to recognize any Cypriot state other than the Republic of Cyprus.[8]

According to this resolution, no symbols, representations, functions, or practices of statecraft employed or undertaken in northern Cyprus are to be recognized. International documents of this sort take great care to refrain from giving any hint of credibility to pariah states. The quotation marks frame references to the "state" and its derivatives, giving the anthropologist clues as to what is considered to constitute proper and improper statecraft according to international law. Study the following excerpt from another United Nations resolution:

> *Gravely concerned* about the further secessionist acts in the occupied part of the Republic of Cyprus which are in violation of resolution 541 (1983), namely the purported "exchange of Ambassadors" between Turkey and the legally invalid "Turkish Republic of Northern Cyprus" and the contemplated holding of a "Constitutional referendum" and "elections" as well as by other actions or threats of actions aimed at further consolidating the purported independent state and the division of Cyprus.[9]

Like "the state," its representatives ("officials," "administrators," "ambassadors") and its functions ("elections," "referendums") are considered fraudulent. The use of the quotation marks in such documents is supported by adjectives such as "purported," "so-called," "pseudo-," "invalid," and "illegal," all putting the existence of the political entity in northern Cyprus into doubt.

We might comment that the producers of such international documents are good deconstructionists, drawing attention to the constructed nature of the state and its functions in much the same way that anthropologists do. However, in the very act of writing off the existence of one state, the producers of international documents inscribe and confirm the existence of other states, and of the intra-state international system itself. In this sort of deconstruction, halted midway, it is possible to validate recognized states in the international legal system against the unrecognized state and its subjects. The quotation marks in these documents may be seen as supporting an international system based on the logic of statecraft.[10] But the quotation marks are a useful analytical device for the anthropologist, as well. When I put legal states, as well as the international system itself, in quotation marks in this discussion, it is to draw attention to the dialectical relation between the legal and the illegal. Jacques Derrida has suggested that "it is in *droit* what suspends *droit*."[11] Arguably, "the law" is well serviced and supported by constructions of "illegality."

In documents produced by the Republic of Cyprus, devices like the quotation mark, allowing for simultaneous reference and erasure, are employed in a similar, sometimes exaggerated, fashion. Observe, for example, the following section from a document published by the Press and Information Office of the Republic of Cyprus:

> The declaration of the so-called "Turkish Republic of Northern Cyprus" which was unanimously declared an independent state by the Turkish Cypriot "Legislative Assembly" on 15/11/83 is the continuation and the zenith of the separatist activities which began on another instigation and with the involvement of Turkey quite openly in '64 but in actual fact covertly from '55. The previous stage was the so-called "Turkish Federated State of Cyprus" which was declared on 13/2/75 and which, in its turn, was the continuation of "The Provisional Turkish Administration" established in 1967. From '63, when the intercommunal friction began and the majority of the Turkish Cypriots, mainly under pressure from their leaders, isolated themselves in enclaves, until '67, the Turkish Cypriots were administered by a General Committee under the Chairmanship of Fazil Kuchuk. . . .

Furthermore, the Turks claim that the Greek Cypriots, unreasonably in their opinion, maintained that they were the legal Cyprus Government and imposed a political and economic embargo on the Turkish Cypriots whom they considered a minority, and at the same time they made recourses to various international fora. That is why the Turkish Cypriot leaders claim the Turkish Cypriots had no other choice but to declare independence without however precluding a final reunification of the island under federal administration. . . .

Recognition of the pseudostate would mean that the legal Cyprus Republic, which is now internationally recognized, would cease to exist and the demand for reunification of the country would cease to be self evident or even completely, naturally understandable. It would be up to the two equal "states" whether they wished to come to an agreement for the federation or confederation and any negotiations for the partnership would begin from the same point for both parties. In other words it would be as if there never was a united and legal state, an invasion, an occupation, refugees; everything would be wiped out. That is the aim behind the declaration of independence in the occupied area of Cyprus.[12]

Here, there is a conflict over statehood and proper international recognition. Hence "officials" in both the south and the north take great care where they place their quotation marks when they produce documents to be circulated for propaganda or administration. In fact, one could get into trouble, under both the northern and the southern administrations, for misplacing or omitting one's quotation marks in official documents or for interacting with institutions on the other side of the border. In documents produced in the south, all of the emblems and practices of the administration in the north are questioned.

Despite this questioning, however, Turkish-Cypriots have been governed by several administrative bodies. They have received birth certificates; they have been schooled at all levels including higher education; they have been allocated housing and title deeds; they have been granted driver's licenses; they have received salaries as state employees; they have applied for pensions and social security rights; they have registered as lawyers and doctors; and they have been conscripted into compulsory military service. Indeed, a state practice of sorts has existed among the Turkish-Cypriots from the period of the enclaves between 1963 and 1974 to the present. And for Turkish-Cypriots who have found themselves subjects of the unrecognized state, an everyday involvement with it has been necessary.

Most documents and titles produced by TRNC institutions are considered invalid by the Republic of Cyprus and the international system.[13] And just as the "state" is unrecognized, so, too, are its "citizens" to the extent that their representation in state-produced documentation is problematic. Those who had only TRNC certificates, diplomas, licenses, or travel papers to show could not (before 2003) reach very far out of northern Cyprus (except to Turkey and, under specific regulations, to other countries). The life histories of individuals in northern Cyprus are marked by documents of the unrecognized state: birth, school, marriage, and death certificates; salary slips; utilities bills; land registry documents; property points; tax forms; and certificates of military service. The Republic of Cyprus considers these transactions in certificates and papers to have a false quality. Indeed, so concerned are they not to recognize administrative practices in the north that statements such as "The pseudo-minister of foreign affairs of the pseudo-state gave a talk at the pseudo-university in the north" are not uncommon. Turkish-Cypriots often joke about this, making up imitations of their own negation in phrases such as "Our so-called artist from the so-called state exhibited his work in the so-called art gallery."

The quotation marks and allegations of illegitimacy in documents coming out of the Republic of Cyprus and the United Nations are countered by similar claims in publications printed in TRNC offices and by their representatives abroad. In a propaganda pamphlet published soon after the TRNC declaration of independence, Zaim M. Nejatigil, "Attorney-General of the Turkish Republic of Northern Cyprus," wrote:

> On 15 November 1983 the Turkish Republic of Northern Cyprus was proclaimed by the unanimous vote of the Legislative Assembly of the hitherto Turkish Federated State of Cyprus. . . .
>
> The Turkish Federated State was set up in 1975 even though no federal structure existed to which it could be federated. The reason behind such a move was to keep the door open for a federation of two federated States. However, in the international field the Turkish Cypriots remained "stateless" because the Turkish "Federated" State did not, and could not, ask for international recognition. Paradoxically, the Greek Cypriot administration claimed to be the "Government" of the whole of Cyprus even though its writ has not run in Turkish areas since December 1963 as confirmed by the then UN Secretary-General in his report S/6228 of 11 March 1965. . . .
>
> All through the process of the intercommunal talks conducted under the aus-

pices of the United Nations since 1975, the Greek Cypriot side assumed, in complete disregard of the present realities, that a unitary "Government of Cyprus" still existed and that the Greek Cypriot administration was that "Government."[14]

However, as much as he attempts to use the same device (the quotation mark) against the Republic of Cyprus, in Greek-Cypriots' actual hands, this act on Nejatigil's part does not produce the effect of "non-recognition" of the administration of southern Cyprus. In other words, Greek-Cypriots do not experience the effects of this particular use of quotation marks in their everyday lives. Internationally, the embargo (economic and political) is on subjects of the administration in northern Cyprus.

Documentary Counter-Reflections

According to a British Home Office document, Derviş Tahsin "arrived in the UK from north Cyprus on 20.4.97 and claimed asylum."[15] "He was in possession of a valid north Cypriot travel document," the immigration officer writes. He was detained, and photocopies of his passport and plane ticket were kept. In the standard first interview, a question-and-answer session, Tahsin was asked what events led him to leave his country. Tahsin said he had been arrested in northern Cyprus because he had refused to participate in a nationalist demonstration. "Why would they arrest you?" asked the immigration officer. "Because of the conflict on the border," replied Tahsin.

> *Question:* These were Turkish Cypriot police and soldiers?
> *Answer:* Turkish soldiers and Turkish Cypriot police.
> *Question:* These are soldiers from mainland Turkey?
> *Answer:* Yes.
> *Question:* Why should they want to arrest their own people?
> *Answer:* Because of the events happening near the border. . . .
> *Question:* What reason did they give you for arresting you?
> *Answer:* Because the Greek-Cypriots were creating problems on the border and they wanted us to go and fight against them. . . .
> *Question:* What sort of trouble occurs on the border?
> *Answer:* Throwing stones and things like that. I am supporting peace not the war in Cyprus.
> *Question:* Are you involved in any political activities?
> *Answer:* No.

After the interview, Tahsin's asylum claim was refused. He received an official letter from the Immigration and Nationality Directorate that read as follows:

Dear Mr. Tahsin . . .

The basis of your claim is that you left North Cyprus because you are frightened of war and only want peace. You also claim to fear arrest from the Turkish security forces because of the conflict between the north and south of Cyprus. You claim that you have been arrested by the Turkish authorities over the years, the reasons being that they want you to go and fight against the Greeks. You claim there is no safety to your life.

The Secretary of State has carefully considered your application but is not satisfied that you are a refugee.

You are the holder of a valid TRNC travel document issued by the North Cypriot authorities in your name. As a holder of a TRNC passport you are considered to be a national of North Cyprus and as such recognised as a citizen of North Cyprus and therefore entitled to all the benefits accruing to any citizens as laid down by the Constitution of 12 March 1985. You do not claim to have any political affiliations, nor do you claim to have had any problems in obtaining a travel document. You do not claim to have had any problems leaving North Cyprus. Your ability to obtain and use this document legitimately indicates to the Secretary of State that you left by normal methods and were of no adverse interest to the North Cypriot authorities. The Secretary of State is therefore of the opinion that you were not at risk from those authorities.

However it is not the North Cypriot authorities that you claim to be afraid of in North Cyprus; it is the Turkish forces in particular whom you claim have harassed you over the years. . . . You also imply that there is no freedom of speech in North Cyprus.

The Secretary of State considers that these claims are not consistent with what is known about the situation in North Cyprus. In forming this opinion the Secretary of State is not satisfied that you have given a true account of events.

The Secretary of State is satisfied that North Cyprus is a fully functioning democracy with respect for human rights. There is no independent evidence to suggest otherwise. Information which is available indicates that in North Cyprus freedom of speech, religion and association with political parties is freely respected. These rights are provided by law. . . .

The Secretary of State is aware that the Turkish Cypriot Army is in North Cyprus at the request of the North Cypriot authorities and these forces work with the North Cypriot authorities. The Secretary of State is of the view that any action that is taken in maintaining law and order would be within the bounds of keeping the peace and that any actions that the security forces take are within the jurisdiction of the legal system as laid down by the Constitution. He is of the view that any complaint you have against the Turkish security forces would be a matter for you to take up through the normal legal channels within your rights as a citizen of North Cyprus. . . .

Having considered all the information available the Secretary of State is not satisfied that you have established a claim to refugee status under the terms of the 1951 United Nations Convention relating to the Status of Refugees. Your application is now refused.

Yours Sincerely,

Asylum Directorate

I would like to place this document from the Immigration and Nationality Directorate of the United Kingdom against the other documents I have presented in this chapter so that they mirror and reflect on one another. The counter-images that will be produced through these multiple reflections is the space in which I will situate my analysis.

Compare, then, United Nations Resolution 541, from which I quoted, with this Home Office document, keeping in mind the reflections of the Republic of Cyprus and TRNC publications I quoted earlier. If the presence of the quotation marks is to be noticed in the references to the TRNC by the United Nations, their absence from the Home Office document is interesting. Britain, like all United Nations member states other than Turkey, does not recognize the TRNC as a "state," And yet, the Home Office document endorses "the law" and validates the "authority" of the TRNC and employs the language of Western liberalism—referring to "democracy," "freedom of speech," and "human rights"—to further grant it legitimacy. Moreover, although the Turkish invasion of northern Cyprus is considered an "occupation" in international legal documents, the Home Office document refers to Turkey's martial law in northern Cyprus to justify its exclusion of the asylum seeker. The immigration officer advises Tahsin to resort to his "rights as a citizen of North Cyprus" and to complain about the army "through the normal legal channels." That the very presence of the Turkish army in northern Cyprus indicates that "normal" measures of legal accountability might not apply is not a consideration that informs the discourse (and action) of the immigration officer. In fact, assuming that a "Turkish" army would protect "ethnic

Turks" in a given territory, and therefore endorsing the ideology of the army itself in its attempt to legitimize its ongoing presence in Cyprus, the immigration officer asks Tahsin, "These are soldiers from mainland Turkey? Why should they want to arrest their own people?" In this ethnicized logic, if Tahsin had been "Greek," his oppression in the hands of the Turkish soldiers would have made sense.[16] Here, although Tahsin has defected from the unrecognized state that he comes from and sought protection in another state, the message of the Home Office is that he ought to continue being a subject of the unrecognized state—hence, the initial refusal of his asylum claim and the order, before his appeal, of deportation to northern Cyprus.

If we once again reflect the United Nations and Home Office documents against one another—documents we might expect to be in agreement within the sacralized zone of "international law"—the construction of the legal international domain, as well as the support and endorsement of the illegal, should be self-evident. Here, then, the anthropologist can easily place the document coming out of the "illegal state" beside the papers produced in "legal states" and analyze them using similar theoretical tools.

Alternative Documents

In the passport section of the Cyprus High Commission in London, the queue is long; the room is full. The passport officers are Greek-Cypriot civil servants. Most of the applicants are Turkish-Cypriots. "All Turkish-Cypriots can apply for Cypriot passports because they are entitled to them," explains a high-level representative of the High Commission. "Cypriot law works," he says, implying a contrast with the unrecognized state in the north that, for him, represents the absence of law. "A Turkish-Cypriot can take the Republic of Cyprus to court for not giving him a passport."

Indeed, since the Republic of Cyprus does not recognize the TRNC, it claims Turkish-Cypriots as its own citizens. "To apply for a passport, you need to show your parents' birth certificates," the High Commission civil servant explains. But birth certificates issued after 1974 under the successive northern Cypriot administrations are not recognized. "If someone born after 1974 has parents who are fifty years old," he says, "he needs to bring their birth certificates." Cyprus was a British colony until 1960, and birth certificates issued by the British are considered valid by Cypriot authorities today if they undergo a recognized revalidation process. "What if a Turkish-Cypriot does not have his parents' birth certificates to show?," I ask. "There are records in Cyprus of all births," the officer explains, "so if someone can't find a document, they can go and check it in the records. Then they have to come and swear that they are the child of so-and-so. Like this, they will be entitled to a Cypriot passport." I do not point out to the officer that at the time (before the opening of check-points in 2003) there was a border that Turkish-Cypriots could not cross to check their records in the south without special permission or connections. But many Turkish-Cypriots went to London to apply for Republic of Cyprus passports through its High Commission in London. Advice and community centers for Turkish-Cypriots acted as intermediaries for such application procedures.[17]

Republic of Cyprus passports gave their holders access to most countries in the EU without a visa. For subjects of the TRNC whose papers were not recognized and who, therefore, had difficulty leaving northern Cyprus, Cypriot citizenship and passports were considered a blessing. From the point of view of international law, their application for Cypriot passports was "legal." The Republic of Cyprus is a recognized state, and Turkish-Cypriots, from the point of view of Cypriot and international law, are its citizens.

However, what looks legal from one perspective is illegal from another. Following the precepts of international law was a dangerous business in northern Cyprus, since it was deemed illegal under the laws of the TRNC. On 12 and 14 April 1998, *Kıbrıs* and *Yeni Düzen*, newspapers published in northern Cyprus, announced a statement by the government that "holders of Republic of Cyprus passports will be charged a fine of 2 billion Turkish liras and given a prison term of 5 months." I was in northern Cyprus at the time of this "passport scandal," as it was called, and Turkish-Cypriots were afraid of being found out for their Republic of Cyprus registration or citizenship. One lower level civil servant said, "I wouldn't get a Cypriot passport because I am afraid. What if they take us in for an embarrassing crime (*yüz kızartıcı suç*)? I am a state employee, I receive a salary from the state. I couldn't take such a risk." This civil servant held a TRNC passport and a passport from the Republic of Turkey. Turkey issues passports to Turkish-Cypriots to use as valid travel documents. This civil servant, however, wanted to help his cousin, who was living in London, to get a Cypriot passport because he could then travel to EU countries without a visa.

As the Denktaş administration was threatening those who would obtain Republic of Cyprus passports, Turkish-Cypriots who were living in northern Cyprus expressed dilemmas about applying for the passports. In popular discourse, Republic of Cyprus passports were called "Greek-Cypriot passports (*Rum pasaportu*)." "I wouldn't want to obtain a Greek-Cypriot passport," said Orhan Bey, a Turkish-Cypriot man, "because I have principles. I wouldn't want to accept Greek-Cypriot policy as it is. But I would like my son to get one so that he can escape from Cyprus and build a life for himself elsewhere." Others who were critical of the TRNC authority, or who lived abroad, were not bothered by such dilemmas and readily applied for Republic of Cyprus passports.

Passports are expensive commodities in international circuits. There is high demand, as well as a large market, for them. Until 1994, the United Kingdom did not enforce visa regulations on holders of TRNC passports. It was easier, at the time, to gain access to the United Kingdom with an unrecognized TRNC passport than with a recognized Turkish one. Therefore, a significant number of individuals from Turkey obtained TRNC passports, paying high prices to the passport mafia operating in northern Cyprus to acquire them. They arrived in the United Kingdom, avoiding the visa restrictions on Republic of Turkey passports, and claimed asylum. The Home Office has since imposed visa regulations on TRNC passports, too. Now it is not possible to embark on an airplane bound for the United Kingdom from northern Cyprus without showing a valid British visa.

Because of these complications, before the opening of checkpoints in 2003 it had become much more difficult, particularly for Turkish-Cypriots born after 1974, to obtain the Republic of Cyprus passports to which they were entitled under Cypriot and international law. The Republic of Cyprus is much stricter toward individuals born after 1974, wanting to distinguish between indigenous Turkish-Cypriots and settlers from Turkey. On one occasion, a young Turkish-Cypriot man born in 1981 in Mağusa (Famagusta) to parents from Baf (Paphos, in southern Cyprus) paid 3,000 British pounds to a passport mafia operating from southern Cyprus to get the Cypriot passport he was entitled to by law. In other words, he had to undertake illegal means to obtain his legal right as a citizen of the Republic of Cyprus. In the border village of Pile (Pyla), to which Turkish-Cypriots were occasionally allowed access by the authorities in the north to meet their relatives from the south, middlemen had sprung up who would escort Turkish-Cypriots to the passport office in southern Lefkoşa (Lefkosia, Nicosia) in return for a fee or who would take documents from Turkish-Cypriots, obtain the passport, and produce it again in Pile in return for an agreed-on payment. There were also Greek-Cypriots who would do this as a favor to their Turkish-Cypriot friends who lived in the north.

Turkish-Cypriots who had worked under the Republic of Cyprus before the troubles were also entitled to pensions. In 1957, under the British administration, a social security law was passed in Cyprus that covered both Greek and Turkish-Cypriots. Those who could document that they had worked in Cyprus between 1957 and 1963, or right before the intercommunal conflicts started, had rights to pensions. In northern Cyprus in 2001, many elderly people were still receiving pensions from the Republic of Cyprus in Cypriot pounds. Applications for Republic of Cyprus pensions were processed by the Dev-İş trade union in northern Cyprus. At a certain point, these applications for pensions from the south were banned by TRNC authorities. Turkish-Cypriots protested, saying that it was their right for having worked under the Republic of Cyprus. The northern Cypriot administration therefore backed down, saying that "most such pensioners will die soon anyway." In 2001, about four thousand Turkish-Cypriots were still receiving such pension payments from the south while living in the north.[18] There were even exchange bureaus advertising that they were able to provide cash in Turkish liras in return for pension checks in Cypriot pounds. The elderly parents of many Turkish-Cypriots still maintained a livelihood in northern Cyprus through Republic of Cyprus pensions.

The Dialectic of Legality

The sorts of transactions that subjects of an unrecognized state have to undertake to obtain legal papers, and the borders they have to cross, over military barricades and legal divides, throw much into question in international legal practices. Viewed with the rationalist logic and rhetoric of international law, the problems for the subjects of the "illegal" state have to do with the anomalous entity, the illegal state itself. This approach, which would isolate and objectify the illegal state for its "piracy," or its breaching of the law, would reproduce the law's mythical representation of itself as an agency that contradicts or counters criminality. I have different suspicions about the law.

If the law were so comfortable with its rationality and legitimacy, why does the obsession with marking the "outlaw" with stylistic devices such as quotation marks and adjectives of negation and doubt persist? The Turkish Republic of Northern Cyprus is interesting as a state that functions outside the accepted boundaries of internationalism. However, the TRNC has been able to maintain itself, I would argue, not against but with the support of international law. This is confirmed by analyses of the complex history of Cyprus that refer to inaction by Britain and the United States vis-à-vis (and therefore their endorsement of) the partition of the island by Turkey's military invasion.[19] I suggest, further, that the TRNC as an illegal state is interesting because it magnifies the international law's underlying support of it by default. To me, as an anthropologist, the TRNC is interesting not because it is an anomaly. I think, instead, that this "state," which appears peculiar, invites anthropological reflection on supposedly normal states. It magnifies the strangeness in "legal" states and in the international system itself.

Paper Bodies

Let us, once again, take a document produced in a legal state and place it beside a document produced in an unrecognized state. Compare, for example, a TRNC and a Republic of Cyprus passport. If we take Jacques Derrida's propositions seriously, we could argue, convincingly, that there is no difference. As a critic of "the metaphysics of presence" as it appears in multiple institutional discourses (including that of the law), Derrida, suggests that "there is no transcendental or privileged signified and . . . the domain and play of signification henceforth has no limit."[20] He questions the very distinction between an original and a copy. Every act of inscription is already a copy, according to Derrida, including that which presents itself as the original. In this sense, there can be no difference between a document written under a legal authority and one produced in an illegal polity. Following this argument, and particularly Derrida's study of "iterability" at the core of the law, Veena Das has argued that the state itself engenders the forgery of its practices.[21] Therefore, one cannot argue that a forged paper contradicts the conditions of possibility set out by the legitimate state authority itself. From a similar theoretical perspective, Brinkley Messick has studied "the existence of tens of thousands of hand-copyists" in Yemen before the advent of lithography and print technology, arguing that "the copy may take on the authority of the original."[22] These anthropological works may be set as precedents for a critique of the "original" or "legal" state, the question that interests me. If we were to deconstruct the notion of the original, in Derridean fashion, we could argue that the documents of both a legal and an illegal state are copies.

As convincing and radical as this argument, derived from deconstruction, may sound, particularly in the way it implicates the authority of legal as well as illegal states, I think it has limitations. I will refrain from making broader claims, for my interest is the ethnographically specific experiences of Turkish-Cypriots as subjects of an unrecognized state. As my account of their experiences seeking legal papers and caught between contradictory documents so far illustrates, for Turkish-Cypriots there is an existential difference between a document of the TRNC and documents of legal states or of the international system. A TRNC passport comes with limitations on access to movement outside northern Cyprus. A Republic of Cyprus passport, by contrast, provides access all over the world. The difference between the two documents experientially is very real for citizens of the TRNC. That is why Turkish-Cypriots have taken such risks, including the possibility of imprisonment under military courts, to obtain Republic of Cyprus passports.

One could argue that the difference, as experienced, is only a difference because international legal discourses would construe an "illegal state," using quotation marks so that there is an effect of difference. True enough. But as Douzinas and Warrington have pointed out, law is the law because it is enforced.[23] In other words, quotation marks are not just artifacts that can be hermeneutically interpreted by the law's critics. The law's enforcing mechanisms have to be studied, too.[24] I will argue that, from the point of view of subjects of the law—in this case, Turkish-Cypriots—there is a difference in the experience of subjecthood under a legal state and an illegal one. Turkish-Cypriots do not experience the same things in the process of applying for TRNC, Republic of Cyprus, Republic of Turkey, and U.K. documents. A document cannot be theoretically abstracted from the historical conditions of its particular production, transaction, and reception. In other words, documents need to be studied and situated in their historical contexts. Even if it can be argued that they are all copies, as copies they do not produce the same effects (or affects) in the experiences of the people who use them.

Legal Forms

Consider the story of Fuat, a Turkish-Cypriot man living in London who felt fear and panic whenever he received a letter from a local British administrative body. He would not open the envelopes on his own; instead, he took them to a community center in Hackney (East London), where Turkish-Cypriot translators deciphered the contents for him.[25] Most of the time, the letters were mundane: a reminder to renew a parking permit from the local council or a form from Inland Revenue to be filled in to claim child tax credit. At the community center, Turkish-speaking social workers mediated between the British state apparatus and the local Turkish-Cypriot community through the process of translation. There was nothing more piercing in Fuat's affective experience of the political than those moments of enforced accountability to the apparently rationalized structure of the British welfare state. The social workers sat in rooms full of forms, files, tea, and smoke, taking immigrants from Cyprus through the steps of filling out official forms.

"We come here to have our forms filled out," Fuat explained on the day I met him at the community center. Shoulders pulled up, his body twisted, he communicated, in cryptic form, how tortuous his experience was of interacting with bodies of the British state. He said he felt rushes of panic each time he was supposed to fill out a document or write a letter to a British authority. He did not fill out the forms; nor did he learn to write letters the way a "proper" British citizen would. He asked the translators to do this on his behalf in periodic attempts to contain his anxiety. The letters to the local authorities were mailed from the community center, and the original correspondence was kept in a file under Fuat's name in a cabinet at the center. Those pieces of paper had such an impact on Fuat's affective experience of the British state apparatus that he did not dare take them back home. Filed away at the community center was all of Fuat's correspondence with the Home Office—his social benefit forms and his household electricity, gas, and water bills—kept for him by the social workers in a safe box.

Correspondence with state bodies via mailed letters, the practice of letter writing to official bodies, and the filing and saving of such documents for future reference may appear ordinary, neutral, or benign activities to those acculturated in Western European complexes of law and statecraft. It may even seem that nothing could be further removed from the spectrum of affect than the clerical side of statecraft. Scholarly works on bureaucracy would have it so, as well, crafting portraits of rationalized Western administrative apparatuses that leave no space for the study of affect.[26]

Community centers that keep files for immigrants who do not know how to engage in writing with bodies of British authority abound in neighborhoods of London where the immigrants live. They are not limited to Turkish-Cypriots. But the filing cabinet in the community center, in my analysis, emblematizes a containment and management of anxious affect in immigrants' interactions with the complex of British law and statecraft. The social worker, who translates, endeavors to mediate the relation between Turkish-Cypriot immigrants and the documents from British state institutions. In the practice of translation by social workers, there is an attempt to calm the affects transmitted by the documents and the ways in which they are interiorized by immigrant subjectivities. The translators assist immigrants in coping with British modes of statecraft by handling their documents for them. The filing cabinet in the community center, as an object this time, serves a similar purpose. Its rational, institutional appearance, a gray container for boring documentation, belies its affective weight for the immigrants. I therefore propose to bear this filing cabinet in mind as an analytical motif, a symbol for the study of contained affect in the domains of European statecraft and bureaucracy. Documents produced by this specific complex of Western European law—or "legal forms," as I tentatively label them—generate nervous affect when they are held and dealt with by immigrant Turkish-Cypriots. It is to this non-rational underside of apparently rationalized state functions that I draw attention.[27]

Ephemeral Papers

Like other people who have to negotiate more than one complex of law and statecraft at the same time,[28] Turkish-Cypriots interact differently with different administrative practices. State apparatuses make themselves apparent in various guises.[29] Here I continue to trace them as they appear in documents and as they are taken in emotively by Turkish-

Cypriots. If the document (or letter) is an emblematic site for the operation of British (and Western European) statecraft, so is it in northern Cyprus, where the self-declared state has mimicked the practices of legal states. Documents are among the primary paraphernalia of modern states and legal systems: They are its material culture. A "wannabe" state has to produce documents to look and act like a state. Therefore, in this section I trace the affective shape that documents take for Turkish-Cypriots when they interact with papers produced by the Turkish Republic of Northern Cyprus.

Papers, especially official written documentation, symbolize permanence in European contexts. Printed or handwritten and signed documentation conveys the image of proof, stability, and durability. In most legal transactions within the Euro-American paradigm, written documents are taken as references for truth or authenticity.[30] I suggested earlier that the TRNC should be analyzed through frameworks used for the study of "modern" administrations. But because the TRNC is unrecognized and considered illegal under international law, there is a peculiarity or difference to documentary practices or transactions under it that any ethnographic study must specify.

When a friend of mine was coming to visit me in northern Cyprus in 1996, I gave her instructions about arrivals, precisely by referring to the unusual aspect of documentary practices here. "When you arrive at the Ercan airport," I told her, "just as you approach the desk of the policeman who checks passports, you will notice a pile of small papers on his stand. Since this state is not recognized, most people don't want to have a stamp of the TRNC in their passports, because with such a stamp you could be barred from entering Greece or southern Cyprus if you ever wanted to travel there." The officials of the TRNC cooperate with passengers through this procedure. They provide visitors with the option of having a piece of paper stamped instead of their passports, thus negating the existence of their state in the very act of asserting it through their uniforms and entry procedures. "Don't lose this paper," I instructed my friend, "because on departure, you will be asked for it again." "What will I do with the piece of paper afterward?" my friend asked me. "You can throw it away," I said, "or if you like, you can keep it as a souvenir." As I was to find out later through my research, this ironic interaction between my friend and me was also felt and experienced by Turkish-Cypriots.

In the entry and exit procedures of their administration, officials of the

TRNC mimic other state practitioners. They check the passports or other travel documents of passengers and prepare to stamp on them the logo of the TRNC. But at that very moment of acting to stamp the documents from other states, the TRNC administrative process interrupts or subverts itself by producing separate pieces of paper for the stamps. I interpret this as evidence of a built-in irony, an ability to be unserious about one's self, in this particular complex of administration, for in the very act of asserting or acting out the existence of their state through the practice of passport control, TRNC officials assist in querying or turning it over. This specific documentary practice reflects the precarious, provisional nature of this particular state practice. An affect of tentativeness and insecurity is reflected and transmitted through its documentary practices.

Similar pieces of paper are provided by TRNC officers at the border checkpoints that have been open between northern and southern Cyprus since 23 April 2003. When they reach the checkpoint on foot or by car, people crossing to the south from northern Cyprus have to produce not only their passport or identity card but also the TRNC piece of paper to be stamped by an officer as a signature of exit. These papers are available at the passport control desks. People write their names, passport number, and citizenship on the pieces of paper, and these are stamped. Similarly, those who are entering northern Cyprus by crossing the border from the south have to fill out or produce these entry and exit papers to the TRNC. Nobody's actual passport, whatever its origin or affiliation, is stamped. When these pieces of paper are full of stamp marks, having been used to cross the border several times, they are discarded. Sometimes, TRNC officers at the border throw away the used papers themselves and ask people to fill out new papers.

Turkish-Cypriots who have lived in northern Cyprus for some time interact with the documentary practices of the TRNC with a degree of nonchalance or indifference. What appears peculiar to anyone not acculturated to this state practice seems normal or familiar to those who are its subjects and live under its sphere of influence.[31] But the same practices arouse the opposite feelings among Greek-Cypriots, inciting anger and frustration. Many Greek-Cypriots criticize the existence of passport control at checkpoints along the border with northern Cyprus, arguing that they assert the partition of their country and the existence of another state in Cyprus that they deem illegitimate. However, numerous Greek-Cypriots have crossed into northern Cyprus since checkpoints were opened in 2003 and have participated in the documentary practices of the TRNC. From the point of view of Greek-Cypriot officers on the opposite side of the same checkpoints, the pieces of paper stamped by TRNC officials are invalid. However, Greek-Cypriot officers have recently been checking TRNC identity cards as proof of Turkish-Cypriot background and status. Therefore, as the rejection of the TRNC—the claim that it does not exist—has become a way for the Republic of Cyprus to assert its own existence, in practical everyday interactions, Greek-Cypriot officers do engage with and, to some extent, acknowledge TRNC documents. In other words, Greek-Cypriots, too, are involved in practices that negate or question the organizing principles of their state, the Republic of Cyprus, in the very moments that they enact its existence. The irony of this situation is appreciated by Cypriots on both sides of the divide.

We could interpret the pieces of paper provided by the TRNC to make travel easier as ephemeral objects. Most documents in Euro-American contexts transmit an affect of permanence. They are taken as proof of authenticity, durability, actuality, and presence. Documents and identity cards of legal and recognized states perform such roles. In the TRNC, in the fashion of Euro-American law and statecraft, documents are taken as proof of existence, too. But the pieces of paper that are discarded once they are full have ephemeral qualities: Now you see them; now you don't. Unlike the documents of so-called legal states, TRNC papers manifest the provisional status of the administrative practice they represent. Rather than being permanent objects of value, TRNC documents transmit an affect of tentativeness. Interestingly, this ephemeral quality is accepted with nonchalance, irony, or indifference by Turkish-Cypriots who are familiar with this documentary practice, in contrast to Western European legal documents, as in the story of Fuat, which incite panic, nervousness, and fear.

Make-Believe Documents

For all of its institutions—for example, the Office of Title Deeds, the Electricity Unit, the Tax Office, the Maps Department, the Post Office, and the Immigration Office—the TRNC has created documents that bear its logo. These documents are highly loaded symbolically because, at each instance of their use and exchange, they not only represent specific identities and transactions but also declare the legitimacy of the TRNC. Because they are not considered legal (and therefore "real") outside the zones of this self-declared polity, I construe them as "make-believe documents" in this analysis.

The population of northern Cyprus has communicated internally for several decades through the medium of make-believe documents and lives in an economy organized around these documents. For example, after 1974, the makeshift Turkish-Cypriot administration allocated houses, land, and property that belonged legally to Greek-Cypriots to Turkish-Cypriots who had arrived from villages and towns in the south. This was done through a point system in which a council of elderly men from each town and village designated the value of the property each family should be allocated on the basis of the size of their previous belongings in the south. The Turkish-Cypriot administrative body was not merely providing temporary shelter. Knowingly defying international law on property and settlement, it considered the transaction permanent and, by allocating property to Turkish-Cypriot refugees, made its subject population party to its operations. In return for the houses and land that were allocated to them—property that still, under international law, belongs to Greek-Cypriots—Turkish-Cypriots were granted title deeds by the Turkish-Cypriot governing body. At a certain point, these title deeds started to bear the logotype of the TRNC, standing as a symbol for the unrecognized state and asserting its very existence. Since 1974, a whole economy has sprung up around make-believe title deeds. Property belonging to Greek-Cypriots has been bought, sold, rented, and otherwise transacted through the use of these make-believe deeds, which are treated as valid documents by the TRNC. So there is a reality, certainly a physicality, to make-believe documents.

Title deeds are only one example of the many documents with which Turkish-Cypriots have been organizing their lives in northern Cyprus. What I want to draw attention to is the Turkish-Cypriots' consciousness or awareness of the make-believe quality of the documents they employ for their transactions. These documents generate a specific kind of affect among the people who employ them. Although many Turkish-Cypriots inhabit Greek-Cypriot property and hold TRNC title deeds, they are not content or completely at peace with this. They often hold the deeds with some trepidation. Many Turkish-Cypriots are acutely conscious that they are living in other people's property and do not feel that they really own it, despite the TRNC deeds. In other words, they hold the TRNC deeds and have conducted transactions with them, yet they do not feel at ease with them. They know that the deeds are not considered legal outside the confines of northern Cyprus, and they are bothered by and even despise these documents.

I want to stress here the affective relations between documents and people. Documents are ideological artifacts. They are not neutral. In some situations, the ideology of documents is not evident to their trans-actors, but under the internationally unrecognized administration in northern Cyprus, the symbolic content of documents is apparent to their users. While Turkish-Cypriots use TRNC documents and everyday life is organized through documentary transactions, Turkish-Cypriots are quite aware of the contradictions in the documents they employ, especially those that hide histories of looting or violence or that have no real security or permanence because the TRNC is not recognized. They relate to the documents they use with a sense of distrust, contempt, and aliena-tion. When documents do not do what they are supposed to—TRNC passports, for example—Turkish-Cypriots treat them with ridicule.

A brief account of the TRNC's Immigration Office and its Passports Unit provides a good example of the nature of Turkish-Cypriots' affective interaction with documents of the unrecognized state. A four-story ce-ment structure painted white inside and out stands close to the bus station in Lefkoşa. This is the unassuming building of the TRNC's Immi-gration Office. It is close to the bus station, because this is where people from Turkey arrive, seeking jobs, housing, and benefits from the TRNC. There is a demand for citizenship in the TRNC on the part of settlers from Turkey, and it is the Immigration Office that processes applications.

The Immigration Office also has a Passports Unit where TRNC citizens can apply for passports. With this passport, one can leave northern Cy-prus only to enter Turkey, because only Turkey recognizes the TRNC as a state. Through a rather complicated process, holders of TRNC passports can also obtain visas to travel to Britain and a few other countries. But because these countries do not recognize the TRNC, they issue their visas to TRNC citizens on separate pieces of paper, akin to the ephemeral papers I explored earlier.

The civil servants in the Immigration Office are all Turkish-Cypriots. In my experience, they are openly ironic, cynical, and humorous about their work. "You are waiting in line to get this passport?," said one to an immigrant from Turkey, dealing with the paperwork as he spoke. "What do you think this passport is good for?" Other civil servants took part in this humorous commentary. "We are trying to get out of this citizenship, and you are flocking in to obtain it? I don't understand!" said one. "This piece of paper is no good outside northern Cyprus, do you know that?," the secretary in the citizenship bureau said jokingly. Thus, in the very act of manufacturing and processing these documents, the civil servants involved in the transactions and authorized to carry them out were turning the documents topsy-turvy by being ironic and cynical about them. These specific documents generated affects of pity, humor, and ridicule among their producers.

Documents of the "illegal" administration incite contempt, evoke unease, and encourage wit among Turkish-Cypriots. Remarkably, they do not instigate fear, panic, or anxiety. Having been used under various transitional administrations, documents of the governing entities in northern Cyprus are familiar ground for Turkish-Cypriots. They have been using versions of such make-believe documents for decades, for all sorts of administrative and other purposes. They know how to interpret and manipulate— or, if necessary, reverse the undesirable effects of—these documents. We could say that through their wit and irony about it, Turkish-Cypriots have made the TRNC a sort of home. We could also say that Turkish-Cypriots have been domesticated by the administration's practices. They know how to read the administration and how to manage their lives within its domain. In other words, this makeshift polity, although unrecognized, has been normalized through decades of administrative practice. And the ironic stance of the Turkish-Cypriots toward their state and its physical representations, as well as their sharp and witty critiques of it, are possible within a context of this sense of familiarity.

Counter-Documents

Turkish-Cypriots have been forced to abandon their rights to internationally recognized and legal citizenship and assume certificates issued by an unrecognized administrative body. Indeed, having been blocked from access to southern Cyprus from the time of Turkey's invasion in 1974 and facing tremendous difficulties in international mobility, they never forgot their entitlement to citizenship under the Republic of Cyprus. It could be argued that in their interactions with TRNC documents, Turkish-Cypriots enact an implicit comparison with Republic of Cyprus papers, which they know are fully and internationally valid. The Turkish-Cypriot community was forced to abandon its subjecthood under the Republic of Cyprus by both discriminatory pressures and attacks by Greek-Cypriots from 1963 and by the creation and enforcement of an alternative administration in the Turkish-Cypriot enclaves and zones. Turkish-Cypriots contributed to the making and sustenance of the successive administrations that have governed them. Yet they have experienced and known their limitations. Turkish-Cypriots' ambiguous relation with TRNC papers has developed within a subtext of knowledge about their rights to legal citizenship in the Republic of Cyprus.

Through the decades when access across the border to southern Cyprus was banned, Turkish-Cypriots found ways to apply for passports from the Republic of Cyprus either through middlemen who secretly operated across the border or by applying for passports through Cypriot embassies and consulates in other countries. In September 2001, for example, when the border was still fully shut, the *Cyprus Mail* (on the Greek side) reported that, "according to officials at the passports office, the number of Turkish Cypriots seeking Cypriot passports usually increases by 10–15 per cent every year, but the rate of increase so far this year has been far greater, with 817 passports already issued in the first eight months of this year, compared to 448 passports for the whole of last year and only 317 in 1999."[32] After 23 April 2003, when passage across the border was allowed for the first time since 1974 through the opening of checkpoints, Turkish-Cypriots began to line up to apply for Republic of Cyprus documentation. The requirements for obtaining Republican passports were the same for Turkish-Cypriots as they were for Greek-Cypriots. Proof of Cypriot parentage or partnership through marriage was sufficient for eligibility. Turkish-Cypriots dug back for Republican documentation that they or their parents had saved through war and displacement. They showed these old birth certificates, which they had not used for decades, keeping them in drawers or lockers, as proof of their Cypriot ancestry or citizenship and right to Republic of Cyprus documents. Those who were unable to locate their old documents, either having lost them during the war or misplaced them over the years, were asked by Republican authorities on the Greek side to take an oath and swear to their Cypriot identity. Having computerized their population files, officers on the Greek side assisted Turkish-Cypriots in locating their personal information. Turkish-Cypriots ran from one state office to the other on the Greek side of Cyprus, obtaining birth certificates or renewing their old ones and applying for

identity cards and passports. Two years after the border opened, the
Greek-Cypriot leader Tassos Papadopoulos declared that about forty thousand Turkish-Cypriots had obtained Republic of Cyprus passports. The
newspaper *Politis*, quoting numbers provided by the Greek-Cypriot gover-
nor of Nicosia (Lefkoşa, Lefkosia), reported in 2005 that since the opening
of checkpoints, 57,291 identity cards and birth certificates had been distributed to Turkish-Cypriots by Republican authorities.[33]

Turkish-Cypriots know that they have rights to obtain Republic of Cyprus documents because the Republic, since its foundation, was meant for
both the Greek and Turkish-Cypriots. The massive move to apply for updated Republican documentation is a way to reclaim these rights as citizens of the Republic. On the one hand, this rush could be interpreted as a
way to retrieve a lost, yet "authentic," identity while simultaneously obtaining "legal" forms to replace or complement the unrecognized and "illegal" documents of the TRNC. However, aside from the elderly population
of Turkish-Cypriots who hold memories of interacting with Republican
papers, for most Turkish-Cypriots—especially young ones—Republican
documents felt less "authentic" (even if they were "legal" and internationally valid) than their TRNC documents, which had been normalized
through decades of use in northern Cyprus. The term "Greek-Cypriot
passport" precisely expresses this feeling of remove from the documents
in the very practice of claiming them. Even as they rush to obtain passports from state offices in southern Cyprus, Turkish-Cypriots feel that the
Republic of Cyprus belongs to Greek-Cypriots. The passport has been
personified and allocated an ethnicity. But the passionate desire to obtain
Greek-Cypriot passports, as well as other Republican documentation, cannot be interpreted as only a pragmatic move on the part of Turkish-
Cypriots. Turkish-Cypriots are not lining up to get Republican passports
simply because the Republic is a member of the European Union and the
passports guarantee international access without visa requirements. For a
group of people whose access to the world was blocked for decades, my
informants told me, "Greek-Cypriot passports" symbolized an opening up
(*açılmak*). "This place has opened up (*ortalık açıldı*)," Turkish-Cypriots
would say in reference to the freeing of access through checkpoints across
the border. The passports also signified a reunion with a time past, before
a bifurcated life. Therefore, we could interpret that, though branded
"Greek-Cypriot" and held with some reserve, Republican documents have
been claimed by Turkish-Cypriots as a way to overcome decades of frustra-

tion and repression. We could even say that for Turkish-Cypriots, applications for "Greek-Cypriot passports" are a political act, a willing or unwilling commentary, through a relation with state objects, on their state of discontent as subjects of the unrecognized regime in the north. For some, the receipt of Republican documents produced feelings of jubilation at the possibilities they would bring, including an opening up to the world.

Counterfeit Passports

In January 2006, the Lefkoşa Chamber of Justice announced that it had identified a ring of dealers who were producing counterfeit passports and smuggling people out of northern Cyprus. The Turkish-Cypriot police searched the suspects, confiscating the tools and technology they allegedly used to fabricate documents in their homes and offices. The *Yeni Düzen* newspaper reported, "The police, after the court procedures, exhibited the objects they had collected during their operations: the computers, laptops, counterfeit identity cards and passports, documents, CDs and diskettes which had been used in the making of counterfeit identities."[34]

In this final section, I explore what it means for an illegal state, whose documents are considered invalid outside its territory, to identify counterfeit documents through a legal procedure. Here is a definition of an illegal domain within an illegal one, throwing the very definitions of legality into question. My intention in bringing the discussion in this chapter to a close is to complicate the differences between what I have tentatively, and heuristically, called make-believe documents, legal forms, and the counterfeit. What affects are generated by counterfeit passports, and how are they similar to and different from make-believe documents and legal forms?

At strategic moments, Turkish-Cypriots call TRNC documents "fake (*sahte*)." For example, Turkish-Cypriots criticize their government's distribution of citizenship certificates to Turkish nationals before elections as "counterfeit citizenship." In October 2003, *Yeni Düzen* reported that the Immigration Office had been allocating TRNC citizenship to Turkish nationals who had never even set foot in Cyprus in the interest of registering them in the voting ballots in favor of the regime's right-wing and nationalist parties. One journalist, publishing on an Internet site, wrote, "Those who know no other way than manipulating the will of the people before the elections, in order to ensure the endurance of the status quo with the coming elections in the Turkish Republic of Northern Cyprus, have been endeavoring to import votes by creating counterfeit citizens."[35] We could say that this is an identification of a fake within a fake, or of a forgery of the forged. However, I suggest a more complicated analysis.

Although considered illegal internationally, a legal system of sorts has been in place in northern Cyprus for decades. And despite the fact that the documentary practices of the TRNC are considered invalid by the international community, a legal system (and understanding) that internally recognizes its own documents, with its own differentiations of the authentic and the counterfeit, has been operating there. In other words, we are speaking about legal procedures (as well as a legal consciousness) within the confines of an illegal state. This makes the distinction between the legal and the illegal more complicated. Through political tensions and rivalries in northern Cyprus, pressure groups on different sides of the political spectrum force one another to face up to the law. Although there is a play on the official counterfeit status of the TRNC in the phrase "counterfeit citizenship," the creators of this framing intend a different nuance. Citizenship certificates handed out to Turkish nationals who have nothing to do with Cyprus are differentiated from documents held by Turkish-Cypriots who regard themselves as the just claimants of rights under the TRNC. In other words, on this occasion citizenship certificates held by Turkish-Cypriots would be internally considered or called not counterfeit documents but legal entitlements. So we have to differentiate between the counterfeit and what I have called, by reference to TRNC documents, the make-believe. Forgery and mimicry are not the same. If the Republic of Cyprus considers all TRNC documents, especially title deeds, counterfeit, the difference between these documents, which have a circuit of operation within the confines of a complex of law and statecraft, and those fabricated completely outside the bounds of any legal practice must be stressed. A counterfeit state defines its own counterfeits, a smaller doll within a larger Russian doll.

A nuanced study of law and the illegal in the domains of document production would ask that we refrain from reproducing the political language of states or international organizations and, instead, invent new frameworks for analysis. With the category of the make-believe, I have attempted to illustrate the performative and phantasmatic, as well as the mimicked, quality of TRNC documents. I have wanted ethnographically to illustrate facets of the assumption of law and statehood in the face of isolation. Although documents produced by the TRNC are certainly counterfeit under international law, especially the title deeds handed out in return for inhabiting Greek-Cypriot property, a legal practice of sorts has existed in northern Cyprus that identifies its own outcasts. In other words, the illegal state has its own others. It is important analytically to differentiate, then, between make-believe and counterfeit documents while also remembering their similarities. What I have identified as mimicry in the state practices of the TRNC, a fashioning of one's self in the model of other legal states, is different from the forgery practiced by those who smuggle people across the border. Yet if we wanted to be more radical in our analysis, could we not argue that all documentary practices, including those under the sovereignty of legal and recognized, established states, have aspects akin to the practice of forgery? Although my suggestion here may appear to negate outright the rule and logic of law, I intend to suggest a subtle critique: In the light of the ethnographic material I have presented, it is difficult to distinguish clearly between the legal and the illegal, the authentic and the counterfeit, the true and the fake. Perhaps TRNC material could push us to consider the "fake" qualities of what I have heuristically, and tentatively, called legal forms, too.

Affective Documents

In an article in which she engages with the work of James Fernandez, Begoña Aretxaga analyzes representations as affectively charged phenomena. Metaphors, in her reading, are not simply constructions or images that are removed from social reality; in her words, metaphors "*do* things." They engender and enact political affects.[36] Here representations and affects are studied as one and the same thing: "Rather than take it for granted, the link between an image and an affective state (of desire, fear, exultation, or contempt) taking hold of people in the theater of politics seems to me in need of interpretation."[37]

In this chapter, I have studied not representations but objects, physical things, as phenomena that generate affect. I argue that state-like structures make themselves evident to the people who inhabit their domains in the form of materialities. Documents are among the most tangible phenomena that induce state-like effects. Here I use the word "tangible" to mean both "that [which] can be clearly seen to exist" and "that [which] you can touch and feel."[38] I carry the study of affect and the political, then, to the study of objects.

Annelise Riles has studied documents, and in fact the law itself, as "an object."[39] Reading such a study of documents, giving due value to the potency of artifacts, one would have thought that it would loosen the potentialities of objects to allow and illustrate their sensual and excessive, affective character. However, Riles prefers to focus on "the form" of documents, its patterns and design.[40] She writes, "I wish to borrow the parallel I observed between the uses Fijian delegates made of documents and mats in order to focus on some dictates of form in international agreements. I wish to consider the way the form of these documents made manifest a reality of levels and levels of realities through a simultaneous and mutual apprehension of the document as pattern and the document as an independent object or unit."[41] Riles presents a methodology for the study of documents. She suggests that we abstract out the structure and composition of these objects: "The character of the pattern—a simple logic that linked words, paragraphs, documents, or conferences— entailed the collection of a potentially infinite number of concrete and distinct entities (words, paragraphs, conferences) into a straightforward digital sequence of numbers and letters."[42] In my reading, this search for aesthetics and form in the document may involve a sterilization and neutralization in that it distracts the analysis from the more poignant potentialities of political objects of this genre. Based on my ethnographic material, I suggest a different understanding of the document. Rather than consider the contoured and formal aesthetics of documents in the manner of Riles, I am interested in exploring the multiple and contingent affects that documents engender in their holders and transactors. I argue that documents, like other objects, have an affective underside. The panic and fear, wit and irony, cynicism and familiarity that documents induce among Turkish-Cypriots in the various situations in which they encounter them is evidence precisely for such an effect. Through this study of documents as affectively charged phenomena, my intention has been to extend the study of affect into another arena: into the study of objects and materialities in a political field.

Documents, among the material objects of law and governance, are affectively charged phenomena. They are not self-contained or sterile; rather, they transmit specific kinds of energy among their users.[43] Documents may become interiorized objects in their transactors. They get transformed; they take other shapes. In Turkish-Cypriots' experiences of Britain, documents are charged with uncertainty and threat. In the TRNC, they are cozily despicable: They provoke irony, cynicism, familiar contempt, and wit. Documents are affective: They produce and effect affect.[44] They take the shape of or transform into affect and become part of their handlers in that way.

Part III   Objects and Dwellings

6. Abjected Spaces, Debris of War

IN 1999, WHEN THE BORDER with the Greek side was still closed, I spent time, lingered, walked, sat, and spoke with people who lived along the border (the Green Line) on the northern side of Lefkoşa (Lefkosia, Nicosia). Rust had infested any metal surface along the border that ran through neighborhoods and streets, as well as houses. Apartment blocks facing the Greek side were covered with bullet holes. Old buildings lay abandoned by their owners, with bushes, grass, and trees emerging through broken windowsills and growing out of collapsed rooftops. Old craftsmen's shops were locked with rusty shutters. Red-colored signposts of a soldier with a gun reading "Forbidden, No Access, No Photography" stood in the middle of every street leading out of the central marketplace (*arasta*). There were few people around: old folks whose families had moved outside the walled city (*surlar içi*) and workers and their families who had recently migrated from Turkey. The middle-class Turkish, Greek, and Armenian-Cypriots who once inhabited these quarters were nowhere to be seen. The border area was full of items thrown aside, things left behind, rubbish rotting away, and abandoned old objects.

On many occasions, while walking alongside the convoluted border area, zigzagging through and around bisected streets, I recorded lists of every item I could see. One of my lists reads:

a rusty fire escape, connecting two stories of an old house [see figure 7]

a plastic water bottle, flattened and thrown aside

children's drawings on the wall separating the Turkish side from the United Nations ceasefire zone

a thin black cat

the half-erect side wall of a ruined old building of yellow stone

a semi-burnt pine tree

spilled piles of garbage

a used tire lying on the ground

an old oven filled with used newspapers

the skeleton of a building, with a collapsed roof-top, broken windows, and no
windowsills

a dirty blanket lying on the side of the road

dog shit

rusty paint tins

broken pieces of wood

a dusty old shoe

clothes hanging over an electric wire

red car parts

the license plate of an old car

bullet holes on the side walls of buildings

the rusty skeleton of an old pushchair

an old mattress, with inside turned out

broken beer bottles on the ground

a semi-broken old wooden balcony

basil leaves growing inside a tomato paste tin

My list goes on, a record of every thing that I could touch, smell, and see.
The border was full of rubbish, debris left behind from the war and the
political stalemate that followed. What was deemed useful was taken and
stored or sold. The remainder was abandoned. Here one could draw an
itinerary of leftovers or collect war memorabilia. Rust and dust covered
every surface.

Few people walked by; even fewer lived there—certainly very few Turkish-Cypriots, and among them mostly the very elderly. Occasionally, one
heard the noise of a car passing by or of the children of immigrants from
Turkey playing ball in the neighboring streets. Ruined old buildings left
behind by Armenian, Turkish, or Greek-Cypriots were now inhabited by
workers from Turkey who had come to northern Cyprus, sometimes with
their families, in search of menial jobs. On Sunday mornings, one heard
the chime of church bells from the Greek side. The skeletal remains of an
Armenian church, with its icons ripped away, windows broken, and marble stones demolished, sat quietly in this once mixed Armenian and
Turkish-Cypriot neighborhood. Piles of litter and refuse had been left
next door (see figure 8).

7. Makeshift staircase leading to a broken balcony on a street blocked by the border in Lefkoşa.

below 8. Border objects.

As I spent time in these spaces and lingered in these surroundings, day in and day out, I experienced a sense of eeriness that spoke through the ruins. Every piece of debris seemed uncanny. It was as if the broken walls, the wrecks of buildings, and the bullet holes had been halted midway in speech; as if they had been stunted, retaining waves of emotion inside them, ready to explode if scratched. The space transmitted an energy of its own, which went through my body. I felt uneasy, disturbed, out of place.

As I walked through these spaces and wrote my notes, I wondered how the old ladies who lived along the border felt about the ruins. Or the immigrants from Turkey who had settled next door. And the Turkish-Cypriots, who had mostly moved out of the walled city of Lefkoşa into newly built middle-class neighborhoods and suburbs. Did this space feel as uncanny to them as it did to me? "We have gotten used to this," said an old Turkish-Cypriot woman living in the border area. "No, these ruins don't disturb me." "I used to feel awful walking by the ransacked Armenian church," said a Turkish-Cypriot man in his late twenties who lived outside the walled city, away from the border area. "But crossing by to go to work every day, I no longer notice." How could this debris not hurt?, I wondered. How could it seem normal? To me the wrecks of the buildings, the walls, and the piles of rubbish seemed so alive, as if they silently spoke their secret memories.

The border area of Lefkoşa, as well as many other areas, seemed to me like an open wound. But if its present inhabitants said they did not feel like that, was it not in the ruins, then, that energy was retained? Was the creepy wave I felt through my stomach only a reflection of my subjectivity, my own projections onto the built (or destroyed) environment, my own constructions, my transference? In time, I was to learn that this need not be an either–or question. I would locate energy neither in the wreckage nor in the people. The specific relationship between the people and the debris, and how this has changed through time, is what I had to study.

Affect and Politics

In this chapter, I study affective interactions between people and a ruined physical environment along a border area. As we have seen, in the psychoanalytic literature, affect has predominantly been associated with subjectivity or the self. Or, the inner world (the unconscious) of the individual has been conceptualized as the kernel through which energy is discharged. For example, the French psychoanalyst André Green argues that "the affect refers to subjective quality."[1] Here, affect is conceptualized as an energy that emerges from, and is therefore qualified by, a person's subjectivity. For something to be called "affect," Green argues, it has to be bound up in the coils of the subjective world, the inner world of the person. Or it is the subjective world that gives a quality to cathectic energy, therefore enabling us to interpret it as "affect."[2]

It follows from this psychoanalytic line of thinking that the affective energy we feel, as we inhabit or move through an environment, is our own subjective transference (or projection) onto that environment. In this reading, we ourselves give this environment a "quality," feeling it in a certain way. Accordingly, to each his own affect; to each her own inner world.

In contrast to this position, let us consider cultural constructionist work on the emotions as developed by anthropologists. In this reading, affect and the emotions are studied under the same rubric (as referring to the same thing) and as a cultural phenomenon. Accordingly, the emotions are culturally constituted, understood, interpreted, managed, and framed. They are contingent and contextual. Numerous ethnographies have been written in this vein, studying the culturally attuned meanings of specific emotions.[3] Many of these studies have taken language as a conveyor of emotional experience and, therefore, as the representation of "culture."[4] In its critique of psychoanalysis (read as a Eurocentric discourse and practice), this body of anthropological literature has brought to light non-Western discourses about the emotions. And yet, while human beings are studied fundamentally as cultural beings, they nevertheless remain, in works in this vein, the main agents (or originators) of affective energy, read as "the emotions."

To be considered alongside this literature, is the long tradition of studying affect and politics in European social theory, particularly critical theory coming out of the Frankfurt School. In works by Theodor Adorno, Elias Canetti, and others, we see a fascination with the political figure of the crowd, the masses, or the mob.[5] Developing a theory of fascism by engaging with Freud's essay *Group Psychology and the Analysis of the Ego*, Adorno sees in the masses a sinister potential for worshipping the father figure, the leader. Such works, emerging out of wartime Europe, have placed affect firmly within the domain of the public sphere, enabling us to now study affect as a political and politically generated phenomenon. Yet in these works, "politics" or "the political" is imagined as a broader category of "the person"—as a crowd, if you will, of human beings. The idea is that when people are massed together as a group, a different kind of energy is projected: Their individuality goes amiss, and they are pulled or directed toward aims or projects in which, if left alone, they would not have gotten involved. Indeed, in this literature inspired by Freud (and Marx), the individual is the main psychical and political agent because the social and the political are conceived as the individual writ large.

More recent work on affect and politics has challenged old associations between the emotions and the private sphere. Building on a long tradition of feminist theory, literary scholars such as Lauren Berlant and Glenn Hendler have studied what they call "public sentiments."[6] They have convincingly argued that, far from being "personal" phenomena, having to do with the privacy of the individual, the emotions are always and already public and political. Studying American novels of the nineteenth century, Hendler argues that sentiments such as sympathy were politically and pedagogically inculcated. Berlant has produced a similar analysis of compassion.[7] The contribution of this work, mostly coming out of literary criticism, is to illustrate the ways in which the public sphere is a source of affect. Yet as in critical theory's imaginings of the political, here, too, politics is conceptualized first and foremost as a sphere of human or intersubjective action and interaction.

I propose, in what follows, to treat affect and politics in a new light, where neither affect nor politics is a singularly human (or subjective) phenomenon. In this chapter, I trace not so much how affect is employed or produced politically as how it is generated out of interactions with spaces and materialities—in this case, a postwar environment. I study war debris, abandoned buildings, looted objects, leftovers, ruins, the border, and the decaying environment of Lefkoşa as spaces and objects that, retaining memories of a political history and specific policies, evoke special kinds of affect among the people who live there. I am interested in how political debris—here, the remains of war—generates conflicted and complex affectivities. I argue that affect is to be researched not only as pertaining to or emerging out of human subjectivity (or the self), but also as engendered out of political engagements with space and entanglements in materialities.

In *The Transmission of Affect*, Teresa Brennan writes:

Any inquiry into *how* one feels the other's affects, or the "atmosphere," has to take account of physiology as well as the social, psychological factors that generated the atmosphere in the first place. The transmission of affect, whether it is grief, anxiety, or anger, is social or psychological in origin. But the transmission is also responsible for bodily changes; some are brief changes, as in a whiff of the room's atmosphere, some longer lasting. In other words, the transmission of affect, if only for an instant, alters the biochemistry and neurology of the subject. The "atmosphere" or the environment literally gets into the individual. Physically and biologically, something is present that was not there before, but it did not originate *sui generis*: it was not generated solely or sometimes even in part by the individual organism or its genes.[8]

Dealing with the kinds of objections that her propositions provoke, Brennan writes, "We are particularly resistant to the idea that our emotions are not altogether our own," and goes on to critique what she calls the Eurocentric notion of the "emotionally contained subject."[9] Her very use of the term "transmission" for a theory of affect encourages the imagination of more fluid boundaries, flow, and passages between individuals (intersubjectively), as well as between human beings and the environment.[10] She writes:

> I am using the term "transmission of affect" to capture a process that is social in origin but biological and physical in effect. The origin of transmitted affects is social in that these affects do not only arise within a particular person but also come from without. They come via an interaction with other people and an environment. But they have a physiological impact. By the transmission of affect, I mean simply that the emotions or affects of one person, and the enhancing or depressing energies these affects entail, can enter into another. A definition of affect as such is more complicated.[11]

In this interpretation, the reference points for affect are not to be found within the individual or her subjectivity and inner world alone. Instead, affect, almost like mercury, is an energy of sorts, on the move, one that knows no bounds—hence, the metaphor of "transmission."

However, having charted the terrain for studying energies transmitted through the atmosphere, muddling the boundaries between the individual and the environment, Brennan then focuses the rest of her study on the transmission of affect intersubjectively, or between individuals. In so doing, she returns to an old question in the psychoanalytic literature on transference and counter-transference and leaves aside what is to me the more interesting (and certainly less studied) field of interactions between the person and her or his environment. She writes: "Visitors to New York City or Delphi testify happily to the energy that comes out of the pavement in the one and the ancient peace of the other. But investigating environmental factors such as these falls outside the scope of this book. This initial investigation is limited to the transmission of affect and energy between and among human subjects."[12] I explore precisely the terrain that Brennan left aside, that feeling discharged by the environment or produced through an interaction between human beings and their material surroundings.

Bordering Ruins, Living with Rubbish

Two soldiers wait on duty, under a tree, to protect themselves from the piercing sun. I park my car in the shade and walk into the walled city of Lefkoşa through a small alleyway. I see a house with an Ottoman numeric inscription, indicating it was built in 1919. The paint on the door has peeled off, and the house is locked. Through the half-broken shutters, I

9. Rubbish along the border.

notice that the house has lost its glass windows. Peeking through, I see a pink plastic wash basin. A small blond child, without shoes, sits on the front steps at the entrance to the house. I learn that he is called Turgay. Does anybody live here? I ask. He says yes.

Many contemporary residents of the walled city of Lefkoşa live in such spaces, immigrants from Turkey who have settled with the hope of finding jobs, as well as old people left behind by their children. Half-torn mattresses, eaten by moths, have been covered with cardboard paper. Patched pieces of cloth have been hung to dry over old, limping Ottoman-style sofas. A plastic sieve here; a wooden spoon there—utensils found here and there have been combined to create a new life. One bottomless chair with torn matting on one side; a worn-out sofa on the other. An old woman pulls a big sack of personal odds and ends with a string behind her on the ground. In her bundle are her belongings—a woolen bed cover, a towel, a pot, a pan—all tied up tightly together with strings.

I walk a little farther and reach the border area again. An open space, right beside the border, has been turned into a garbage dump (see figure 9). Bones of recently butchered animals lie on the ground, covered with flies. Watermelon husks and other food remains, plastic bags, bottles, and cans are all scattered about. I make my way through half-eaten figs and crushed tomatoes to reach the other side of the road.

In front of a house right along the border, two women sit, cutting red peppers to dry under the sun. I approach the house, which is leaning to one side from structural damage. One of the women warns me to come no farther, saying, "This is the border." She also volunteers her opinion on the border. "In fact," she says, "to tell you the truth, they don't do us any harm. We hear no sound from the other side. But it is our people, the ones on this side, who hurt us. The other day, they wanted to throw us out of this house." I ask the woman where she is from. She tells me her story of arriving in northern Cyprus from Hatay in southern Turkey, from a village that borders Syria. She tells me how her main problems are with her Turkish-Cypriot landlords and employers. Then, seeing that I am curious about the border, she says: "Have you climbed to the top of that building? You can see the other side well from there."

I walk to the block of apartments next door. The empty-looking building does not appear very solid as I climb it. It is a structure from the 1960s, abandoned to its fate. But I notice that some apartments have inhabitants. Mud and dust have grown on the steps leading to the top floor. To my amazement, the entire top floor remains as it was in the days of war, as a shooting point. Sacks of sand were placed on top of one another to hide and protect the soldiers. Through decades of ceasefire, no one had removed the sand sacks.

I speak with an old Turkish-Cypriot man who lives with his wife in a house very close to the border. His children, now grown up, have moved out of the area and to the suburbs. "A shroud (*kefen*) has been draped over Lefkoşa," he says. "Lefkoşa is now deceased (*Lefkoşa ölmüştür*)."

Old People, Workers, Old Things

I met Naciye Aba in 2001. She was in her late seventies and lived in an area of old car workshops neighboring Lefkoşa's border area. She looked after a saint's tomb, the Tomb of the Seven, facing the mostly shut craftsmen's workshops. Her home, right across from the tomb, was an old coffee shop, a lengthwise rectangular structure built of cement. It had no windows, only an iron gate that she kept open for sunlight and air. Naciye Aba told me the story of how she ended up living there: "I used to work for the owner of this coffee shop. Then the fighters [*mücahitler*, referring to TMT fighters] gave it to me to live in. Thank God for that, too. It doesn't have a bath. I heat water and clean myself in this corner. It doesn't have a toilet, either. Thanks to God, they gave me the key to the Seven's Tomb, so I use the toilet in there. But that is across the street, so I have problems going out there at night. I have no kitchen, either. We put a small stove over here, and that's where I cook my food."

On the shelf that Naciye Aba had turned into a kitchen, there were about thirty empty plastic Coca-Cola and other soda bottles in a pile. Odds and ends had been piled on top of each other, things that had meaning and use for her. Above the gas cooker was a newspaper clipping of a photo of Rauf Denktaş in his youth. Naciye Aba had collected mallow leaves for cooking. "I gathered these from the field behind the hospital," she said. She sat, separating the good leaves from the bad ones. She would then boil the leaves and make dinner out of them.

"During the war," Naciye Aba said, as she broke some mallow leaves away from their stalks with a knife, "I worked at the military station (*mevzi*) next door. Every day, I baked bread and cooked tea for the fighters (*mücahitler*). My general liked me very much. . . . One day, I fell ill from sadness (*maraz*). Somebody reported me, asking that they kick me out of the job. I went to a doctor. The doctor checked me over. He said to the fighters, 'Have you no shame? This woman has suffered so much and has looked after you and now you are going to kick her out?' This way I stayed at the military station for another seven years." When the Greek-Cypriots left, she continued,

> I was given this coffee shop to live in. The coffee shop used to belong to a Greek-Cypriot man who was my employer (*usta*). All the other shops from here to the Arabahmet neighborhood belonged to Armenians. But after 1963, this place became the border with the Greek side [and the Armenians left]. This cement building, next to the lathe operator, didn't exist, either, so I was left right in the crossfire. One day, my son arrived, wearing his fighter's clothes. He came inside. They saw him from a shooting point on the Greek side and shot right through into the shop. Can you see [showing me the wall]? The bullet holes are still there. What can I do? Do I have the money to paint over them?
>
> Then, one day, my daughter and my new employer's daughter were sleeping at the back, side by side. At nighttime, there was shooting in this area. Bullets hit all four walls of the shop; one of them just missed the leg of my employer's daughter. After that incident, we dug a hole through the wall at the back of the shop so we could go in and out through there, without being noticed by the Greek-Cypriots at their shooting points. The fighters used to come in and out of that door, too.

The makeshift back door was still there, now covered with a zinc plate. So were the bullet holes. "I covered one of them," said Naciye Aba. "If you lift that picture of Ajda Pekkan [pointing to a magazine clipping of a Turkish actress], you'll see there is a bullet hole under that."

> Every day I hear the chime of church bells from the other side. We don't hear the sound of people, but we hear bells. Especially on Saturday and Sunday, they ring their bells every fifteen minutes. . . . All of this area used to be full of [Turkish-]Cypriots. But they all found housing and property elsewhere and moved out; others died. There are only five or six of us [Turkish-]Cypriots (*Kıbrıslı*) left here; all the rest are from Turkey, from Hatay. Those who came from Turkey, I don't know where they work, but they find jobs and get salaries from somewhere. They don't disturb me.

I looked around Naciye Aba's home. I saw:

Plastic bottles to store water
A portrait of Mustafa Kemal Atatürk
A framed picture of Rauf Denktaş

Framed photographs of the Turkish and Turkish-Cypriot national heroes
    Namık Kemal, Dr. Küçük, and Atatürk

A framed photograph of the first martyrs, wrapped in red star and crescent

A framed photograph of Naciye Aba's son in a fighter's uniform

A framed photograph of Naciye Aba's mother wearing the black veil

Magazine clippings of actresses from Turkey

A second portrait of Atatürk

A framed verse from the Qur'an on the wall

A clipping of Bülent Ecevit, Turkey's prime minister in 1974, when Turkey
    invaded Cyprus, pasted to the door of a cupboard

A picture of Naciye Aba's daughter in a fighter's uniform

Pieces of cloth in plastic bags

A half-broken bicycle

Bullet holes in the walls

A makeshift door at the back, covered with a zinc plate

"The roof next door has collapsed; a lot of cold air comes through that door," said Naciye Aba. "There is a lot of humidity in here; upstairs, one of the walls has been almost completely destroyed by humidity." There are no windows in Naciye Aba's dwelling, no toilet, no bath. "If I want to go to the toilet at night, I do the small one here and the big one at the Seven's Tomb. Thank God there aren't any bad people in this neighborhood," she said. And looking at her walls, she said, "I had pasted the photos of my brothers and sisters on the cupboard and they got angry with me, so I replaced them with pictures of actresses." Showing me around, she said, "I keep olive leaves in these plastic bags to burn as incense [against the evil eye]. They also brought me some bread from the village; it's in that other bag. When I have a headache, I boil eucalyptus leaves or sage. I put them in plastic bags, because I have nothing else to put them in."

I walked out of Naciye Aba's house, kissing her hand as I left, through the car workshops in the neighborhood of the Seven's Tomb (see figure 10). I spoke with the mechanic there. "This car is left from 1976. That one is from '78. . . . But we also have cars left from the Greek-Cypriots (*Rumdan kalma*)," he said. I passed by another '60s car, sitting with its parts torn out. That one was also "left from the Greek-Cypriots," he said. "We sell the old parts of some of these cars; others we repair."

Across from the workshop, I visited Ali and his family, who lived in a room that was part of an old shoe factory, right beside the ruins of the Armenian church. Ali, in his mid-thirties, had settled here in 1983, having immigrated from Adana in southern Turkey. He worked on construction sites for a Turkish-Cypriot employer. In the space underneath the old shoe factory, families who had settled from Turkey had crafted chicken coops out of garbage they collected here and there. There were rusty car parts, old iron rods, and garbage everywhere. An old-fashioned bathtub sat in a corner in the space under the factory where small children were playing. Ali told me how he and his family ended up living in the old shoe factory:

> Those who came before us say they found shoes everywhere. When we arrived, there were no more shoes left. We split the rooms of this factory by building makeshift new walls. We erected these walls to make more living space and like this we made a home. [He showed me the wall he had constructed to create two rooms for his mother, his brother, and his brother's family who had come with him from Turkey.]
>
> My wife was a [Turkish-]Cypriot. We separated. I have three children from her; they live with her family. Our cultures don't match with the [Turkish-Cypriots]. They lived under the British; they lived with the Greek-Cypriots. They are different. . . . The [Turkish-]Cypriots speak well to our face, but they speak badly about us behind our backs. I told my wife there would be problems between us because of her friends. If there is a crack in the inner wall of a house, you can't fix it. If there is a crack on the outer wall, you may be able to paint over it. And there were cracks in our relationship.

I asked Ali about the rundown Lusignan-style building of yellow stone next door, which stood in ruins (see figure 11). "When we first arrived, that building was in good shape," he said. It now had no shutters, windows, doors, or windowsills. Its balconies had fallen off. "You see, one of us needed a door, so we went and took one. The other one needed a window and ripped one out of there. This way, in time, this building became a ruin."

Dust, Abjected Neighborhoods, and the Middle Classes

"The [Turkish-]Cypriots look down on the walled-city areas of Lefkoşa," said the *muhtar* of the Kafesli neighborhood when I visited him one day. "They don't like to come here. They say they wouldn't set foot here after nine in the evening. Ministers and party men, too, only come in here before election times, to solicit votes. And the only thing the municipality does here is collect garbage twice a week."

Before the troubles between the Greek-Cypriot and Turkish-Cypriot

above 10. Cars left behind by the Greek-Cypriots since 1974.

11. Vandalized Lusignan building close to the border in northern Lefkoşa.

communities, Lefkoşa (Lefkosia, Nicosia) was a cosmopolitan town inhabited by Turkish, Greek, Armenian, and Maronite-Cypriots, among
others. In 1963, when the troubles began, the city was divided into ethnically segregated enclaves. Between 1963 and 1974, Turkish-Cypriots
lived within the enclave designated for them, protected by their fighters.
Likewise, the Greek-Cypriots lived in separated sections of the city. In
1974, the Turkish army took over almost half of the town of Lefkoşa,
erecting a border, with barrels and barbed wire, right through its center.
The Greek, Armenian, and Maronite-Cypriots who lived in the sections
invaded by the Turkish army had to move south, to what was refashioned
as the "Greek side." In turn, the Turkish-Cypriots who were caught in the
south of Lefkoşa had to move north, to what was declared the "Turkish
side." At first, in 1974, Turkish-Cypriots who were refugees from southern
Lefkoşa, or elsewhere in southern Cyprus, were allocated housing that
belonged to Greek and Armenian-Cypriots in northern Lefkoşa. Some
Turkish-Cypriots who were unable to live in their own homes in the
1963–74 period because they were in areas controlled by EOKA were able,
after 1974, to return and reclaim their properties. In the place of their old
Greek or Armenian-Cypriot neighbors, some of these Turkish-Cypriot
families from Lefkoşa acquired new Turkish-Cypriot neighbors who were
refugees from villages in southern Cyprus.

Meanwhile, the Turkish-Cypriot administration, bent on increasing
the "Turkish" population of northern Cyprus, invited immigrants from
Turkey to settle down, with promises of jobs and housing. Entire communities from various places in Turkey were relocated all over northern
Cyprus. At first, immigrants from Turkey were allocated homes in villages
left behind by Greek-Cypriot escapees of the war of 1974. But, in time
more immigrants arrived, including many who had not been specifically
invited by the administration and who therefore were not given proper
housing or jobs. From the 1980s on, and especially in the 1990s and
2000s, unrecorded immigrants from Turkey arrived in northern Cyprus
and settled wherever they could find shelter. Many rented housing from
Turkish-Cypriots who had either inherited property from their elders or
obtained Greek-Cypriot property through the allocation and distribution
system of the administration. Some illegal workers, as they were called,
stayed in workers' rooms. Others transformed abandoned buildings and
spaces in the northern walled city of Lefkoşa into dwellings.

Gradually, the Turkish-Cypriots started to move out of the walled city of Lefkoşa into newly built, modern suburbs. The city began to expand northward. New apartment blocks were erected, with air-conditioning and modern furnishings, intended for middle-class Turkish-Cypriots, particularly newly married couples. Parks were constructed in these neighborhoods by the municipality of northern Lefkoşa. The pharmacists, doctors, shop owners, and traders of the walled city also moved their shops and clinics to the new neighborhoods outside the walled city. Supermarkets were built, selling local produce as well as imports from Turkey in sterilized, air-conditioned environments. Turkish-Cypriots began to organize their everyday lives in the suburbs of northern Lefkoşa, setting foot in the walled city only for work or business in state offices.

A Turkish-Cypriot doctor whose clinic overlooked the border area of Kermiya on the outskirts of northern Lefkoşa said, "You know how disturbed I am by the sight outside my window? It's as if the war is going on. There are war remains everywhere. You see [pointing out a site closed off with barbed wire], that area is held by the military. Everywhere here is full of ruins left over from the war. It feels as though it is still wartime. People who have taken over Greek-Cypriot property don't have their houses painted. Everything is stalled. For this reason, I have moved to Girne (Kyrenia). I live in a modern purpose-built residential complex. The [Turkish-]Cypriots clean their houses there; they look after their gardens. It's a proper area. The environment affects me very deeply, you see."

The doctor went on to reflect on space in northern Cyprus: "You know, the earth under our feet here is full of corpses. All Turkish-Cypriots know this; Greek-Cypriots know this, too. The Muratağa and Sandallar mass graves were left on this side. But we also know that the mass graves where we buried the Greek-Cypriots are on this side, too. That's why some Turkish-Cypriots don't want an agreement with the Greek-Cypriots. They think the Greek-Cypriots will return and look for their graves. You see, Turkish-Cypriots know that the underneath of this space is full of corpses."[13] He continued:

> I have a patient who comes and tells me he is worried there will be an agreement with the Greek-Cypriots one day and that the Greek-Cypriots will return. He told me he wakes up in the night to the thought of Greek-Cypriots lying dead in the fields close to his house. Few will talk about this, but the anxiety is there. So in order to find a rationale or cover for this, people embrace the nationalist ideology, because without that ideology, their identity and integrity would be at risk.

In 1974 and 1975, right after the war, and when they were settled in Greek-Cypriot housing, people constantly spoke about what had happened to the Greek-Cypriots who used to live there, to their Greek-Cypriot neighbors in mixed villages: Who died in what way; how the Greek-Cypriots were forced out of their villages by Turkish soldiers. . . . But nowadays, thirty years after the war, it's very rare for Turkish-Cypriots to mention the death of their former neighbors or what they found when they first came to the village they ended up inhabiting. . . . They only speak of what they buy, what they consume: their new car, their new refrigerator, their children's new clothes.

A lot of spaces in northern Cyprus were left unattended, the marks of war remaining and rust and dust allowed to grow. It was as though these spaces had been left to die by the Turkish-Cypriots or were pushed to the backroom of consciousness. At times, this was the façade of a house, the front walls, or a secret back room, with the belongings of the former Greek-Cypriot inhabitants locked away. "The bullet holes on the outer walls of the house we took over from the Greek-Cypriots remained in place all the way until my brother got married," said a Turkish-Cypriot woman from a well-to-do family. "Those holes were there all through my childhood. And it's not because my family didn't have the means to fix or paint over them."

But the walled-city area of northern Lefkoşa is an especially neglected space. Generally, the Turkish-Cypriots, most of whom have created middle-class lives for themselves, do not visit the walled city of Lefkoşa unless they have to for work in a state office or for bureaucratic business. "We don't go there," said numerous middle-class Turkish-Cypriots. "I go there only once a year, for nostalgia," said a woman in her twenties. "I do all my shopping outside the old city."

One summer evening in 2001, Atiye, a lawyer in her fifties, invited me to take a stroll. Atiye had grown up in the walled city of Lefkoşa and was proud of having been born and bred there—of being a *Lefkoşalı*. She now lived in a middle-class suburb with her husband and daughter. "Lefkoşa appears dusty to me," she said as we walked beside houses in her neighborhood on that light summer evening. "It's as if it has gotten old; as if it is peeling, acquiring wrinkles, crippling. In the old days, this place used to glitter. The houses, the trees, everything. But even the trees now look to me as if they have collected dust." She told me how she had once received permission to cross to the Greek side for a bi-communal event, and "the Greek side seemed so glittery to me, clean, no dust, the way all of Cyprus used to be in the old days." As we continued walking, Atiye overheard old songs being sung by young people in a bar under a circle of tall eucalyptus trees. The bar was called Sinema Nostalji. Indeed, the space evoked nostalgic feelings in Atiye. She started singing along to the tunes. "It used to be so lively in Lefkoşa in the old days, you know," she said. "Even during the troubles, between '63 and '74, there was singing along the city walls, lights, tables and gardens for sitting. We used to take strolls in the evenings, and everyone was outdoors. There were pastry shops everywhere, and we could go out at night as young women on our own. . . . Now, there is no life here."

Atiye then talked with disdain about the immigrants from Turkey who had settled in northern Cyprus. "They don't clean in front of their houses," she said. "You see how the Turkish-Cypriots wash their pavements and water their gardens every evening? I've never seen someone from Turkey doing that. They let their children run, with bare feet, on the city streets. A car could hit them. The children play in filth; they splash their feet in dirty water, in mud. . . . Since the people from Turkey arrived here, Cyprus has changed. It didn't used to be this way. It was so well taken care of."

Atiye said she wanted to take me to an old pastry shop in the walled city area, the only one left, still functioning, since the old days. She seemed excited, as if she had found a way to connect with her memories of the once lively Lefkoşa, to redeem her nostalgia. The owner of the Budak pastry shop said, "People come here for particular tastes. Usually they come to locate a taste in their memory, which they associate with a visit to this shop. They ask for *kok* [a sort of creamy cake with icing on the top] or for *sütlübörek* [a dairy sweet]." For Atiye, the names of these desserts had a Proustian effect.

Upstairs in the pastry shop were tables and seats in wood and leather from the 1970s, dusty and unused. The shop was no longer frequented very much, only on occasional nostalgic excursions by the Turkish-Cypriots. "In the old days, lovers used to carve their names on these tables," said the shop owner. "My father painted over the carvings, but still some people come, searching for traces of their names under the paint. . . . Look, you can see some letters here." But nothing much had changed in the Budak shop since the '70s, he said. "People like to come here because it's frozen in time. If they wanted to see it changed or updated, we would have done that." Atiye's eyes shone as we ate our *sütlübörek*s. She seemed happy, like a child.

Affect and Abjection

It should come as no surprise that a border area might be filled with ruins and rubbish. Much of the literature on the abject, the grotesque, base matter, and filth is based on an imagination of a "border," in its various metaphorical connotations, that defines the contours around the subjective or the socially symbolic realm and separates it from that which threatens it. Julia Kristeva, for example, locates abjection in the psychical mechanisms of subjectivity, in the othering processes through which the individual attempts to define and protect his or her identity. Kristeva reads abject as "other." "The abject," she writes, "has only one quality of the object—that of being opposed to *I*."[14] To create a seeming integrity of being in the face of actual fragility, the subjective self defines certain things and realms as abject and distances himself or herself from them. According to Kristeva, abjected domains are representations of psychical spaces within the inner world of individuals against which one has defined one's identity. She writes:

> If the object, however, through its opposition, settles me within the fragile texture of a desire for meaning, which, as a matter of fact, makes me ceaselessly and infinitely homologous to it, what is *abject*, on the contrary, the jettisoned object, is radically excluded and draws me toward the place where meaning collapses. A certain "ego" that merged with its master, a superego, has flatly driven it away. It lies outside, beyond the set, and does not seem to agree to the latter's rules of the game. And yet, from its place of banishment, the abject does not cease challenging its master. Without a sign (for him), it beseeches a discharge, a convulsion, a crying out. . . . A massive and sudden emergence of uncanniness, which, familiar as it might have been in an opaque and forgotten life, now harries me as radically separate, loathsome. Not me. Not that. But not nothing, either. A "something" that I do not recognize as a thing. A weight of meaninglessness, about which there is nothing insignificant, and which crushes me. On the edge of non-existence and hallucination, of a reality that, if I acknowledge it, annihilates me. There, abject and abjection are my safeguards.[15]

Subjectivity is conflicted. On the one hand, a distinction from abject seems essential to its making, but on the other hand, abject intrigues. It has a drawing force. If the subjective self is formed through a banishment of that which is considered filthy, dirty, or dangerous, then its identity must be very fragile. At least, it must be vulnerable to the challenges of abject or must protect itself against abject, as if with force of arms, constantly, continuously, and repeatedly.

In Kristeva's work, abject is border, tout court, a boundary that protects and challenges identity at one and the same time. Therefore, as she meditates on the subjective meaning of the corpse, she writes:

> These body fluids, this defilement, this shit are what life withstands, hardly and with difficulty, on the part of death. There, I am at the border of my condition as a living being. My body extricates itself, as being alive, from that border. Such wastes drop so that I might live, until, from loss to loss, nothing remains in me and my entire body falls beyond the limit—*cadere*, cadaver. If dung signifies the other side of the border, the place where I am not and which permits me to be, the corpse, the most sickening of wastes, is a border that has encroached upon everything. It is no longer I who expel, "I" is expelled. The border has become an object. How can I be without border?[16]

Drawing on Kristeva, we could construe the border area in Cyprus in such terms, not merely as an actual military blockade, but also as a spatial materiality that stands for that practice of abjection in the attempted constitution of a kind of subjective order in the aftermath of war. The abjected quality of the border. The border as an abjected space. The border area as the representation of that construed difference between the abject and the self. The border area (and the walled city of Lefkoşa) might have become, for the Turkish-Cypriots, something they wanted to abject out of themselves. But what could that thing be? Abject, according to Kristeva, is the representation of an uncomfortable aspect of psychical space imagined and represented as filth. If so, what could this "thing" (the abject, the abjected space) stand for in the psychical experiences of Turkish-Cypriots? Why might it have been desirable, even necessary, to maintain certain marks and remains of war intact in northern Cyprus? In line with Kristeva's study of distancing from the corpse—corpses that Turkish-Cypriots knew, as the Turkish-Cypriot doctor said, to lie under the ground in northern Cyprus—did certain spaces have to be associated with death, ruins, or old age in order, after wartime, to create "life" elsewhere?

Kristeva engages with Mary Douglas, for whom "defilement is an element connected with the boundary, the margin, etc., of an order."[17] In Douglas's work, filth is read as constitutive of society. It is against filth that society is formed by defining and identifying that which should be excluded. But Kristeva criticizes Douglas for overlooking the subjective process (and language) as a fundamental aspect of the process of abjection.[18] In her psychoanalytic reading, abjection is an affective dynamic that emerges from the subjective need to define and protect the ego. Abject is constitutive of the ego by negation: "I am not that." As I ponder my field notes, it seems to me that there has indeed been an attempt by Turkish-Cypriots to define a new social structure against the abject, and these spaces where I have dwelled along the border and the walled city of Lefkoşa might be the abject against which the new socially symbolic order has wanted to define itself. Yet I think that other interpretive possibilities are blocked by this reading. What else could the ruins stand for? What else might they imply?

Other scholars who have worked on abjected matter have also associated it with order-making mechanisms, whether subjective or social. Social class and the bourgeois public sphere (including law and the state) have been constituted by defining, identifying, and banishing the abject. In their work on "transgression," inspired by Mikhail Bakhtin's studies of carnival and the celebration of "the grotesque," Peter Stallybrass and Allon White have interpreted base material ("the lower bodily stratum, the sewers, the underworld") as fundamental to the making of the bourgeoisie, along with its social classifications and discourses.[19] They read differentiations between "lower" and "higher" matters, in domestic and urban architecture, in language, as well as in relations between the social classes, as social demarcations. Such bordering mechanisms, essential to the making of higher social class, depend on the association of "the grotesque" with the lower classes, in their reading. They argue that "the carnivalesque was marked out as an intensely powerful semiotic realm precisely because bourgeois culture constructed its self-identity by rejecting it."[20] Comparably, we could say that in *History of Shit* (2000), Dominique Laporte studies the elimination of feces, or personal cleansing practices, as constitutive of civilization, including the making of bourgeois law and the state. The very notion of "the public," in Laporte's reading, was generated by defining excrement as filthy and, therefore, as a "private" affair.[21] Some of this work on the making of the bourgeois public sphere against the abject is helpful in coming to understand the manner in which the Turkish-Cypriots, in reconfiguring themselves as a middle class after the war, have defined the walled city now inhabited by migrants from Turkey and the elderly as that space where they will not go, the border of their identity, that abjected other side, the counterpoint to their newly established middle-class sociality.

In much theoretical writing on the abject, abjected material is imagined as that which is excluded from the social order yet is constitutive of it by negation. The abject is that against which the subjective self, the social class order, or the public sphere has been defined. We might say, then, that the abject is necessary for the constitution of personal, social, and political orders (and "orderliness"). It may therefore have been necessary to maintain that abjected space I had been observing, along the border area, untended and unattended, war marks and ruins in place, to demarcate a space for new Turkish-Cypriot subjectivities, a new social class system, and a new polity.

Georges Bataille offers another understanding of what he calls "base matter."[22] In contrast to structuralist, psychoanalytic, or Marxist interpretations of excrement, where shit is considered in a dualist fashion as that which is anti-system, Bataille perceives in excessive material a specific potentiality.[23] Base matter has its own energy, its own possibilities. It is a totality in itself, not just material against which a subjective, social, or political system is to be defined.[24] "Base matter," writes Bataille, "is external and foreign to ideal human aspirations, and it refuses to allow itself to be reduced to the great ontological machines resulting from these aspirations."[25] Much further than standing for anti-system, base matter is a reality that lies in the beyond; "a black hole, its negative and creative energy discloses the gift of unknowing, the decapitation of the summit and the eruption of other forces."[26] Bataille's work might assist us in studying the energy discharged by ruins and rubbish in their own right. If we follow Bataille, rather than standing for something (in psychical-subjective or social-political space) against which an order or integrity is constituted, the abject might be something wholly and entirely different, an "other" reality.

Writings on abject, filth, and excrement assist me in interpreting and understanding the material that literally got tangled around my feet while living in and researching northern Cyprus. Through Kristeva, I am able to consider what the ruins, the rubbish, and the war remains in northern Cyprus stand for in Turkish-Cypriots' subjective and internal psychical mechanisms. I think along with Stallybrass and White, to consider the extent to which the walled city of Lefkoşa has been practically abandoned by the Turkish-Cypriots in the interest of creating a new middle-class identity. Indeed, that the neglected spaces, the old city, should be associated by middle-class Turkish-Cypriots with poor immigrants from Turkey is no coincidence. Turkish-Cypriots have certainly defined their identity in the past couple of decades against the settlers from Turkey (and their perceived lifestyles). "We are not them," they will argue, using racialized metaphors for the abject to characterize people from Turkey. As they attempt to separate and distinguish their lives and identities from the immigrants, the Turkish-Cypriots have also defined the old city of Lefkoşa as out of bounds, socially demarcating their own neighborhoods and suburbs.

However, based on my northern Cypriot material, I have other and further speculations (or suspicions) about the abject. In studying the abject as that which is anti-system (subjective, social, or political), constitutive of the system in its very negativity (an "anti-thesis"), or as utterly external to system (a "non-system"), these scholars of abjection have overlooked the extent to which the abject may be systemic—that is, inherent in the (subjective, social, or political) system in itself and in its own right. In other words, I would like to argue, again based on my ethnographic material, that the banishing of the abject might be an ideological, performative, or rhetorical move: We will act as if the abject is only "there" (or about "that") and not elsewhere, everywhere, and about everything.

In studying Cyprus, I cannot but perceive abjection within an economy of violence. Walter Benjamin has proposed that there is violence at the foundation of every legal and political system.[27] In his famous article "Force of Law" Jacques Derrida says that according to Benjamin, "There is something 'rotten' at the heart of law."[28] The reference point for that rottenness (or the abject) is violence. There is violence at the origin of every legal system, according to Benjamin.[29] Derrida interprets:

> Every juridical contract, every *Rechtsvertrag* ("legal contract") is founded on violence. There is no contract that does not have violence as both an origin (*Ursprung*) and an outcome (*Ausgang*). Here a furtive and elliptical allusion to Benjamin is decisive, as is often the case. The violence that founds or positions *droit* need not be immediately present in the contract. . . . But without being immediately present, it is replaced (*vertreten*, "represented") by the supplement of a substitute. And it is in this *différance*, in the movement that replaces presence (the immediate presence of violence identifiable as such in its traits and its spirit), it is in this *différantielle* representativity that originary violence is consigned to oblivion. This amnesic loss of consciousness does not happen by

accident. It is the very passage from presence to representation. Such a passage forms the trajectory of decline, of institutional "degeneracy," their *Verfall* ("decay"). . . . The first example chosen is that of the parliaments of the time. If they offer a deplorable spectacle, it is because these representative institutions forget the revolutionary violence from which they are born.[30]

Following this cue, I would like to suggest that, were we to conceive of abjection as violence (or violation), that which founds and that which is glossed by (legal and political) system, other interpretive or analytical possibilities might come to the fore. Abjection might serve a political purpose. Why did the Turkish-Cypriots tell me they were not disturbed by the ruins? Why did they say they were used to them? Here, further ethnographic elaboration is necessary.

The Economy in Ruins

Ruins, rust, dust, and garbage are not material sui generis. They do not just emerge on their own. Rather, they are generated through specific social relations between people, materialities, and the built and natural environment. To put it differently, people participate in the making of ruins. Both Turkish-Cypriots and Greek-Cypriots, supported by armies from Turkey and Greece and led by local guerrilla fighters on each side of the intercommunal conflict, as well as other communities who have inhabited Cyprus (such as immigrant-settlers from Turkey), have had their share in the shape of the present environment—the bullet holes in buildings, dwellings without roofs and windowsills, houses looted of their belongings. Cypriots know and remember their agency in the ruination of the environment during the troubles and the war. Therefore, in this section I study agency and complicity in the making and abandonment of what I call *abjected spaces*.

Turkish-Cypriots often told me, "Everyone has looted objects in their households." The term for loot in everyday Turkish-Cypriot folk language is *ganimet*. An old Turkish word (with an Arabic root), *ganimet* was used by the Ottomans to refer to property or material objects appropriated from the "enemy," or from occupied territories, during and in the aftermath of war. While retaining this reference to plunder, like a residue from the Ottoman period, the notion of ganimet in contemporary Turkish-Cypriot usage means symbolically and metaphorically much more. In my observation, ganimet was an affectively charged concept used by Turkish-Cypriots to signify a form of violence against the material properties of the other party in the troubles (the Greek-Cypriots). When Turkish-Cypriots used the term, they implied a form of self-criticism; they were commenting on their own involvement, as a community, in the appropriation of material objects and property belonging to the Greek-Cypriots and left in northern Cyprus after the war. Ganimet stood not simply for specific things appropriated from the Greek-Cypriots in the aftermath of war; it also signified a broader and morally problematic social practice, an institutionalized form of stealing and destruction with which they symbolically charged or criticized not only themselves, as human beings, but also, more particularly, their administration. In this social-symbolic world, the term implies a self-critical moral discourse. In my reading, *ganimet*, in the Turkish-Cypriot usage of the term, is a word that signifies violence committed against other people by violating, appropriating, or trading in their property. This discourse, as well as the actual economy around looted items and ruins, should therefore figure in any depiction and analysis of the affect of the built environment in the aftermath of war.

The story of Hatice Hanım is worth telling in this respect. A middle-aged Turkish-Cypriot woman originally from a village that is now south of the Green Line, Hatice Hanım lived in a village taken over from the Greek-Cypriots in the north of Cyprus. In the village, Turkish-Cypriots had been allocated Greek-Cypriot land and dwellings by the northern Cypriot administration. But in one part of the village, over the mountain slopes and right across from houses inhabited by Turkish-Cypriot families, stood a whole neighborhood in utter ruins (see figure 12). The rooftops of old village houses had collapsed. The plaster and painting on the old dwellings had peeled off. The internal mud walls had been eaten away by the rain. Windows were broken or had disappeared. Doors and balconies were nowhere to be seen. Fig trees and thick bushes had grown in the small rooms. Here, the present inhabitants of the village herded their goats. The old village church had been turned into a sheepfold; icons had been ripped from the church walls, and there was dirt all over the outer and inner walls of the once cherished sacred site.

"How do you feel," I asked Hatice Hanım one day, "living across from these ruins?" "We have gotten used to seeing these things," she replied, almost too easily or in an apparently nonchalant manner. "How did these places look when you first arrived in this village in 1974?," I asked. "They were in very good (*mısmıl*) condition," she said. She then gave me an account of how this neighborhood had turned into ruins over the years:

When we first arrived [from our village in the south], we weren't able to warm to this place. We were allocated this house by the administration. When we first entered it, we couldn't move. We sat in one place for three days, unable to do anything. You feel sorry. You see all the furniture that belongs to other people, another family, you feel sad. . . . Then someone came in through the back door saying they would take the kitchen table, since it seemed we weren't using it. Imagine, we had been staying there for three days already and we hadn't noticed that the house had a back door. I was fifteen years old at the time. My sisters were twenty and thirteen. Then we saw and heard everyone talking about something called *ganimet*. We didn't know what ganimet meant. Everyone spoke of ganimet here, ganimet there. Then we understood that ganimet meant taking something and running away with it. When we first arrived here, we constantly saw objects being moved from one place to the other: furniture, household utensils, refrigerators. The entire village was full of things left in front of houses, carried from one to the other, or exhibited outdoors for sale. Already some people had started trading in ganimet things.

This neighborhood across the street was in very good condition when we first arrived. We took four sofas from the houses in there and one mattress.

12. Ruins of Greek-Cypriots' homes with spring flowers on the Beşparmak (Pentadaktilos) Mountains.

Everyone took something when they needed it. We took tiles from the roof-tops, wood out of the windowsills. Someone who needed a door for his house went to that neighborhood and obtained a door. The rain, too, ate into the mud walls of these houses, and in time they turned into ruins. . . . No, I don't feel bad seeing them. I don't notice. We got used to these ruins.

In telling the story of the ruins, Hatice Hanım also recounted her, her family's, and her fellow villagers' part and agency in their making. But perhaps due to this involvement, the affect generated by these ruins, which appeared like a shocking war zone to my eyes and senses, had been repressed and abjected over the years.

After border checkpoints were opened in 2003, I visited Hatice Hanım again. She had just returned from visiting the village she and her family had left behind in 1974 when they became refugees and moved to the north. "My heart is burning," she said. "My inside is hurting." She then told me how she had found her family home in their original village in the south. "The Greek-Cypriots placed a wire fence around a whole neighbor-hood in our village. They turned that whole area into a sheepfold. Our home was left in there; we couldn't go in. It was full of sheep shit. The windows had been ripped out, and there was no door or roof any longer, either. I couldn't see a sign of any of our furniture or things. The Greek-Cypriots must have looted everything after we left. It feels so bad." For a long time, Hatice Hanım was unable to recover from that heavy feeling of having found her ancestral home on the Greek side looted and in ruins.

"There was a whole surge in ganimet after the war," said Servet Hanım, a Turkish-Cypriot woman in her forties who lived in Lefkoşa. "There was something called 'going out for ganimet.' After most of the items left by the Greek-Cypriots had been appropriated and distributed, people would go on excursions, especially on the weekends, into abandoned Greek-Cypriot villages or neighborhoods in search of further ganimet." This woman, like many other Turkish-Cypriots who recounted this period, had a moral judgment of her own and her fellow Turkish-Cypriots' involve-ment. "Everyone acquired some kind of ganimet," she said, but she por-trayed with particular disdain the people whom she, like other Turkish-Cypriots, called the "1974 rich," who acquired wealth by trading in looted goods or by investing in looted property. "We call them the *ganimettos*, those who became rich through ganimet," she said.

In local moral discourse about looted property, Turkish-Cypriots dis-tinguished between those who had obtained Greek-Cypriot property after the war due to need (referring to refugees from the south, for example, who had lost their own property) and those who traded in ganimet and acquired wealth by looting. "A lot of these people, the 1974 rich, are in the administration now, you know. Anyway, those who were involved in patronage networks (*torpil*) obtained the best ganimet properties."

The economy in loot and leftover items in the midst and aftermath of war did not develop on its own: An administrative procedure was in place that supported the appropriation of Greek-Cypriot property as a policy and sanctioned practice.[31] The Turkish-Cypriot administration in northern Cyprus allocated Greek-Cypriot property (housing and land) to Turkish-Cypriot refugees who had lost their property in southern Cyprus. But the administration also allowed and explicitly supported and organized the appropriation and exchange of items and objects that belonged to the Greek-Cypriots. Some of this was done as charity for the elderly and refugees from the south who were left without anything. Hatice Hanım recounted that members of the administration would drive trucks loaded with ganimet goods through the village, distributing furniture and clothing left by the Greek-Cypriots to the needy Turkish-Cypriot refugees. Likewise, the elderly Ahmet Bey, who ended up in Lefkoşa after the war, said, "The garages behind the thread factory had been turned into ganimet sale areas. Ganimet goods were sold cheaply there to families who hadn't been able to obtain any for themselves, or to the elderly. Some of these goods were used; others were not. The shops and storage places left by the Greek-Cypriots had also been emptied and the items in them put up for sale."

Numerous Turkish-Cypriots recalled their involvement in the ganimet economy with shame and criticized the administration that supported it. Doğan Bey, who was a young man in the aftermath of war, recounted that his father had refused to take any items left by the Greek-Cypriots, while almost everyone else in their village was going on ganimet excursions. "One day, Denktaş came to our village," he said. "All the people in the village gathered to hear his speech in the village coffee shop. Apparently, someone had told Denktaş the story of my father, who would refuse all ganimet goods. 'Who is that fool (*enayi*) who wouldn't take ganimet?' Denktaş screamed in front of everyone in the village. After this, our villagers ridiculed my father."

Turkish-Cypriots recounted many such memories of the northern Cypriot administration's involvement in the appropriation, allocation, sale,

and distribution of looted property. They suggested that their administration had encouraged looting and even organized it. "The Turkish Republic
of Northern Cyprus is a state built upon ganimet," said Osman, a Turkish-
Cypriot man in his thirties. This symbolic ascription or representation of
polity referred not only to the expropriation of Greek-Cypriot properties
and belongings. Turkish-Cypriots extended the notion of the "ganimet
state" to imply that their state had established theft as a generalized
practice. "You see how this state still loots us?," said the elderly İbrahim
Bey in reference to his household bills. "What do you expect? This government was built on ganimet, lives with ganimet. Look at the fees they
charge for electricity, for water, for the telephone. . . . Is this not stealing?"
More than a simple reference to items appropriated in the aftermath of
war, *ganimet* has been turned into a politically charged metaphor through
which Turkish-Cypriots characterize and critique themselves and their
administration.

Affective Ruins

To return to the original question of this chapter: Does the ruined environment transmit affective energy, and if it does, how? Or, if it does
not, why is that so? I walk, again, through the ruins around the border
area in Lefkoşa and wonder. I remember what it looks like from the
window of an airplane: a visibly dark area cutting through the circle of old
Venetian walls, with high-rise buildings on the Greek side of the city and
low-built yellow stone structures on the Turkish side. The border area
stands out as an abjected space. But it is not only here that the abject is to
be located, sensed, or studied in northern Cyprus (or, for that matter, on
the Greek side in the south). Turkish-Cypriots refer to the walled city in
Lefkoşa, now largely inhabited by immigrants from Turkey, using metaphors of abjection, invoking filth, dirt, and decay. The Turkish-Cypriots
have mostly moved out of the walled city and organize their lives, as
much as possible, in its outskirts. They have marked the walled-city area
along the border as an abjected space. They say, "We don't go there." They
have carved it out of their lives and attempted to shove it out of their
consciousness. But why? What does this signify?

Many spaces in northern Cyprus are like this: rust grown over the
skeleton of an old coffee shop overlooking the sea in the Karpaz (Kar-
pasia) region; dust over olive trees around a military no-go area close to

Kormacit (Kormakitis); ruins of churches and Greek Orthodox cemeteries on the outskirts of villages; military stations and shooting points along the crowded seashore. The abject is everywhere, yet within this broader abjected space, certain areas have been particularly marked and shoved off as the abject itself, against which homely spaces have been carved out as markers of cleanliness, orderliness, coziness, and intimacy. "We don't go there," said a Turkish-Cypriot about the walled city of Lefkoşa. "I rarely set foot in there." It is an abjected site within a broader environment of abjection. Elsewhere, in the suburbs, the Turkish-Cypriots have created specific living areas for themselves, with newly built and modern neighborhoods, with watered gardens, air-conditioned cars, shopping centers, and clean households. How do we interpret this?

Consider how certain Turkish-Cypriots characterized their political system during this period: "a state of looting (*ganimet devleti*)." I read here a self-critical moral discourse that associates abjection with the violation of the property of others; a characterization of a political system as morally problematic. In such representations, it is not only specific sites, places, or areas that are associated with abjection; a political system itself is described through metaphors of the abject. We have wronged others. Those ruins remind us of that, so we dare not go there. Wrong has been done to us. Those bullet holes are like wounds in our bodies, so we keep them there. We have committed violence, and violence has been committed against us. We dare not see; we do not like to see; we would rather not go; no, it does not feel bad. Could the areas abandoned by the Turkish-Cypriots, especially abjected and left to their fate, represent to them the originary violence (in Walter Benjamin's sense) at the foundation of their system, in which they were also involved? Could that projection of abject qualities onto specific sites in northern Cyprus, and the maintenance of the abject in those spaces (through sheer abandonment), be an attempt to protect one's self (and one's system) from abjected memories of violence done to others, as well as violation against one's self? That originary violence at the foundation of law, in Benjamin's sense, is all too close to the skin for Turkish-Cypriots—closer, perhaps, than for others who appear to live comfortably in other states; other locations where that foundational violence is more effectively glossed and buried. The abject represents violence. So if that abjected space, those ruins, do not appear to make the Turkish-Cypriots feel bad today, perhaps it is because that memory of violence and violation has been projected onto them, and an attempt has been made to create against them a counter-space of apparent integrity, conviviality, life, cleanliness, order, and ease.

I started this chapter with a critical engagement with works that have privileged human subjectivity as the originator of affective energy. I hope my material has illustrated how affect is not merely intersubjectively mediated (among people) but is specifically charged between people and their material environments. My original question—Is affect transmitted by the ruined environment, or do we perceive the environment by projecting our subjective worlds onto it?—was, perhaps, misplaced. Affect is produced neither by materialities nor by the inner world alone; it is produced through their interaction. In this chapter, I have studied politics as a domain of interaction between people and their material environments.[32] The affect transmitted by the ruins, to build on an idea suggested by Teresa Brennan (2004), has to be situated within the contingencies and historicity of those specific interactions between spatial materialities and human beings that change through time.[33] I suggested that, for the Turkish-Cypriots in the period just before 2003, ruins in northern Cyprus did not apparently "feel bad" because they had been abjected, both spatially and consciously, as reminders of the community's and the state's involvement in their making. Ruins also reminded Turkish-Cypriots of their own internal destruction, the violence done to them by the Greek-Cypriots. Did they maintain the bullet holes intact since 1963 and 1974 for that reason? Did the buildings with the bullet holes represent their having both committed violence and been violated? Buildings with bullet holes; bodies with internal wounds. Carnage outside; shambles inside.

I have studied what I call abjected spaces as affectively charged sites within a political domain and delineated abjection as a particularly fruitful arena for the study of politics. Abjection has mostly been studied as that which contradicts or goes beyond a system or structure (whether that is the subjective self or the socially symbolic order). But in northern Cyprus, the sociopolitical system itself was perceived and represented through metaphors of the abject by its own subjects. If certain spaces in northern Cyprus are specifically abjected (and declared marginal or out of bounds), this is only an effort to create seemingly clean environments within a broader environment of abjection at many levels. That act of abjecting—"We don't go there"—is the ideological gloss, the way in which a memory of violence, as well as a broader reality of abjection, is pushed out and repressed. Theorists who have studied the act of abjection as the nature of abjection in itself may have confused the ideological move for the thing itself. In my reading, some spaces have to be left filthy or wounded so that the whole system does not appear to be so. This is a performative act. My northern Cypriot material has led me to another conceptualization of the abject: the political system as the abject, an abjected political system. Through these notions, I propose that we conceive of the abject not as that which is anti- or non-system (that which stands against or is kept outside the personal and sociopolitical order), but as a representation of the system (both political and personal) in itself.

7. Affective Spaces, Melancholic Objects

MANY OF THE TURKISH-CYPRIOTS I worked with reflected a melancholic interiority in the period when I did the research for this book in northern Cyprus. The term they often employed to express their condition, feeling, or inner state of being was *maraz*.[1] Their use of the term was ethnographically distinct and different from its mainland Turkish understandings. In the Turkish-Cypriot dialect and usage, *maraz* refers to a state of mental depression, deep and inescapable sadness and unease, which I explore, in English, through the concept of melancholia.[2] Many of my informants said that it was the Cyprus problem that produced maraz in them, thus historically locating or situating their inner lack of calm and happiness. They referred specifically to their state of confinement in northern Cyprus, with checkpoints closed and access to the south denied, the economic blockade and political stalemate, as well as the lack of resolution of the Cyprus problem. This was a historically specific and subjective interpretation of an inner state of being and feeling. I am interested in understanding this melancholy not only as an expression of the inner worlds of my informants, but also as the mark of the energy (or affect, as I am calling it) discharged on them by the dwellings and environments they have now lived in for decades. "This space feels melancholic," my informants often said, referring to the rusty and dusty surfaces of buildings left unkempt and un-maintained since 1974. They were naming the feeling their environment inflicted on them. I therefore propose an anthropology of melancholia in this chapter by way of studying the affects generated by space and the non-human environment.

What, I ask, is the role of the outer environment in engendering subjective feeling? Or, how are subjective feeling and environmentally produced affect intertwined? More specifically, are we to speak of subjectively felt or spatially effected melancholy? What concerns me is that the theoretical tools we have in hand to study such an ethnographic problem would have us tilting to one side or the other of these questions. My use of the either–or form in posing these questions is therefore rhetorical. Later in this chapter, I study the privileging of one side or the other of these questions as a problem in regimes of knowledge production, one that I will explore through the metaphor of ruination. By "ruination," I refer to the material remains or artifacts of destruction and violation, but also to the subjectivities and residual affects that linger, like a hangover, in the aftermath of violence. With the metaphor of ruination, I shall also explore what goes amiss in attempts by anthropologists and scholars in associated disciplines to discard old conceptual apparatuses with the introduction of new ones.

Objects of Violence

Let us highlight, once again, the core question of this chapter: Is the affect of melancholy experienced in relation to looted objects and properties a projection of their users' subjectivities onto the objects or an energy discharged out of these objects themselves? Here I find it helpful to think about my material through the exercises proposed by Actor-Network Theory (ANT). One of its greatest proponents, Bruno Latour, has written against the privileged ascription of agency to human beings, arguing that, as "actants" of sorts, "non-human entities," too, may be interpreted as effecting a kind of agency.[3] In a recent work on politics, Latour writes: "It's not unfair to say that political philosophy has often been the victim of a strong object-avoidance tendency."[4] "*Back to Things!*" is the motto of Latour's work, as well as of others working with ANT.[5] The point of this dictum is to effect a shift from a subject-centered (or human-centered) to an "object-oriented" philosophy.[6] So, Latour writes, "The 'Body Politik' is not only made of people! They are thick with things: clothes, a huge sword, immense castles, large cultivated fields, crowns, ships, cities and an immensely complex technology of gathering, meeting, cohabiting, enlarging, reducing and focusing. In addition to the throng of little people summed up in the crowned head of the Leviathan, there are objects everywhere."[7] Thinking through my material from northern Cyprus, I agree with Latour that there is a need to attend to the centrality of objects in the making of politics. The northern Cypriot polity is a great example of the embroilment of subjects with objects—in this case, significantly, objects seized from other subjects. Arguably, a new body politic has been fashioned in northern Cyprus out of appropriating, using, and exchanging objects captured by violation from other people. I am therefore interested in the object quality of politics.

Yet I find that Latour's work is limited in its *qualification* of objects and their politics. Latour argues, without ethnographic specification or historicization, that subjects and objects are always and already engaged with and entangled in one another, imagining a flat or horizontal network of assemblages between human and non-human entities, transcendentally and at all times, without qualification or interpretation. In fact, flattening is a methodology that Latour intentionally prescribes in an attempt to generate symmetry between different modes of agency.[8] I shall argue differently. The relation people forge with objects must be studied in the contexts of historical contingency and political specificity. If people and objects are assembled in a certain manner, I argue that this is not because they always, already, or anyway are so. Rather, assemblages of subjects and objects must be read as specific in their politics and history. In my case, the Turkish-Cypriots' relations with looted objects is an assemblage of sorts forged in the aftermath of an act of sovereignty: a declaration of war in the aftermath of long-term intercommunal conflict, the erection of a border to delineate distinction between two ethnically defined communities, and a long-term state of emergency.[9] Reading sovereignty in this specific arrangement of people and things qualifies the network and locates it historically. This particular assemblage of human and non-human entities—the one I have been studying—is no neutral assembly. Rather, it has been created by keeping certain people and things out, by excluding them, in this case with the erection of a border as a mark of sovereignty. The meeting of people with certain categories of other people is banned; the union of humans with their own non-human belongings is disallowed. Many people are excluded from this network altogether because they have been killed. Therefore, the network cannot be theorized as an all-inclusive or pervasive, transcendental phenomenon. Marilyn Strathern has suggested a methodology of "cutting the network."[10] She writes, "If networks had lengths they would stop themselves," identifying a problem in the limitlessness of Latour's notion of the network.[11] In my research, it is sovereignty that does the cutting. Latour's horizontal and two-dimensional imaginary of the network, then, should be complemented with a theory of sovereignty and history that introduces qualified verticality and multiple dimensionality.

With his emphasis on objects, Latour wants explicitly to urge a post-linguistic and post-hermeneutic shift in social theory. In fact, I read ANT as a direct attack on the "linguistic turn" associated with poststructuralism and deconstruction.[12] Arguably there is an attempt to define the contours of a new "paradigm" (in this case, quite akin to Thomas Kuhn's sense of it) against the dominance of social constructionism in the human sciences, with its emphasis on language and subjectivity. If language is predominantly what identifies the subject and differentiates him or her from other entities, then I read ANT as a critique of the anthropocentrism of social constructionism. So, as the object (or visible matter and evidence) takes primacy, language, representation, the imagination, interpretation, and the subjective are "mopped up" (in Kuhn's sense) in this new methodology. I study this as a form of ruination in knowledge production.

Objects are not involved in relations with human beings in a linguistically or symbolically neutral arena. Objects are, rather, qualified through language. They can be neither pre- nor post-linguistic. Nor can they be non-symbolic. Remember what my Turkish-Cypriot informants called the objects they used: "Greek-Cypriot property (*Rum malı*)" or "loot (*ganimet*)." Likewise, recall the moral discourses and ideologies that battle over the representation of objects in northern Cyprus. Latour would like to situate the political in objects. But with his attack on the linguistic turn in the social sciences, he mops up (or ruins) theoretical vantage points that suggest that objects are discursively qualified, as well.

As welcome as its emphasis on the agency of non-human actants is, in its paradigmatic efforts to reconstitute the object of social analysis (identifying it literally and materially as an object), ANT has so tilted the balance toward studying non-human entities that all methodologies for studying the human (including non-essentialist theoretical approaches) are deemed antithetical to its efforts. Or, if the human has not altogether disappeared in ANT frameworks, accounts of it have become extremely impoverished. Here, I certainly do not mean to call for a return to the philosophy of the subject or to humanist philosophy by reinstating the highly problematic notion of "the human." I am, rather, reflecting on what gets mopped up, once again, with declarations of theoretical turns. As they ardently keep at bay any inferences to the human (or anything associated with human subjectivity or interiority), so do ANT theorists limit themselves in their imagination of any agency that is also or especially human in its associations, such as the imagination or the emotions.[13] If we were to limit ourselves to an ANT framework or methodology, we would have to call off any query into affect as referring to human factors, too.

The British geographer Nigel Thrift has developed what I think is a crucial critique of ANT along these lines. He writes:

> In their surely correct insistence that action is a property of the whole association, actor-network theorists tend to recoil with horror from any accusation of humanism. Quite rightly, they fear the taint of a centred human subject establishing an exact dominion over all. But the result of their fear is that actor-network theory has tended to neglect specifically human capacities of expression, powers of invention, of fabulation, which cannot be simply gainsaid, in favour of a flattened cohabitation of all things. But human expressive powers seem especially important in understanding what is possible to associate, in particular the power of *imagination*, "the capacity to posit that which is not, to see in something that which is not there" . . . , which is the fount of so many non-preexistent relations. Imagination might be thought of as having a number of components. . . . Though these processes are ineluctably linked to the object world, they cannot be reduced to it.[14]

I agree with Thrift on this point and think that tendencies in knowledge production that would identify their object of analysis and methodology by way of negation (the refuting or discarding of other theoretical approaches) have a way of bringing the anthropologist to an impasse vis-à-vis his or her ethnographic material. The same is true of recent emphases on non-human agency. As significant as its contribution is to social theory and ethnographic methodology, ANT, through its rhetoric, makes it difficult to imagine reconciliation with other theoretical approaches that would include a consideration of (non-essentialist) human capacities for imagination and affect. But reconciliation is exactly what I mean to achieve through this discussion.

Affective Spaces

Picture a wide plateau in the midst of the island, appearing rather dry, burned by the sun, showing various shades of yellow and brown. The plain appears endless to the eye up to the point where it is spotted with a few trees in the mountain on the horizon. Thistles, prickly bushes, and dry plants cover the surface of the plateau. "This whole area on the skirts of the mountain used to be so green," said Hasan, a Turkish-Cypriot, "before the big fire in 1995, which is said to have been ignited by mistake from one of the army's storehouses for ammunition. All the fruit trees, carob, olive, and pine trees burned up. For a long while, I didn't want to visit this area, as it aroused immense melancholy in me. And look, now it looks like a desert." I looked in one direction, and the yellow plain appeared dry as far as the eye could see, until it got caught by a wave of heat. On one side, there was a cemetery of used cars. "All those cars and car parts you see over there," said Hasan, "are left from 1974." He was locating what I was observing, rooting it with a specific date, a significant event. "They are cars that were left from the Greek-Cypriots when they were fleeing from the war. . . . Many of us used Greek-Cypriot cars (*Rum arabası*) which we found parked here and there in villages, in towns, everywhere, for a long while. Some turned the sale of looted cars into a business. But now most of these cars have gotten old; they are like museum pieces. They have been dumped here. Maybe somebody is still making a living out of selling their spare parts." The rusty car skeletons and the shards of the used cars lay on top of one another on one side of the plateau, reflecting the sunlight.

I turned my face toward the other side of the plain. A number of white cement structures had been erected here and closed off to access with barbed wire. Red signposts on the wire read "Military Area: Access Forbidden." "That is a residential neighborhood for Turkish officers and their families," said Hasan. "We cannot walk that way; it is blocked." And recalling what this place was like in the old days, he said: "This used to be a picnic area adjacent to a village." We walked through the thorns and bushes on the plateau, and I asked, "Why is this space left so unkempt? Why is it not taken care of?" Hasan said:

> What we are walking on is Greek-Cypriot owned land (*Rum toprağı*). A lot of Greek-Cypriot land was allocated to Turkish-Cypriot refugees, but some who appropriated land did not develop it, out of worry that the Greek-Cypriots would claim it back one day. Everyone knows the status of this land as "loot." It is illegally assumed property. But you know, there are a number of shrewd people among us who have started to develop such looted land and sell it to British expatriates. Otherwise, who would want to invest in land that legally belongs to the Greek-Cypriots?

The space through which we walked exuded a melancholy that I could feel intensely. From Hasan's account, I understood that the plateau had taken this dry, unkempt, and prickly shape through time. "Had these fields been owned with proper [legal] title deeds," said Hasan, "this area would have been lush and green." Hasan was suggesting that the space would not feel the same had its ownership been straightforward and uncontroversial. He was saying, for one, that the fields would be ploughed, planted, and maintained and would produce an affect of freshness and liveliness. Instead, in the prickly fields through which we moved, the atmosphere discharged a feeling of the uncanny, a strange feeling derived, in this instance, out of a sense of impropriety, haunting, or an act of violation.

I would like to ask the reader to keep this description of an ethnographic field in mind as I move on to discuss recent theoretical work on affect. I will be referring to what scholars in geography and cultural studies have called the "affective turn," following the work of Gilles Deleuze.[15] This turn to study affect has been represented by scholars in associated disciplines as the movement that follows, critiques, and moves beyond the "linguistic turn" in the human sciences. Significantly, Thrift has developed "non-representational theory" along these lines.[16] Thrift correctly argues that much of cultural theory in the past couple of decades has been dominated by an interest in texts, semiotics, and discourse, which he identifies as approaches centered on studies of "representation." He is referring to poststructuralism and the way it was taken up in the human sciences, including, significantly, cultural geography and (cultural) anthropology. Instead, and in place of the primacy of language in such approaches, Thrift would like to open researchers' imagination to a study of non- or pre-linguistic registers of experience, which he studies via the work of Deleuze through the rubric of affect. But what is affect?

"Affect is not simply emotion," writes Thrift, "nor is it reducible to the affections or perceptions of an individual subject."[17] Affect *does* refer, broadly, to an emotive domain, but its scope goes far beyond that of human subjectivity or the self. In this approach, too, as in ANT, there is a welcome move to go beyond the philosophy of the subject. Compare this, for example, with how Bruno Latour, in a very interesting statement, has suggested that ANT is about "redistributing subjective quality *outside*."[18] The point with which I very much agree is that most theoretical work on affect, before this particular affective turn, has focused on the inner world or interiority of the human subject, referred to as subjectivity. In turn, emergent theories of affect illustrate that it can be studied in sites and spaces beyond the scope of the human subject, her subjectivity, or her psyche.

Thrift's spatial theory of affect goes straight to Deleuze for its inspiration. Gilles Deleuze developed his theory of non-subjective affect by way of rereading the works of Benedict de Spinoza. Therefore, there is a huge Spinozist influence, via Deleuze, in the emergent theories of affect I am discussing. Against the subject-centered philosophy of Descartes, which privileges the thinking and fully conscious human being as its main and singular object of analysis, Spinoza wrote about the unity of the mind and the body. Any philosophy that imagined cognition to be devoid of corporeality was amiss, according to Spinoza. Thought, in his reading, was embroiled in the passions, or what he called *"affectus."*[19] If sentiments, emotions, or feelings refer to subjective experience (or senses that can be put into discourse), affectus, in Spinoza's sense, refers to a sensation that may move through the subject but is not known to it (i.e., it is unmediated by the cognitive, or the thinking and knowing, and talking subject). There is a "lack of subjectivity" in Spinoza's philosophy.[20]

Deleuze's own theory of affect follows this post-subjective trajectory. "Affects are not feelings," writes Deleuze. "They are becomings that go beyond those who live through them (they become other)."[21] Deleuze is referring to sensual intensities that may move through human bodies but that do not necessarily emerge from them. The reference point for affect (which used to be, singularly, subjectivity) has been radically altered and multiplied in this approach, making it possible to read many other things, such as space and the environment, as affective.[22] The notion of affect in the Deleuzian interpretation, then, is diametrically opposed to any theory of subjectivity, including, and especially, the psychoanalytic notion of the unconscious.

Just as ANT could be read as a critique of the linguistic turn in the human sciences, as I argued earlier, so is the Deleuzian turn to affect a reaction to the centrality of discourse analysis in the human sciences. In fact, as Deleuze's and Guattari's works can be read as a direct attack on psychoanalysis, so are they as explicitly critical of linguistics.[23] Guattari has specifically argued that "affect is non-discursive."[24] It is not about language but is pre- or extra-linguistic. Guattari speaks of a sensation being "scenic or territorializing [in its] dispositions."[25] Affect, in his terms, is "hazy and atmospheric."[26] It is the non-discursive sensation that an environment generates. So, he writes, "An affect speaks to me, or at the very least it speaks through me. The somber red color of my curtain enters into an existential constellation with nightfall, with twilight, in order to engender an uncanny effect that devalues the self-evidences and urgencies which were impressing themselves on me only a few moments ago by letting the world sink into an apparently irremediable void. On the other hand, other scenes, other existential territories could become canvases for highly differentiated affects."[27] Guattari calls such affective sensations mapped across space and time "*ritornellos*," or "reiterative discursive sequences that are closed in upon themselves and whose function is an extrinsic catalyzing of existential affects."[28] Ritornellization is about the emergence of an "aura" in the sensory world. So, akin to Latour's suggestion to "redistribute subjective quality outside," Guattari suggests that psychoanalysis would have much to learn from letting go of its subject-centered reductionism to allow for a multiplication and differentiation of possibilities in the study of affect.[29] Affect might be about things other than subjectivity.

Deleuze's and Guattari's notion of affect is as open in orientation as is their theory of spatiality. In *A Thousand Plateaus* (2004), the two philosophers differentiate the "root" from their preferred notion, the "rhizome." Their metaphor for what they call the "root book" is the tree, which, well installed downward into the ground, sets out branches upward and vertically.[30] For Deleuze and Guattari, the root book emblematizes Western modes of thinking. The root refers to genealogy, to the skyward branching out of the tree. In its verticality, the epistemology of the root refers to memory, including to the psychoanalytic notion of the unconscious. Deleuze and Guattari observe rooting tendencies in most of the modern human sciences—not only in psychoanalysis, but also in biology, archaeology, linguistics, and history. The root traces, locates, creates a grid, defines structures, in this reading. Instead, Deleuze and Guattari propose the imaginary of the "rhizome."[31] Above all, rhizomes are about multiplicity; they cannot be sited, cornered, controlled, curbed, or located. Nor can they be given any shape, structure, or hierarchy. And going especially against what Deleuze and Guattari perceive as modernity's vertical or perpendicular imaginary, a rhizome moves smoothly in a plain, in an endless surface, that knows no bounds or limits. The rhizome is "a map and not a tracing," they write, associating the trace with structure, determinacy, and genealogy.[32] In turn, "the rhizome is anti-genealogy."[33] Such remarks imply that Deleuze and Guattari conceptualize affect as rhi-

zomatic, or see affect as the rhizome itself, which is everywhere, in constant motion, and un-siteable. This is a distinctly different imagination
about affect from the psychoanalytic notion of the unconscious, for
which the two authors' metaphor would be the root.

So Deleuze and Guattari are asking us to reverse the orientation of our
thinking, from a verticalist imaginary where things are grounded and
rooted to the metaphor of the endless and limitless "plateau." "A plateau
is always in the middle, not at the beginning or the end. A rhizome is
made of plateaus," which allows for multiple possibilities.[34] Thrift studies
this Deleuzian horizontality as a "cartographic" (against an "archaeological") imagination.[35]

I referred earlier to the Mesarya (Mesaoria) plain in northern Cyprus,
which, from the point of view of geography, is a plateau, or flat land that
lies, in this case, between two mountain ranges: the Beşparmak (Pentadaktilos) on one side, and the Trodos (Troodos) on the other. In Deleuze
and Guattari's view, the plateau, like "nomadology," is an analytical fiction. This plain is associated with openness and limitlessness, as well as
with potential and creativity.

The "plateau" I described in northern Cyprus is similar and yet different. The Mesarya plain is bisected, right through the middle, by a
military border that has been in place since 1974. My informants who live
in villages, inherited or appropriated, on the plain have spoken of feeling
confined, entrapped, and suffocated in this slice of territory, especially in
the period that I did fieldwork, before the opening of checkpoints on the
Green Line in 2003. Deleuze and Guattari associate the plateau with free
roaming, movement, multiplicity, and potential, rhizome-style. The thistles, thorns, and bushes I described that grow on the northern part of the
Mesarya plain may have flourished rhizomatically, shooting off weeds in
every direction, crossing over barricades and barbed wire. So has the rust
grown on the surfaces of abandoned cars, dumped refrigerators, and
farming tools, as well as bullets that one finds on the plain, cast aside or
left behind sometime after the war. Rust is rhizomatic, and so is dust,
which can accumulate over time, especially if a space is kept un-maintained for some reason.

Yet I prefer to describe my ethnographic material—these prickly plants
and wastelands—in terms of ruins, shards, rubble, and debris (à la Walter
Benjamin's imagination) rather than the rhizome. What is the spatial
orientation of ruins? Horizontal or vertical? Are ruins about "roots," in

Deleuze's and Guattari's sense? They may well, partially, be so. My informants "traced" the ruins around them, not just passing them by, but locating them in time and space. "Those bullet holes are from 1963," they would say, "whereas the bullet holes over there are from '74." Every abandoned or seized object was sited and dated. The affect discharged by the bullet holes was historicized, symbolized, and interpreted.

My ethnographic field is full of borders and fences erected vertically as emblems of sovereignty. The landscape of northern Cyprus reveals a huge load of ideological paraphernalia: the star and crescent of the Turkish and TRNC flags inscribed by soldiers on mountain slopes and lit up at night to be visible from every point on the island, including the Greek side; the words "How Happy Is the One Who Calls Himself a Turk" written in mega-characters on hills overlooking the plain; entire areas cut off from access or circulation with barrels and barbed wire. Rhizomes?

Rather than casting roots against rhizomes, I suggest, through my preferred metaphor of the ruin, another kind of orientation. We said that the root is vertical, whereas the rhizome is horizontal. The ruin, however, which describes my ethnographic material, is both and neither. A ruin is rhizomatic in the sense that it grows in uncontrollable and unforeseen ways. For example, a village mud house abandoned during the war slowly loses its painted surface over the years, with rain and wind and lack of maintenance. The objects inside the house are looted; its windows, windowsills, and doors are removed to be used elsewhere. A ruin is further ruined through time if it is not used, assumed, or inhabited. Therefore, we could say that a ruin is rhizomatic in some senses. But a ruin is also about roots, because it is sited as a trace of a historical event. It is remembered, kept, lamented, and cherished in the memory of those who left it behind; it is sited and noticed by those who uncannily live in it or in its vicinity. It leaves marks in the unconscious. The ruin, then, works against Deleuze's and Guattari's paradigm setting (or what I have called ruination). It is vertical and horizontal at the same time; it is both root and rhizome.

Back to our core question: How do we theorize affect? I would rephrase this as follows: How would affect be theorized were we to work with the metaphor of the ruin rather than the rhizome? Are certain affects projected onto the ruins by the subjects who make them or who live in their midst? Or, do the ruins exude their own affect? Once again, I would argue that both are evident. Paradigm setting has cast subjectivity against affect, as though one cancels out the other and as if one has to choose between camps of theoretical approach: a subject-centered *or* an object-orientated one. But neither the ruin in my ethnography nor the people who live around it are affective on their own or in their own right; rather, they produce and transmit affect *relationally*. An environment of ruins discharges an affect of melancholy. At the same time, those who inhabit this space of ruins feel melancholic: They put the ruins into discourse, symbolize them, interpret them, politicize them, understand them, project their subjective conflicts onto them, remember them, try to forget them, historicize them, and so on. I would very much endorse the lead of contemporary theorists of affect who, in reading Deleuze, have argued that affect must be studied in domains that are not limited to subjectivity and registers that are not only linguistic or symbolic. But reflecting on what emerges from my ethnographic material, an observation of the affect transmitted through the rusty environment of northern Cyprus does not lead me simply to discard language and subjectivity, for I also observed that my informants' subjectivities were shaped by and embroiled in the ruins that surrounded them. They expressed melancholic interiorities. They put their heartbreak into discourse by speaking of maraz. They talked or kept silent about the ruins. So the affect of the ruins had a subjective quality, too. My material pushes me, therefore, not to simply follow a new paradigm that would have us cast away or turn a blind eye on observations or an imagination provided by other theoretical approaches. Instead, I want to maintain the scope provided by both theoretical orientations, even though they are being presented as antithetical. I propose to ruin neither of them.

Melancholic Objects and Spatial Melancholia

In the spirit of what I have proposed, I ask: What would an anthropology of melancholia look like? The reader will see that my material calls for a conceptual merging of affect and subjectivity, object and subject, root and rhizome, verticality and horizontality, asking for three-dimensional rather than two-dimensional analysis. Ethnography works against the grain of paradigm setting; it asks for all scopes of the imagination to be kept on board.

Classically, Freud studied melancholia as an inner state of being—a psychical condition generated out of the loss of a loved object who could not be grieved.[36] Although mourning allowed for grieving, and therefore an overcoming of the feeling of loss through the lapse of time, melancholia resisted such closure.[37] While in mourning the mourner was conscious of his grief and aware of the object of his feeling of loss, the melancholic was ambivalent about the target or origin of his pain, feeling the loss more unconsciously.[38] What is significant in Freud's seminal essay "Mourning and Melancholia" is that melancholia is studied fundamentally as a psychical condition referring to subjectivity, to the interiority of the human being. In (classical Freudian) psychoanalysis, melancholia is an inner state of personal feeling generated out of loss in an intersubjective relationship. So the only kind of relation that counts is that between people.

Judith Butler has famously expanded on Freud's theory, developing the notion of "gender melancholy."[39] Here, the intersubjective relation Freud talks about, by reference to loss, is studied as gendered. The loss, in Butler's reading, refers to gender identifications, specifically homosexual love and attachments that are prohibited in cultures of compulsory heterosexuality. According to Butler, we live in "a culture of gender melancholy" insofar as we are not allowed to grieve the loss (or un-consummation) of love for people of the same sex.[40] Like Freud, Butler studies "melancholia as a specifically psychic economy," although in her reading it is embroiled in gendered forms of subjectivation and power (via Foucault).[41] Hence, as a student of "the psychic life of power," in her words, Butler is primarily a theorist of subjectivity.

Reflecting on my material, we could imaginatively expand on Butler's theory by reference to situations of so-called ethnic conflict. When the person who has been lost (or spared) is one who belongs to the community of the so-defined enemy, the loss is not symbolized as a loss and therefore is not grieved. Sovereignty and the making of distinct political communities (as well as the identification of "internal enemies" or "traitors") does not allow for the ritualized mourning of people lost to the other side of the divide or those of a different political affiliation. The feeling of loss, not cognitively registered, can therefore generate melancholia, a psychical-subjective state in which the object of loss is largely unconscious to the identity of the mourner and in which, therefore, the loss is irredeemable, ambivalent, and lingering. I find that this analysis of melancholia in the spaces where I have been working—in Turkey, as well as in Cyprus—would be appropriate: deep and unrecognized sadness arising out of the inability to name what has been lost because the "who" who has been lost (people from the community of the so-called enemy, external or internal) cannot be officially known, named, recognized, or grieved.

Yet reflecting on my Cypriot material, I find that this analysis of melancholia, which would register it singularly in the field of subjectivity or the psyche, is as limiting as it is enlightening. In its centeredness on the subject, or the interior experience of the human being, it misses significant aspects of the relations that generate melancholia and loses out on possibilities of analysis. As in my ethnographic account of looted objects and ruined spaces in northern Cyprus, the "lost object" is not only a person (a Greek-Cypriot). Rather, in this case, the lost object (the person) is present in the life of the melancholic in the form of an actual material (or non-human) object, such as a household item, fields of olive trees, or animals. This object (whether it is a piece of furniture, the house, or the land on which the house was built) reminds the people who use or inhabit it that it itself is a loss to the people who were its original owners. The affect of that loss experienced by members of the other community (in this case, Greek-Cypriots) lingers uncannily in the spaces and objects they have left behind. Turkish-Cypriots inhabit many of these spaces and still employ many of these objects. Here, melancholia is mediated through objects and non-human environments. Therefore, we can speak in such instances and historical contingencies of *melancholic objects*, things that exude an affect of melancholy, and *spatial melancholia*, an environment or atmosphere that discharges such an affect.

The melancholy the Turkish-Cypriots said they felt, then, and the affect of melancholia that the space of northern Cyprus exudes can only be interpreted three-dimensionally. This melancholy refers exclusively to neither affect nor subjectivity; it refers to both. On the one hand, Turkish-Cypriots inhabit the melancholy of the other community through their left-behind objects and spaces, because the environment effects this affect. There is the Turkish-Cypriot refugees' own melancholy, having lost their personal belongings and homes in southern Cyprus, as well as members of their community in shootings by Greek-Cypriots during the intercommunal conflict and the war. But there is also another order of melancholy that has to do with violence done to others through appropriating their objects. The melancholy experienced—in this case, via the everyday presence of objects that belong to others—is a loss of a sense of moral integrity. This is articulated and consciously symbolized (put into discourse) by the Turkish-Cypriots through decades of appropriation and right up to this day, as in my analysis of moral discourses around ganimet. In this final interpretation, melancholy is the loss of the self to the self, the loss of a sense of the self as clean and pure. This is a feeling of an abjectified self, of abject inside the self, of subjectivized or interiorized abject, to the point at which the abject is inhabited and no longer recognized as separate from the self. Melancholia, then, is both interior and exterior. It refers to subjectivity and the world of objects at one and the same time. Here, beyond paradigmatic shifts and wars, theories of affect and subjectivity, as well as of objects and symbolization, demand to be merged.

8. Home, Law, and the Uncanny

"I NEVER WARMED TO THIS HOUSE," said Latife Hanım, of the house she and her family had been living in since 1974 in the village of Taşkent (Vouno) in northern Cyprus. "It's not our house," she said. "It's left from the Greek-Cypriots." Latife was originally from the village of Anadiou in the Troodos range viewing the Baf (Paphos) region, now in southern Cyprus. At nineteen, she was married and moved to the village of Dohni (Tochni) in the Larnaca region, again in the south.[1] She and her husband settled in a house passed to them by her in-laws. "We put a lot of labor into that house," she told me. "When it's your own home, you make an effort without thinking."

Three years into their marriage, Latife and her husband had a year-old son and were expecting another child, when her husband was advised by his Greek-Cypriot employer to leave his village as soon as he could, warning him that there would be troubles. It was April 1974. Latife and her family decided to move to her family's home in Anadiou for a while. On 20 July 1974, Turkish troops landed in Cyprus, invading towns and villages in the north of the island. A couple of weeks after Turkey's invasion, Latife and her family heard of troubles in Dohni. Several Turkish-Cypriot men had been rounded up and killed by Greek-Cypriots from the same village. Had they remained behind, Latife could have been widowed.

Months after the incidents in Dohni, which are remembered to this day by Turkish-Cypriots as one of the biggest massacres committed against them by the Greek-Cypriots, Latife and her husband learned from the radio that the villagers of Dohni were being settled in the village of Vouno (later named Taşkent) on the Beşparmak (Pentadaktilos) mountains viewing Lefkoşa in the north of the island. The pregnant Latife and her young son were transported to Vouno on United Nations buses. Her husband joined them later, crossing the mountains on foot to reach northern Cyprus. "We weren't allowed to carry any of our belongings," said Latife. "We lost everything. I had about twenty handwoven bed-sheets in my dowry chest. I had given these to one of our relatives, before leaving Dohni. But when our relatives escaped for the north, all my belongings were left behind, too. I have no idea what happened to my bed sheets."

Latife spoke about the relationship she had had with things. "I used to keep things (*eşya*); I used to give a lot of value to things," she said. "In Dohni, I even had things that I had brought there with me from my childhood in Anadiou. I remember I had brought a copy of *Snow White* with me in my dowry chest. This book had been given to me as a gift by a lady from Ankara who had wanted to adopt me as a child. I kept this book as a precious item all the way until we had to leave Dohni. But then . . . we lost everything."

In Vouno (Taşkent), Latife and her family first moved in with her in-laws, who had been allocated a Greek-Cypriot house. Almost all of the houses in Vouno had been distributed among Turkish-Cypriot families from the village of Dohni. Latife and her family had arrived late, when nearly everything in their adopted village had already been appropriated by their fellow villagers. They had to wait several months until Greek-Cypriot houses that were being used by Turkish soldiers were evacuated and made available. Meanwhile, Latife's second child died soon after he was born. "There were many eyes on this house," said Latife, meaning that many people were interested in settling in the house that she and her husband were finally allocated. "We had to argue and say that we had a small child and had lost another; we had to fight until we were allowed this house." There was moral negotiation among the villagers of Dohni as to which family should be given priority of settlement. The relative needs and extent of suffering of each interested party were collectively evalu-ated. Latife and her husband were given the rights to inhabit a Greek-Cypriot home on the outskirts of Vouno. "The Settlement Office sent three keys to the village for the three neighboring houses here," she said. "Each family would move into the house with the matching key." The key that was given to Latife's husband opened the door of the house that became their home.

The Cypriot House as a Political Institution

In this chapter, I explore the experience of inhabiting a home that belongs legally and sentimentally to other people. The story of Latife and her family that I just recounted is one of many such stories. Thousands of Turkish-Cypriots had to evacuate their original homes in southern Cyprus to move to northern Cyprus as refugees and settle in houses in villages and towns there. Most of the houses they were allocated in northern Cyprus even today belong to Greek-Cypriots under international law. Latife's story will form the centerpiece of this chapter, along with the stories of other Turkish-Cypriots, as I study how, having lost their own, they continue to use other people's homes and belongings. What interests me is the affect generated by the built environment and by material objects that have been appropriated. I study the energy transmitted through houses and things that are charged with the traces of other people's lives.

In *Home Possessions*, Daniel Miller has studied what he calls "the agency of the home itself," analyzing not people's symbolic worlds, cultural constructions, and social relations as they are mediated through their homes but what the houses in themselves, as material properties with agencies of their own, "do" to their inhabitants.[2] In a chapter on British estates and London council blocks, Miller studies people who relate to their dwellings with a degree of alienation, whether through a literary imagination of being haunted by the previous owners of the estate or through a sense of deficient agency in altering a space allocated by the state.[3] My analysis in this chapter follows from Miller as he engages with the work of other scholars who have theorized the agencies of inanimate objects.[4] However, while such works on the entanglement of people with the animacy of things stress the agencies of material objects and situate such entanglements in the cultural (or "ontological") systems they study, none of them studies things as objects of another, political, sort. In the analysis that follows, I study the built environment and material objects in northern Cyprus as vessels for a contingent and contemporary politically induced affect. The energies transmitted by the materialities used by Turkish-Cypriots can be abstracted to make anthropological or theoretical comparisons, but they are more interesting in this regard when they are studied as objects of political and legal substance. In other words, they are not to be studied only as exemplars, in another culture, of the enmeshment of people with things.[5] These objects testify to the embroilment of politics and law in the most intimate spheres of existence: around people's most private and personal belongings. I would like to suggest, therefore, that the properties that people use are charged not only with a "cultural" agency (as in the agency of ghosts, spirits, or ancestors, as studied by anthropological students of material culture), but with the agencies of politics and law. The built environment and material objects are transmitters of politically and legally mediated affect. In this sense, political and legal institutions can be studied as producers as well as loci of affect. Bruno Latour's "non-human" entities,[6] then, must be studied as politically contingent. Non-human entities are politically charged. Political and legal institutions (such as administrations, bureaucracies, courts, and state structures) can be analyzed as "non-human" objects of sorts: not just as vessels that transmit the human energies that went into their making, but as objects with agencies in their own right. In this sense, I regard the Cypriot house not only as a cultural institution (as it would be studied with the existing anthropological repertoire on the house), but also as a political and legal institution. In fact, I would argue that the Cypriot house has been a centermost political and legal institution. Politics and law in Cyprus have been centrally negotiated around people's personal homes and belongings. It is in this sense that I study the Cypriot house as charged with affect.

Collected Items

Latife showed me the objects around her house. Her living room was cluttered with furniture. The various sofas, cupboards, and buffets had not necessarily been placed with a seating arrangement in mind. Two tall buffets had been pushed to one corner of the living room and covered with sheets to prevent them from getting dusty. On the floor were several plastic barrels full of olive oil, which Latife and her family had produced. So part of the living room was being used as a storage space for the family's produce and excess household items.

"We found this *divan* in the neighborhood above the hill," said Latife, showing me a traditional wood-carved Cypriot sofa. "It's left from the Greek-Cypriots; I only changed its upholstery." She continued:

> When we arrived in this house in 1974, we didn't find any furniture. There were
> only four iron beds without their mattresses, as they had been used by the
> Turkish soldiers who had stayed here. But there was nothing else. Since we

arrived late in this village, all the good furniture had already been taken away by our fellow villagers who had come earlier. The objects left from the Greek-Cypriots—I mean, the loot (ganimet)—had also been distributed. When we didn't find anything, what were we going to do? We started going around and searching. From here and there we collected the things people thought were broken or useless and we brought them to the house. Not much loot (ganimet) had been left in this village when we arrived. I remember that we didn't even have mattresses to sleep on, so when I found a mattress in the neighborhood on the hill, I carried it home. All of our villagers had taken the good belongings of the infidel (gâvur). What they didn't want, or what wasn't in good condition, they threw away. When we arrived, we only had the clothes on our bodies to wear, so I went around the village and collected clothes that had been thrown on the ground. I washed them and like that we wore the infidel's clothes. Let God not show such days to anyone. That was a very difficult time.

Latife's husband, Kemal, joined our conversation: "War is a terrible thing. Let God not show it to anyone." He recalled what the village of Vouno (later Taşkent) looked like when they arrived four months after July 1974: "There were things left from the Greek-Cypriots everywhere—on the sides of the roads, on the ground, on the hills." Imagining how the Greek-Cypriots of Vouno must have escaped, he said: "We found suitcases full of personal belongings. The Greek-Cypriots must have packed their things to run away, but finding them too heavy to carry must have left them on the side of the road. One night, as I was walking through the village, I noticed something shining on the ground. I picked it up. It was a golden engagement ring with the year 1971 inscribed on it." "That's also the year we got engaged," said Latife. "I still wear the ring sometimes."

Latife went on to describe how they got the items in their house. "I found this buffet [of carved wood] in that neighborhood above the hill, and this long buffet was in the house we stayed in before moving to this one, so we carried it with us. . . These armchairs with iron legs, we changed the upholstery and still use them." Thirty years after the event, Latife and her family were still using the furniture and other things they had collected in various parts of the village of Vouno (Taşkent) in 1974. Large pieces of cloth and drapery in reds, greens, and navy blue had been thrown over a couple of sofas in the living room. "I didn't have a chance to change the upholstery of these," she said.

"We are used to using other people's belongings," said Latife. "As long as it's clean, I don't mind wearing something someone else has worn."

Latife still had an eye for things that had been thrown away. One day, as we were walking together in Lefkoşa, she noticed a pair of old shoes among garbage thrown on the side of the road. She kneeled down and picked them up. "I like these. They are flat shoes, I can wear them," she said and took them home with her. Latife enjoyed receiving donations of used clothes; she looked through a bag of old clothes that her employer in Lefkoşa had given to her and identified which of her children and grand-children could use which garment. She was used to using things marked by other people's lives.

A few pieces of furniture in Latife's house were not "left from the Greek-Cypriots," as she put it. On the three significant walls of the living room were black-and-white as well as color photographs of her family members. The photographs had been placed in old wooden frames and hung at the center-top of the walls. Among those shown in the photo-graphs were Latife's parents, sisters and brothers, and in-laws, as well as Latife with her husband and children and her grandchildren. It is a con-vention in traditional Cypriot homes to display family photographs in living rooms, but when this is done in a house owned by Greek-Cypriots, I interpret it as an effort to personalize space that has been appropriated, an attempt to turn an adopted house into a home by linking it with the adopting family's kinship network and genealogy. The Turkish-Cypriot family's photographs on the walls of the Greek-Cypriot house, in my reading, represent attempts to include a family's own sociality in the history of the adopted property. The photographs included Latife's ances-tors and descendants in the genealogy of the inhabited house. They represented an effort to transform the adopted dwelling into a more homely space.

The Unhomely

In the essay "The Uncanny," Freud explores the kinds of psychic situations that arouse a feeling of eeriness, fear, or dread.[7] He studies such situations in literary examples as well as in his psychoanalytic case material and classifies them under the analytical category *unheimlich*, in German. Se-mantically, "unheimlich" translates into English as "the uncanny," but Freud notes that etymologically "unheimlich" corresponds to the English "unhomely."[8] I am more interested in this etymological equivalent of unheimlich for my analysis in this chapter, because when interpreted that way, "unheimlich" can be read as a commentary on the home. Studying such manifestations of unhomeliness (by reference to Freud) in architecture, Anthony Vidler has developed the concept of "the spatial uncanny."[9] It is precisely this generation of an anxious affective state through the built environment and domestic space that I study in this chapter. But my topic is specific: Since this is a particular history of expropriation, I study the relative "homeliness" of a misappropriated house.

According to Freud, "*unheimlich* is clearly the opposite of *heimlich, heimisch, vertaut*."[10] Turning to a German dictionary published in 1860, Freud provides passages that refer to the feeling of homeliness (heimlich). From these, I extract a few that I find most relevant to the discussion in this chapter: "Heimlich, *heimelig* . . . 'belonging to the house, not strange, familiar, tame, dear and intimate, homely, etc.' . . . 'belonging to the house, to the family, or: regarded as belonging to it, cf. Lat. *familiaris*, familiar' . . . 'intimate, cosily homely; arousing a pleasant feeling of quiet contentment, etc., of comfortable repose and secure protection, like the enclosed, comfortable house' . . . 'cosy intimacy' . . . 'I shall probably feel nowhere more at home than here.'"[11] Later, Freud suggests that "heimlich is also used of a place that is free of ghostly influences."[12] In turn, in the antonym of "heimlich," "unheimlich," Freud identifies feelings of being "uncomfortable, uneasy, gloomy, dismal, uncanny, ghastly, (of a house): haunted, (of a person): a repulsive fellow."[13] He also notes that "the German phrase *ein unheimliches Haus* ['an uncanny house'] can be rendered only by the periphrasis 'a haunted house.'"[14]

On reading selections from Freud's interpretation of the "heimlich" (or homely), the reader might at first sight think that there is nothing about Latife Hanim's home that could classify as such. The house belongs not to her or to her family but to Greek-Cypriots. Almost all of the furniture and objects in the house belonged originally neither to the house nor to its present inhabitants. They are items that were dispersed and are being put to different uses in a new context.[15] One might be led to think that a feeling of "unhomeliness" pervades such Greek-Cypriot homes inhabited by Turkish-Cypriots (or vice versa) in the south.

However, I propose another kind of analysis. Let us consider whether the opposition "heimlich–unheimlich" is a false antonym. Or, to put it differently, does the unheimlich have to be conceived as a necessary contrast to the heimlich? Do the meanings for heimlich provided by Freud presuppose an originary bourgeois notion of coziness and comfort in the home derived from original or sole ownership? What if we did not take this notion of "homeliness" or "the home" as the baseline against which to compare other experiences of "home"? What if "the unheimlich" is placed right at the center of a conceptualization of the home?

As I read carefully, I find out that this is, in fact, what Freud intended. As categorical and classificatory as the German dictionaries of his time were, in his analysis Freud challenged the distinction between heimlich and unheimlich: "Heimlich thus becomes increasingly ambivalent, until it finally merges with its antonym unheimlich. The uncanny (*das Unheimliche*, 'the unhomely') is in some way a species of the familiar (*das Heimliche*, 'the homely')."[16] With this interpretation, Freud negates the antonymic meaning implied by the opposition homely–unhomely.[17] He goes further to the heart of his analysis by arguing that something will be perceived as uncanny only because it used to be familiar (or homely) and was repressed: "The uncanny is that species of the frightening that goes back to what was once well known and had long been familiar."[18] Freud is interested in detecting traces of the unconscious in uncanny material.

But I would like to attempt another kind of analysis out of this, to suggest that Freud has taken the heimlich as his central or main reference point, an experience of the settled and comfortable bourgeois European home.[19] It is out of this imagination that he projects his notion of "the unhomely." And notice that in his interpretation the unhomely refers back to the homely (or, in his reading, the unconscious, that which is most familiar). We said he cancels out the opposition via this interpretation. But what if we took another route? What if we presupposed the uncanny or took that as our locus and estranged ourselves, for conceptual purposes, from notions of the homely as a reference to coziness and comfort? I think such a tack would take us to other arenas of interpretation from those Freud explored. In fact, I argue that Freud interprets the uncanny from a secular-rationalist position. In his work, something can be perceived as uncanny only if it is in the realm of nonfiction. Fiction cannot arouse a feeling of uncanniness by definition, according to Freud, because the reader expects the writer to use his fictive imagination.[20] Something is uncanny only if experienced in the realm of rationality because it is unexpected, it does not fit, or it jars. In turn, I argue that, if we were to center the uncanny in our analyses, the uncanny would not appear so strange.

This is what I suggest has become of the uncanny in northern Cyprus. Imagine three decades of living significantly in houses owned by others, using the personal belongings of others, and plowing and caring for land and trees registered in other people's names. Latife Hanim told me that she had "never warmed to this house." However, she did not find the presence of Greek-Cypriots' objects in her home as strange as I did. Home was this uncanny space for her and her family. "Home" did not arouse feelings of the heimlich as defined by Freud. Home contained aspects of the unheimlich, and this was experienced as normal. In such expropriated Greek-Cypriot homes inhabited by Turkish-Cypriots in northern Cyprus, the unheimlich is part of the everyday experience of homeliness. Rather than being a counterpoint to the homely, the uncanny is an aspect of the home for Turkish-Cypriots who were allocated Greek-Cypriot land and property. Or, the unhomely has been rendered homely. This analysis will lead us to an anthropological reconceptualization of the home in the following sections of this chapter.

Household Habits

Latife's home was always immaculate. Whenever she was not working, Latife cleaned her house, balcony and verandah, and garden. She mopped the floors at least once a day. She used old pieces of cloth to wipe the kitchen surfaces several times before and after meals. She used bundles of cloth, again, to clean and dust furniture in the house. She and her husband carried buckets full of water to the balcony and verandah at least once a day, and they washed the water away with a broom, leaving the space clear of fallen leaves or petals. Likewise, they assiduously cleared their garden of unwanted roots, thorns, or thistles.

Such special interest in and concentration on order, cleanliness, and neatness is evident in almost all of the Turkish-Cypriot homes I have known and visited. Latife's home and her household habits were not an exception. Washing, cleaning, wiping, and dusting were activities done habitually, over and over, several times a day. The women of the house took primary responsibility for domestic orderliness. However, men also took part in maintenance, particularly of the gardens (or the *avlus*, as the Turkish-Cypriots called them). The avlu—the inner or back garden—was regarded as semiprivate space. Avlus were well kept, tended, cared for. Cemented sections of the garden space were swept clean of earth every evening with a broom, and at night, before going to bed, Turkish-Cypriots watered the plants, flowers, and trees in their gardens for long periods of time with a hose.

Turkish-Cypriots arranged seats (usually plastic chairs) in the evenings to face either their avlus or the front doors of their houses, with backs turned to the road. They positioned themselves to look into or toward their homes. Sitting like this, with their backs to the outer world and in a semicircle facing their houses, Turkish-Cypriots cut vegetables for their evening meals, un-leafed stalks of the molokhia plant, or peeled fruit for their children. Coffee was served on such occasions to neighbors, relatives, or other guests, as well as to household members. Sweets made of fruit preserve were offered, too, to any guest who arrived in the morning or afternoon. Often a household member or a guest was asked to read fortunes in the coffee grains of others sitting in the semicircle. News was exchanged, gossip circulated, and people made political commentaries. At one end of this seating arrangement was invariably the television, which was positioned at the door of the house or the garden, facing outward so it could be watched by the company facing the house. Turkish-Cypriots talked, looked after their children, and, at the same time, watched the news or other television programs and interpreted their daily or political predicament. It was as if the Turkish-Cypriots had turned in toward their homes, had hidden themselves inside, turning their backs on the outside world, focusing on maintaining order and cleanliness inside their dwellings. Having less agency in the domain perceived to be outside their homes, Turkish-Cypriots attempted to lay a special hold over their household units. I interpret the daily and what seemed to me excessive routines of cleanliness in the homes and gardens of Turkish-Cypriots as an attempt to create subjective order within an objective world that had been adopted in the aftermath of utter disorder. The embodied repetition of daily household rounds and duties, and especially its extreme thoroughness, asks to be studied as a commentary on the context of Turkish-Cypriot sociality and subjectivity. Such everyday routines carry a philosophy with them, in Eduardo Viveiros de Castro's sense of "ethnophilosophy,"[21] although they were not intended as such. It falls to the anthropologist to decipher the philosophy in our informants' seemingly mundane everyday practices. In Turkish-Cypriots' special attentiveness to household cleanliness, I detect unarticulated efforts to make a "home" out of the "unhomely," an order out of disorderliness, intimacy in a hearth of memories of violence or violation experienced by one's self and by others.

Turkish-Cypriots who inhabit Greek-Cypriots' homes know that they do not legally own the houses. They live in the houses with an awareness of their original Greek-Cypriot owners. They are conscious of using other people's belongings. But they keep these belongings clean and in good condition. One of the renderings Freud provides for the concept of homeliness (*heimlich*) reads: "a careful housewife, who knows how to create a pleasant homeliness (domesticity) with the meagrest of means."[22] Turkish-Cypriots', particularly women's, endeavors to order their homes deserves a more poignant analysis of homeliness. Here, domestic household work figures as the primary agency in an attempt to overcome feelings of the uncanny, to render the uncanny less visible or less effective, to pacify its affects. Here, the uncanny is a domestic item, and it has been normalized or rendered homely. However uncanny this home is, it is nevertheless home for Turkish-Cypriots. So in spite of all their trepidation vis-à-vis their expropriated homes, Turkish-Cypriots always asserted, "This is also our home," referring to their post-1974 livelihood there and the fact that their children had known or seen no other space of homeliness.

Household Maintenance

Turkish-Cypriots who inhabit Greek-Cypriots' property maintained their homes with some trepidation while I did the major part of my fieldwork in 2001–2002. Household maintenance in this period reflected the nature of the affective relations Turkish-Cypriots had forged with the houses they lived in. "If I knew this house could remain with us, I would maintain it beautifully," said Nezih. "I would do major building work." Nezih and his family had been living in a house in a village in the Güzelyurt (Morphou) region since 1974. His family had moved to the village, along with their fellow villagers, as refugees from a village south of the border. Nezih was twelve at the time, and he remembered how his family had been allocated the house and the orange groves that surrounded it in place of the house and land they left behind in their ancestral village in the south. With the passing of Nezih's parents, the house was left to Nezih, his wife, and children.

"If I invest in this house, I don't know whether we will be able to keep it in the long run," said Nezih. Consequently, Nezih fixed only what was essential. He and his family had not altered much of anything in the house since they started living there in 1974. They had built a fireplace in the living room. Nezih joked that this was their contribution to "Christina," the name of the Greek-Cypriot owner of the house, which Nezih had discovered while sifting through the photographs and personal belongings left behind by the original owners. Aside from the fireplace, Nezih and his family had had the house painted a couple of times over the years. When I visited them, the inner walls of the house were crystal white. "We also had the iron bed frames polished," said Nezih's wife. "But we didn't paint the legs of the beds; they still make creaky sounds when we turn in our sleep." If tiles fell off the kitchen walls, they did not replace them; nor did they make any changes to the floors, balcony railings, or other features. They did not buy new furniture, either. Showing me the sofas in their living room, the long chair, the kitchen table and chairs, the beds, and the children's study desks, Nezih said, "We still use what is left from Christina."[23]

Nezih and his wife lived in their house with the knowledge that it still legally and sentimentally belonged to its previous Greek-Cypriot inhabitants. Nezih wondered about the owners of his house; he tried to imagine what they were like and who they were. He had even queried their whereabouts through friends who were able to cross the border. One day, when I was visiting them, Nezih brought out a whole package of photos from storage in the basement. He first showed me the photo of Christina, whom he imagined was the owner of the house. He then took out Christina's driver's license, dated 1972. "Christina was twenty-two years old in 1974," he said. "Her parents had built this house for her." Nezih developed the story his own curiosity and research had suggested. He believed that the house was Christina's dowry and that her mother had lived in the house next door until 1974. "Christina and her husband had two small children," he said. He showed me small black-and-white photographs of Christina in a school uniform, in her wedding gown alongside her husband, with a baby, posing in front of her balcony and under her orange trees. "Do you know where she might be living right now?," I asked. "If she is alive . . ." said Nezih. He had heard of troubles and killings in this village in 1974.[24] "Other people got rid of the photographs and personal belongings they found in the houses left from the Greeks. They threw them away or burned them. Maybe we should have done that, too; but we didn't."

Nezih and his family imaginatively cohabited their home with its Greek-Cypriot owners. Christina was imaginatively present in the marital home she had left behind. The Turkish-Cypriots who adopted this house were in a social relation with her in her absence, as they used her furniture and kept her personal belongings. They construed an imaginary relationship with her through the personal objects she had abandoned. And they inhabited her domain with trepidation. They were conscious of using her items, and they transferred this awareness to their children. They organized their household habits and maintained the house through an imaginary relation with Christina, considering what she would find pleasing or upsetting and trying to keep her home in a reasonably good state. They dwelled here with a level of anxiety, uncertain of their future rights to maintain this house as their property. They related to what had become their family home with a sense of guilt toward Christina, a feeling they only rationalized by referring to the property they had left in their ancestral village, now administratively in southern Cyprus. They even expressed gratitude to Christina for the use of her belongings.[25]

The specific and contingent affective relation to one's home I have described here should be distinguished from the alienation studied by Daniel Miller among inhabitants of London council estates. It should also be studied in terms that differ from tenancy contracts. Even though many Turkish-Cypriots refer to the Greek-Cypriot owners of their homes as their "landlords (ev sahiplerimiz)," there was no direct agreement between parties about this living arrangement. Turkish-Cypriots also have not been paying rent. Both public housing and tenancy, in their Euro-American renderings, usually take place under ordinary circumstances and within the accepted confines of the law. In the case I am studying, however, there is an enduring uncertainty in the aftermath of a war and a long-term failure to reach a political agreement between two sides to a conflict. There are also legal battles or disagreements over rights to property and settlement. Therefore, the notions of homeliness, house ownership, and property ask to be conceptualized differently. This is a kind of living arrangement that does not fit neatly within the parameters of Euro-American notions of dwelling in the confines of recognized law and contractual agreements.

The House as a "Psychic State"

In his book *The Poetics of Space* (1994), Gaston Bachelard writes philosophically about the house.[26] In a book that should be read more for poetic inspiration than for empirical reference, Bachelard derives from the house what he calls "a phenomenological study of the intimate values of inside space."[27] He creates an imaginative portrait of "the childhood home" as it is embodied in the person who grows up in it:[28]

But over and beyond our memories, the house we were born in is physically inscribed in us. It is a group of organic habits. After twenty years, in spite of all the other anonymous stairways, we would recapture the reflexes of the "first stairway," we would stumble on that rather high step. The house's entire being would open up, faithful to our own being. We would push the door that creaks with the same gesture, we would find our way in the dark to the distant attic. The feel of the tiniest latch has remained in our hands.

The successive houses in which we have lived have no doubt made our gestures commonplace. But we are very surprised, when we return to the old house, after an odyssey of many years, to find that the most delicate gestures, the earliest gestures suddenly come alive, are still faultless. In short, the house we were born in has engraved within us the hierarchy of the various functions of inhabiting. We are the diagram of the functions of inhabiting that particular house, and all the other houses are but variations on a fundamental theme. The word habit is too worn a word to express this passionate liaison of our bodies, which do not forget, with an unforgettable house.[29]

Bachelard writes about the house as a "psychological diagram," a "primal image," a space that holds "cosmic" power over its inhabitants, and a "psychic state." He gives the name "topoanalysis," a word derived from psychoanalysis, to this "systematic psychological study of the sites of our intimate lives."[30]

This chapter is intended, in line with Bachelard, as a spatialized study of affect or a study of affect as experienced through space and material objects. However, unlike Bachelard's, an anthropologist's philosophy must emerge from her empirical ethnographic material. In his phenomenology of the house, Bachelard paints a picture of psychically and phenomenologically experienced warmth, stability, and peace. He writes of the house as our "original shell," "our corner of the world," "our first universe, a real cosmos in every sense of the word."[31] He writes about "well-being" in the house: "Within the being, in the being of within, an enveloping warmth welcomes being. Being reigns in a sort of earthly paradise of matter, dissolved in the comforts of an adequate matter. It is as though in this material paradise, the human being were bathed in nourishment, as though he were gratified with all the essential benefits. . . . This is the environment in which the protective beings live. We shall come back to the maternal features of the house."[32] Reading Bachelard, one is left with an image of the home as a space of unproblematic quietude, of intimate tranquility, of basic centeredness, of an unarticulated feeling of peace. As pleasing as it is poetically to imagine such a space, I would argue that Bachelard's imaginary of the home is situated in a specific European middle-class experience, even if he writes in a manner that would make it appear universal. Bachelard writes about people who symbolically, physically, and psychically feel at one with their homes. In other, non-European contexts, anthropologists have written of such senses of bodily and relational completeness in one's home. Houses have been studied, by anthropologists, as emblems of culture, as reflections of the social world around them. For example, Janet Carsten and Stephen Hugh-Jones suggest that "the house and the body are intimately linked. The house is an extension of the person; like an extra skin, carapace or second layer of clothes, it serves as much to reveal and display as it does to hide and protect. House, body and mind are in continuous interaction, the physical structure, furnishing, social conventions and mental images of the house at once enabling, moulding, informing and constraining the activities and ideas which unfold within its bounds."[33]

Likewise, in his study of the Maori house, Alfred Gell studies the house and the person as a unit. This is why, he writes (with Claude Lévi-Strauss in mind), "so many social groups are referred to as 'houses.' "[34] In other words, houses embody or stand for social collectivities. The Maori house in Gell's reading, was an entity in union (or "at one") with Maori being. Gell describes an ancestral presence, a continuity between the past and the present of a house, a symbiotic or organic relation between Maori house, mind, and body: "To enter a house is to enter a mind, a sensibility, especially if it is such a house as the Maori were accustomed to make. Like many traditional psychologists, the Maori located mind and intention in the viscera. To enter a house is to enter the belly of the ancestor and to be overwhelmed by the encompassing ancestral presence; overhead are the ribs of the ancestor, in the form of the superbly decorated rafters which converge towards the ancestral backbone, the ridge-pole—the fountain-head of ancestral continuity."[35] I suggest that such anthropological imaginaries about "houses" are situated, too. It is strange that such anthropological renderings of houses, inspired by the study of non-European contexts, should be so similar to Bachelard's Europeanist representation of household phenomenology as an unproblematic union between a person and his dwelling. Do these anthropological and philosophical studies of the house lack an imagination of other kinds of experiences of the home?

Cypriot houses that have been abandoned, changed hands, and been appropriated by refugees provide us with another notion of the house. Here there is uneasiness between a person and his dwelling, a conflict, anxiety. As they embody embryonic warmth and maternal encapsulation in the intergenerational relations forged between their present inhabitants, expropriated Cypriot houses also, and at the same time, provoke worry, discontent, and nervousness. Rather than being repressed and subliminal, as in Freud's rendering, uncanniness is on the surface, tangible, and visible in Cypriot homes that have changed hands. It is there to be seen, touched, and observed in furniture appropriated from the house's previous inhabitants, in the only half-maintained use of the space, in the personal belongings of the original owners of the house. Rather than being a space of fetal coziness, such Cypriot houses are always tinged with anxiety, arising from their past ownership and unknown future. Unlike the Maori house described by Gell, where there is an ancestral presence and continuity (including a visceral sense of union with the house), in the Cypriot houses I have studied and described, there is guilt over having appropriated someone else's ancestral property and an attempt, through hanging family photographs on living-room walls, to inscribe the incoming family's ancestral links and genealogy in the space of the home. Such anxiety experienced in the very space of domesticity should incline us to another analysis of the house. In the Cypriot house, the uncanny is not to be excavated but is out in the open, there for the seeing. The uncanny, rather than being ghost- or phantom-like,[36] is tactile and evident: It can be held, touched, used, sat on, slept on. The uncanny is a foundational experience in expropriated Cypriot households. In the next sections of this chapter, I study why this is so by reference to the political and legal charges weighed on the house in Cyprus. I argue that the Cypriot house is a political and legal institution. It is charged with what I call politically and legally induced affect.

Property of Equal Value

Greek-Cypriots' property was not appropriated and distributed arbitrarily. Instead, Turkish-Cypriot administrators invented a system or procedure for the allocation of property to Turkish-Cypriot refugees from southern Cyprus and to immigrants from Turkey who were given rights to settle in northern Cyprus. The idea was to give an appearance of administrative order in an attempt to disseminate an affect of fairness or justice done to the Turkish-Cypriots. This intended affect, projected by the creators of the property-allocation procedures, was never unproblematically internalized by Turkish-Cypriots, not even by the administrators themselves. Instead, practices around this system of expropriation can be likened to a dramatic play in which all of the actors are aware of the farce in which they are involved yet continue to act as if they were not.

Greek-Cypriot property was allocated to Turkish-Cypriot refugees and immigrants from Turkey after 1974 under a façade of law. It is important to note this for a proper ethnographic understanding of the specific way and conditions under which Turkish-Cypriots obtained the Greek-Cypriots' houses they have been living in since 1974. It was not the case that anyone could go and settle in any property he or she took a liking to. Rather, there was a specific and explicit attempt to create an administrative procedure (a policy, in fact) through which Turkish-Cypriot refugees could claim property in northern Cyprus in return for property they had had to abandon, because of the war, in the south. The policy created by Turkish-Cypriot administrators was called İskan, Topraklandırma ve Eşdeğer Mal Yasası (Settlement, Land Allocation, and Property of Equal Value Law; iTEM).[37] It is interesting to observe how an illegal appropriation was framed and presented in the guise of "law (yasa)," and even more intriguing to know how this law and its implementation was recognized as a farce by administrators and beneficiaries alike.

Property is one of the most fundamental components of European and international law; accordingly, property abandoned by Greek-Cypriots in northern Cyprus in 1974 still legally belongs to its original Greek-Cypriot inhabitants, as does Turkish-Cypriots' property in the south which counts as the legal private property of Turkish-Cypriot individuals or families. All property in Cyprus, north and south, is registered in the Office of Title Deeds of the Republic of Cyprus (now in the south), and Greek-Cypriots can show documents for their property in northern Cyprus. These documents are recognized under international law. It is against these documents and this legal ownership of northern Cypriot property by Greek-Cypriots that the iTEM law was created. Turkish-Cypriot administrators took advantage of the military border between northern and southern Cyprus in the manner in which they allocated property to Turkish-Cypriots. The border was heavily guarded militarily, and access across was not allowed (for almost three decades) to Cypriots of either side. Therefore, it could be argued that the iTEM law is dependent on Turkey's military presence in Cyprus. In Walter Benjamin's terms, this could be studied as the "originary violence" at the foundation of law.[38] Under these conditions, where a separate administrative entity was established in northern Cyprus, which had seceded from the Republic of Cyprus, a legal procedure that negates Republican, European, and international law was invented.

iTEM is a sophisticated system of property allocation, with clauses regulating specific situations and conditions, including property sharing and inheritance. First published in 1977, iTEM was approved by the High Courts (Yüksek Mahkeme) of northern Cyprus and revised several times thereafter. Like other legal procedures in northern Cyprus, iTEM mimics or models itself on European legal practices. The Turkish-Cypriot lawyers, judges, and administrators who created it were all trained in places where Euro-American legal systems have been in operation—Britain, Turkey, or Cyprus. In other words, the law in northern Cyprus cannot be studied as an anthropological anomaly, a case to contrast with Euro-American law in the classical fashion of legal anthropology, because it imagines itself as, and was conceived within the realms of, a Euro-American legal culture. What is interesting here—and this is what I analyze and draw attention to—is how the iTEM law, like other laws of northern Cyprus, takes issue with Euro-American law from within: It mocks Euro-American law while copying its medium and style. In other words, northern Cypriot law is an illegal system that is fed by European and international law. Although Cypriot, European, and international legal systems ardently declare its illegality and do not recognize it, I argue that iTEM is in the style of European and international law, or has been "mothered" by it.

I find it ethnographically appropriate to convey how iTEM was implemented through the experiences of a Turkish-Cypriot rather than as a generalized account of a procedure, because I am interested in the affect generated by law among those subjected to it or operating within its domain. Nezih, whom we encountered earlier, described the several stages in which the property allocation system was created. "First they invented something called the 'T-ruler (T- cetveli),'" he said. He showed me his T-ruler document. It had the shape of a large "T" in the middle of the document, with the tail of the "T" dividing the form into two sides. "This is to compare property left in the south with property obtained in the north," he explained. The left-hand side indicated Turkish-Cypriot property abandoned in the south, either in 1963 or in 1974, and the right-hand side documented Greek-Cypriot property appropriated after 1974.

"They created a Regulating Commission (Tanzim Komisyonu), and this commission created the concept of the point (*puan*) and that of value (*değer*)." Every property (including dwellings and land) would be assigned a numerical value in points. Councils of elderly members of every Turkish-Cypriot village left in the south gathered to declare the value of the property left behind by each Turkish-Cypriot family or individual. In this way, people were able to fill out the left-hand side of their T-rulers, indicating the value in points of the property they had had to abandon. In turn, the Regulating Commission assigned value in points to Greek-Cypriot properties in the north. The idea was to allocate property according to the Eşdeğer Puan Sistemi (Property of Equal-Value System). An example of social engineering in the aftermath of war and displacement, this system ideally or apparently meant to reproduce, in northern Cyprus, the social structure of Turkish-Cypriots as they had lived in the south. The concept of equal-value would symbolically create an appearance, if not a reality of social justice.

The Turkish-Cypriot administrators wanted to please their subjects to guarantee their complicity, since a social structure gone haywire after the war could create feelings of injustice. The system of property allocation would ensure that the rich would remain rich and the poor would remain poor and that no one would obtain more property value in the north than he or she had previously owned in the south.

"By subtracting the value in points on the right-hand side from [those on] the left-hand side of the T-ruler, each party can calculate how many points he or she can still claim from the state," Nezih explained. Showing me his T-ruler document, he illustrated how he and his family had 5 million points still owed to them by the state. This meant that the value of the Greek-Cypriot property he and his family had been allocated in northern Cyprus amounted to far less than the property they abandoned in the south.

Most properties in northern Cyprus were allocated for the settlement of Turkish-Cypriot refugees and immigrants from Turkey under a population policy in 1975. Nezih told me that in 1985 and 1986, all citizens of the TRNC were called to the Settlement Office (İskan Dairesi) to have their property values compared. Everyone had to have a completed T-ruler. "People objected to the value in points that had been assigned to their properties," he said. "There were many misappropriations and a lot of injustice in the way in which property was distributed." Therefore, although the property allocation procedure was invented to create an appearance of justice by reproducing a previous social structure, this system in practice, according to Nezih, delivered the opposite results. "Those who had *torpil* [referring to the system of gaining benefits by exploiting social connections] got more property than they had the equal-value right to."[39] These are the people whom the Turkish-Cypriots refer to as the "1974 rich," or those who became rich after the war by obtaining far more Greek-Cypriot property and land than they had ever owned in the south. Another term that was often used among Turkish-Cypriots to refer to those who advanced in social status after 1974 was "*ganimetçiler*," or "the looters," a moral judgment of those who, by exploiting their social networks (torpil), obtained large amounts of Greek-Cypriot property. The Turkish-Cypriot administrators who created the property-allocation system were often themselves accused of being looters for withholding the best Greek-Cypriot property for themselves. Such discourses of morality in relation to property allocation were also used by Turkish-Cypriots in their characterizations or evaluations of specific politicians, administrators, political parties, and even the TRNC state as a whole. "Can there be justice in a country of loot?," said many Turkish-Cypriots I knew. "Can there be peace of mind in a society of loot?," said Nezih. "If you want to study this country, you have to study property and settlement. There were many injustices (*haksızlıklar*)."

By "injustice," Nezih was referring mainly, or on the surface level, to injustices in the allocation of property among Turkish-Cypriots. Beneath that, I believe he was also referring to the original injustice, the appropriation of Greek-Cypriots' property. But within the realm of the Property of Equal-Value System and the T-rulers, Nezih recounted stories of Turkish-Cypriots' obtaining much more property than they were due. He considered this an injustice. He believed the property allocation system was corrupt. This was a moral evaluation of the property procedure within the terms set by the procedure itself. However, there was also an implicit sub-commentary in Nezih's remarks, a moral evaluation of the property procedure in the first place or at the outset, referring to the original idea of appropriating land that belonged to others.

"At a certain stage, they created something called the Table of Sources (Kaynak Paketi)," said Nezih. "They declared the value in points of all the property left in the hands of the state. For example, the state has so many dönüms of land in the village of Edremit in the value of so many points. . . . These tables were published, and people could approach the state to buy this land by showing the extra points they had the right to claim on the right-hand side of their T-rulers." But a very interesting practice was introduced at this stage whereby the TRNC administration asked Turkish-Cypriots to renounce their right to ownership of their property in southern Cyprus and to cede that property to the state if they wanted to benefit from the Table of Sources. This practice was called "renunciation (*feragat*)." The renunciation document that had to be signed by every Turkish-Cypriot who wanted to buy land with the value in points they had in excess read: "I cede all my property in the south to the government of the Turkish Republic of Northern Cyprus." Turkish-Cypriots were transferring all rights to their legally owned property in the south to the TRNC administration, which could now act on their behalf in any negotiations with the Republic of Cyprus, take unilateral decisions about Turkish-Cypriot property, or act as the owner of all that property. When the law of renunciation was introduced, the border was closed, and Turkish-Cypriots did not perceive any possibility of returning to reclaim their original property in the south. Their arms were twisted. Therefore, there was a rush to claim property from the Table of Sources by going through the property renunciation procedure.

"Our old man refused to sign the renunciation documents," said Nezih, referring to his grandfather, who had been a major landowner in their ancestral village in southern Cyprus and did not want to cede his rights to ownership of the land to the TRNC administration, believing that wrong would be done to him. "There were others who did not sign the renunciation documents, but only one in a thousand. But if you don't sign, you are stuck without any property. So we told my grandfather: 'The whole country is getting property, and we are unable to, because you won't sign the document.' We took my grandfather to the Settlement Office and had him sign the document. That way, we were able to apply to be allocated property through the Table of Sources." Nezih further explained that, despite signing the renunciation documents, he and his family could not get further property in the north. "The best land was distributed among the supporters of the regime," he said. To illustrate the corruption in the property allocation system, Nezih told me that most Table of Sources property was announced at the time of elections in northern Cyprus, and people were promised good property out of the table in return for voting for the parties of the TRNC establishment (the DP and the UBP at the time). Likewise, to distribute property to their supporters, the DP and the

UBP created new notions of property points, which they called the "fighter points *(mücahit puanı)*" for those who had fought under the TMT during the intercommunal conflict, and "damage points *(hasar puanı)*" for those whose property had been damaged during the war. "With such concocted categories of point and value, they [the administrators] distributed property to their collaborators," said Nezih. "Many people who were given useless land in return for signing renunciation documents took the state to court for this."

There was, therefore, an internal moral and political battle, as well as legal struggles, among Turkish-Cypriots and their administrators about how Greek-Cypriots' property was allocated in the north. Legal procedures of sorts were undertaken within a realm of illegal property appropriation. Turkish-Cypriots challenged their administrators about the legality of the procedures they introduced and implemented, and the only way they could do this, under conditions of subjection to the TRNC and confinement to the borders of northern Cyprus, was to use the courts of the TRNC to take the TRNC itself to court. Here, the legal and the illegal are intertwined and indistinguishable, one within the other, every act being both one and the other.

"At first there were no title deeds *(koçan)*," said Nezih when I asked him which documents were given to Turkish-Cypriots for their use and inhabitation of Greek-Cypriot property. "In the beginning, they gave us all what they called documents of appropriation *(tahsis belgesi)*." These documents showed that property had been granted to a Turkish-Cypriot party in return for property of equal value left in the south. But documents of appropriation were also given to immigrants from Turkey. "Then they invented what they called documents of definite possession *(kesin tasarruf belgesi)*. And finally, they transformed these documents into title deeds (koçan)." At first, the state granted TRNC title deeds only to Turkish-Cypriot holders of Greek-Cypriot property. But immigrants from Turkey organized demonstrations asking for title deeds for themselves, too, Nezih recounted. "Then they [the administrative supporters of the TRNC regime] also gave title deeds to the immigrants from Turkey before elections, in order to gain their votes. When such things happen, you lose your value judgments. The worst thing in this country is injustice. How can one live contently with injustice?" Turkish-Cypriots like Nezih considered the acquisition of title deeds by immigrants from Turkey an even further injustice, as the immigrants obtained Greek-Cypriot property against no equal-value counterpart. This would often be characterized as "having gained property from the air (*havadan mal sahibi olmak*)" by people who did not experience the war and displacement in Cyprus and who therefore lost no property in the south against which their expropriation of property in the north could be rationalized.

I wondered what Turkish-Cypriots thought of the title deeds the TRNC administration state had given them for the Greek-Cypriot properties they lived in. Latife Hanım said, "This is not our house. The state distributes title deeds. They gave us a title deed for this house, too. It says on the title deed that it has been granted in return for property of equal-value. But it is fake (*sahte*) what they have given us. These are fake title deeds. Anyway, even if they aren't fake for us, they are fake for the Greek-Cypriots."

Turkish-Cypriots who lived in Greek-Cypriot property and held TRNC "title deeds" were in full cognizance of the "fakeness," as they called it, of these documents. Regardless of this, an active economy around northern Cypriot property has been in place, using these deeds. Greek-Cypriot property has been bought, sold, and transferred with deeds and documentation supported by TRNC law. But Turkish-Cypriots handle or use their property documentation, including title deeds, with trepidation. It is as if these documents were both present and absent at the same time—now you see them, now you don't. The permanence and sense of security associated with writing, signatures, official letters, and documentation in Euro-American and international law need to be re-evaluated in this context. Here, documents do not evoke a sense of confidence in their holders and handlers. Instead, documents, and especially those produced by the state, transmit an affect of insecurity, tentativeness, violation, greed, and injustice. These documents are modeled on European and international law. They cannot be interpreted as completely other to Euro-American law, and any anthropological endeavor to find that which counters or contrasts with Western law would be doomed to failure. Nevertheless, they provoke different kinds of affect.

As I have illustrated, TRNC law has been enormously modifiable. Of course, this is true of any legal system, but it is more poignantly so under the TRNC because the illicitness of its practices in the face of the international community are known to its administrators and its subjects. The tentativeness, malleability, and manipulability of TRNC law, including the iTEM, has led to conflicts about property among Turkish-Cypriots, including among members of the same family. "Our neighbor cheated on us," said Latife Hanım:

He is my husband's nephew. His son was working in the Office of Title Deeds, and he diminished the inner courtyard (avlu) of our house by half in the maps and registered the other half under his name. In fact, the whole of that courtyard had been allocated to us by the administration. But my husband's nephew wanted to put up a fence to divide the courtyard. We brought the fence down and called the police. He wasn't able to put up a fence. Now it remains without a fence; we didn't allow him that. We also parked our car on what he registered as his side of the courtyard. And then we brought the Settlement Office to court. The court proceedings are still in process. It has been one and a half years and there is still no result. We also hired a lawyer. Now that we have also had this courtyard incident, I developed even more coldness towards this house. And I feel disgust to call this neighbor our "relative."

Law and the Uncanny

Earlier in this chapter, I developed the notion of the unhomely home as a motif to describe Cypriot houses that have been appropriated. I also suggested that the Cypriot house should be studied as a political and legal institution. We are now in a position, given the material I have introduced, to analyze this better. Here, I would like to suggest that uncanniness does not emerge sui generis. Rather, uncanniness is a legal and political form. The uncanny has been studied within the confines of individual psychology in psychoanalytic writings. In such writings—significantly in that of Freud—the uncanny is a reflector of material in a person's unconscious world. But it may not be only individual psychical energy that produces uncanny effects. I argue, based on my Cypriot material, that politics and law are also generators of feelings of uncanniness. As Turkish-Cypriots relate to their houses and property with a sense of anxiety and uneasiness, so do they hold, keep, and handle their documents and approach the law of their state and its administration, practices, procedures, and implementations with a sense of trepidation. Here I develop the concept of the *legal uncanny*.

The term "the legal uncanny" does not designate the illegal. The notion of the illegal could only be a criminological category of analysis, or perhaps a legal one, not one for anthropological conceptualization. It comes with a positivistic epistemology that would assume that the distinction between the legal and illegal can be rationally or even scientifically determined and that these domains and categories are distinct and incommensurable. Indeed, full-fledged scientific disciplines—criminology and law—have been established precisely to objectify the illegal. Likewise, governing practices are in place all over the world—the police, the legal system—to identify and control that which is defined as illegal. I consider the illegal a problematic analytical category and do not use it as such, especially because it is a particularly politicized or "native" category in Cyprus. In the Republic of Cyprus and among Greek-Cypriots, the illegality of the TRNC (which is a fact in international law) is a paramount concern, and every practice in northern Cyprus, including such mundane activities as eating, drinking, or swimming there, are evaluated under the rubric of illegality. In other words, the notion of the illegal is ideological in Cyprus and cannot therefore be a category for anthropological analysis. Now, the concept of the *legal uncanny* that I here propose does not designate the illegal. I am not suggesting that northern Cypriot spaces, including houses, feel uncanny because they are administered by an illicit system of governance. It is another kind of analysis I am after in developing the concept of the *legal uncanny*. Uncanniness is not paramount in appropriated Cypriot houses simply because the administration in northern Cyprus, which allocated these properties in the first place, is illegal. Although I have not studied abandoned Turkish-Cypriot properties in southern Cyprus now inhabited by Greek-Cypriots, I imagine a similar uncanniness must be there, as well, even though the property-allocation practices of the Republic of Cyprus (a legally recognized state) were different from those of the TRNC.[40] Rather, I invite readers to consider the case I have described as a motif that might challenge the way we envision law and politics more generally. Under the administration of an illegal state, uncanniness is more apparent. My argument is that studying this illegal state only makes more evident the uncanny aspects of law and politics that can be studied in all state practices, including those considered legal. It is with such a course of thinking—which is not one that would make illegality relative—that I propose the analytical concept of the *legal uncanny* as different and distinct from the notion of the illegal. I argue that the legal uncanny could also be studied in spaces and sites deemed legal under national and international laws.

Freud studied how, like a déjà vu, the uncanny reveals unconscious material already unknowingly familiar to the individual psyche.[41] Inspired by Freud, as well as by artistic and literary renderings of the uncanny, scholars have explored the uncanny as revealed in space and the built environment, as well as in aesthetic forms.[42] Others, such as Julia Kristeva, have begun an analysis of the uncanny in political space, in her

case studying the figure of the stranger or foreigner as an uncanny remi-
niscence of the familiar in cosmopolitan spaces.[43] This chapter, and others in this book, follow from these studies in an attempt to specifically
theorize the uncanny as a political and legal form. "Such a move," as
argued by John Welchman in reference to Hal Foster's work, "also takes
us to the limits of psychoanalysis, prompting us to look to the uncanny in
its wider social and historical contexts, where it may be said to arise not
just as a kind of symptom, but also as a metaphor for various ideological
and political effects."[44] In this chapter, I have looked at the space of the
home, and of property, not just as a site of "the spatial or architectural
uncanny," as theorized by Anthony Vidler in a tradition of aesthetic and
psychoanalytic renderings of the uncanny,[45] but also as a legal and political institution that in itself transmits an affect of uncanniness. The appropriated Cypriot house, as I have analyzed it, should be conceived as a
microcosmic magnifying glass, a lens onto political and legal practices not
just under the illegal state in northern Cyprus but in administrative
practices more broadly.

9. Collectibles of War
and the Tangibility of Affect

IN THIS CHAPTER, I TELL THE STORIES of three amateur collectors in northern Cyprus who have amassed objects left behind in the aftermath of war and created distinct indoor spaces out of them over the years.[1] The odds and ends they have gathered and displayed in their homes and personal surroundings produce and emit specific kinds of affect. By reflecting on the affects discharged by these material remains of war and the ways they have been collected and exhibited by the three men, I explore affect in this chapter in a way that considers its tangibility and visibility.

Affect has generally been theorized through metaphors that invoke abstraction, imaginaries of immateriality, and conceptualizations of invisibility. Insofar as affect has been a central query in the Freudian psychoanalytic tradition, for example, the unconscious has been the primary rubric through which the affects have been considered.[2] In this classical reading, affect refers to an invisible primary core in the interiority of the human subject or it emerges out of this immaterial abyss. This subjective core is non-organic: It is not supposed to be conceptualized as physical, physiological, or embodied. In psychoanalysis, not only are the affects invisible to consciousness; they also emanate necessarily out of a human subject and his or her inner world. Affect is projected out of a human subject onto an outer environment and world of objects. In other words, in psychoanalysis affect is studied and explored only or mainly through a theory of subjectivity.[3]

In the sociological tradition, too, affect is abstract, though in this case it is not about subjectivity but, instead, has been reduced to the category of the social. Arguably, Durkheim bases his theory of society on a notion of affect. He writes about society as "some current of energy [that] . . .

come[s] to us from without," as a force from the outside that dominates as well as sustains a group of people.[4] This energy (i.e., society), in Durkheim's imagination, is "effervescent," intangible, like an invisible gas. Totems are only representations of this abstraction; they hold no significance in their own right. This exterior force generates what Durkheim calls "a state of exaltation, [in which] a man does not recognize himself any longer. Feeling himself dominated and carried away by some sort of an external power."[5] In that affective moment of collective exaltation, Durkheim studies the emergence of the social, tout court.

In this chapter, I contest the manner in which affect has been theorized through metaphors of intangibility—the unconscious, the effervescent—in both the psychoanalytic and the sociological traditions. I do this by considering the war remains collected by three men in northern Cyprus and exploring how the affects transmitted by these objects are mediated and qualified. Affect is shown to be both contained and emitted through these objects' very solidity, presence, visibility, and tangibility. Affect is also shown to be entangled in regimes of politics, meaning, and morality.

Building on the works of Marilyn Strathern, Alfred Gell, and Bruno Latour, we are now able to conceptualize the potency of objects, the agency of things or non-human entities in their own right in relation to human subjects.[6] My exploration of the tangibility of affect follows from these works. However, since language, subjectivity, and textuality have been bracketed (or cast away) in these studies, it is difficult to know how this potency (what I explore in affect) would be qualified and mediated or how it could be entangled in meaning. We could argue that what emerges is the possibility of studying affect not as an interpretation (in the Geertzian sense) of the social environment and the object world as projected out of a human subject and his or her cultural world, but through the qualities, texture, and potentialities of the objects themselves. The very affect transmitted by objects could be explored: the qualifications that might emerge not from the interpretive, symbolic, or cultural mediations of human-centered practices but through tangibilities in themselves. In this chapter, I illustrate how the affect of objects only becomes felt and known to us, as human beings engaging with them, via mediation and qualification. Theories of materiality that would bracket out mediation or qualification, then, could be considered limiting.[7] So could theories of affect that would construe it diametrically against the hermeneutic tradition.[8] My questions, instead, are: How is affect qualified? How is meaning given to the affects transmitted by objects? How do the affects emitted by materialities come to mean anything?

Here I find it useful to discuss the work of Gabriel Tarde, as he assists us in qualitatively exploring affective transmission—that is, in qualifying affect, giving meaning to it. Few have read Tarde as a theorist of affect.[9] Other aspects of Tarde's work—those more amenable to Actor-Network theory—have received greater emphasis.[10] In this chapter, I engage specifically with Tarde's notions of "imitation," "contagion," and "suggestibility." In these Tardean concepts, I, like Lisa Blackman, read a theory of affect. Blackman has written:

> In *Psychologie Economique* Tarde (1902) stresses the importance of understanding the subjective aspects of the economy through engaging with understandings of psychological matter which were prevalent at the time of his writing. This was not a matter of studying individual psychology, characterized by the abstracted, self-contained individual, but rather an "inter-psychology" . . . which recognized that subjects were open to affecting and being affected. *Economic Man*, which epitomized for Tarde the alien and abstract concept that economists were mobilizing, was one that created "a man with nothing human in his heart." . . . It was the question of the heart, of the realm of feeling, affect and desire which was central to Tarde's formulations and which led him to take seriously the interplay and interpenetration of the psychological and the sociological.[11]

Tarde is a theorist of intersubjectivity. In other words, insofar as he centers relationality in his queries, the relations he studies are between human subjectivities or, more precisely, between the mental states and psychologies of human subjects—hence, his notions of "inter-mental activity" and "inter-psychology."[12] So we could argue that, for Tarde, affect is an energy that is transmitted only between human beings. The environmental, spatial, or material worlds do not figure in Tarde's picture.

I have already argued that Durkheim has a theory of affect; in fact, I went so far as to argue that Durkheim's notion of the social is based on a concept of affect as the cohesive glue that brings and holds a group of people together against the forces of *anomie*. Tarde conceptualizes affect rather differently. As Latour has proposed, in Tarde there is no theory of the social as some sort of context for human activity.[13] Instead, as I have noted, Tarde's sociology emphasizes interactivity. It focuses on what he calls the inter-mental or inter-psychological, on what is transmitted, through imitation, between one human subject and another. These multiple imitations never amount to any massive or cohesive group of any sort or to anything like a "society," as in Durkheim. Instead, in Tarde we are kept at the micro-ethnographic level of interactivity. Affect, in Tarde, is what is transmitted through these inter-mental or inter-psychological influences between one human being and another and through infinitesimal links to other people.

What, I ask, is the quality of this affective transmission? How is this inter-mental relationality to be qualified or understood? I argue that in Tarde's work, a qualification is assigned to affect as transmitted between human subjectivities. Consider Tarde's notions, or his choice of words, to represent his theory: "imitation," "contagion," "suggestibility." In transmissions of affect between human subjects, Tarde generally imagines mimicry, resonance, harmony, and agreeability. David Toews has studied this in Tarde's interest in the influence that one individual holds on another that eventuates in a "following," what Tarde calls an "imitation."[14] Similarly, Terry Clark has analyzed the centrality of the concept of "imitation" in Tarde's sociology:

> What remains are the "inter-mental" aspects of men, or man insofar as he is influenced by other men. The basic process by which this inter-mental influence takes place, and the basic social fact for sociology, Tarde holds, is imitation. Social relations are essentially imitative relationships. But sociology need be concerned with only those aspects of the psyche which are transmitted between minds. Here, the two basic psychic units, the two elementary particles of imitation, are what Tarde isolated in an early essay as "belief" and "desire," the one cognitive, the other emotive. The final result of imitation for the individual is a "mental imprint," an impression on the mind similar to the imprint on a photographic plate.[15]

I shall explore this quality of Tarde's notion of affective transmission in more depth later in this chapter, but suffice it for the moment to say that I find an element of conservatism in Tarde's theory of affect insofar as transmission through relationality is primarily analyzed through the terms of influence, following, repetition, and reproduction. Durkheim the conservative and Tarde the radical?[16] I would not quite agree. If in Durkheim affect functions as the social glue—affect is what conserves society or what makes everyone conform and stick together—in Tarde affect is no less conservative: It is about being under influence, imitating, and reproducing; about following the ideas of the one who is most powerful. In both of these analytical or theoretical conservatisms, as I would like to call them, I detect possibilities for qualifications of affect that have gone unexplored or astray.

Let us now return to the subject of the ethnography in this chapter: the war remains collected by three men living in northern Cyprus. What is the significance of these collections of objects? What do the collections say? What do they mean? What can they tell us about how affect can be qualified? And how, if at all, do they challenge Tarde's imaginary of imitative or suggestible, what I call agreeable and cozy, affect?

Collection 1

I am visiting a village in the Mesarya plain in northern Cyprus that used to belong to Greek-Cypriots, and is now inhabited by Turkish-Cypriots. In the village lives a man in his forties, whom I will call Metin, who says he inherited an antiques business from his father. Metin has invited a group of Turkish-Cypriots and me to his home. He wants first to show us his garage. We peer through the darkness and see that the garage is packed with objects. Among them I notice a large marble stone with a carved-out center that looks like a washbasin. Metin tells us he found the piece in a field on the outskirts of the village. "Apparently, the Greek-Cypriots used to give water to their animals in this thing," he says. It was pitch dark outside, and there was no light in the brick garage. We could barely see the objects, so Metin ran to fetch a gas lamp, which he used to light up the objects one by one.

First, he showed us an old wooden buffet. The cupboard's glass doors were broken, and it looked worn; its varnish had completely disappeared. "Where did you find this?" we asked Metin. "From the houses," he said, with no more words. He moved the gas lamp to another item. An old, Cypriot-style wooden chest appeared. The lamp moved on again, making visible a painting of horses running in a field, a dresser, a carved-wood cupboard, and one household item after another, furniture, paintings. We were stunned at the quantity.

Metin led us out of the garage and into the side garden of his house, a two-story building left by the Greek-Cypriots. The garden was another collection site. Metin had placed and arranged objects on the ground of his garden, things he had found here and there on his walks through the village and on his excursions in northern Cyprus. There was an ancient-looking amphora, which he said he had dug up from under the sea while he was diving. There were seashells covered with mold, an old sewing machine, a small flower vase. Metin pointed at the trees in front of his house. "That tree is left from the Greek-Cypriots," he said. "The other one was planted by us. It is twenty-six years old [referring to the number of years, at the time, since 1974]."

We walked up the three steps from the garden into Metin's house. The entranceway was cluttered with things Metin had collected. In the left corner stood an ivory chest. "This one is Ottoman," said Metin, as if guiding us through a museum collection. On top of the chest stood a box full of old liquor glasses. On the wall of the entrance hall was a framed embroidery made out of colorful thread, with Greek writing. On a stool, we noticed a volume of a Greek-language encyclopedia with pictures. On another wall was an old poster representing the suffering of the Turkish-Cypriot people.

Metin turned on the lights in the small living room. We walked in and found ourselves in the midst of yet more of what Metin called "antiques." Metin did not mention that the objects belonged to the Greek-Cypriots who used to live in the village unless we asked. This knowledge was assumed, not necessary to articulate. If we asked, however, Metin nodded his head, matter-of-factly, and said "yes."

In the middle of the living room stood a 1970s-style wooden table with a plastic cover. Under the window, lay an old *divan*. On the wall hung a framework of silken Cypriot embroidery. Among the leaf patterns woven out of silk were the photos of a young couple in romantic poses. "Are these photos of Greek-Cypriots?" I asked. "Yes," Metin said, nodding. Under the frame was a fine dresser of carved wood; in the corner, an old buffet full of pretty glass items. We kneeled down to peer into the glass case. There were thin glasses in red and blue, vases, ceramic bowls, plates, and other objects. "Where did you find these?" we asked Metin. "From the houses," he said, again. "Are they all from this village?" I asked. "Yes," he responded. "They are all from this village."

Picking out a glass item from among the collection, he said, "This is Ottoman glass, blown in the Beykoz style." On an old wooden table were more things: decorative statuettes, silverware, spoons for fruit preserves, vases. Metin pushed a glass case and opened a cupboard. There we saw more ceramic plates and bowls, all hand-painted. In the corner of the room was a cushioned armchair, and on it Metin had placed an imitation statue of Aphrodite. Interspersed among all of these things were Metin's family photographs: framed images of his brothers and sisters at their weddings, a photo of Metin as a little boy with his parents and older sister, and other shots of his family.

"These objects are crying," said one Turkish-Cypriot in our company of visitors. Metin said nothing. As we walked out and departed, another Turkish-Cypriot commented on the eeriness and uncanniness of the objects in Metin's collection. He said he found the experience of seeing the collected objects extremely disturbing. He commented that the objects were loot (ganimet). It was indeed hard to shake off the uneasy feeling the objects had discharged or brush away the strange mark they had left on us.

Collection 2

I am visiting the village of Gemikonağı (Xeros) along the coast of northern Cyprus for fieldwork. Here, a young Turkish-Cypriot woman and I look for a place to sit and talk. We notice an old hotel building that seems to be functioning as a coffee shop. Huge waves from the Mediterranean hit the sea-viewing walls of this rundown building. The exterior paint has washed away over the years. We turn the doorknob at the main entrance and enter a large space with windows looking onto the massive sea. A middle-aged woman greets us, and an old man sits on a chair by the window. We order Turkish coffee, and the lady disappears along a corridor into what we guess is the kitchen. "Everything here has collected dust," says my Turkish-Cypriot friend as we look up at the cobwebbed items hanging from the ceiling in the old hotel lobby. Spider webs link one object with another.

I approach the old man by the window and ask him about the objects. "I collected them after the war," he said. "How did you collect them?" I asked. "I went from village to village and collected every farm tool I could find left behind in the fields." "Why especially farm tools?" I asked. "I had a special interest in farm tools," the old man replied, "and I hung all the things I could find up here." Most of the farm tools on display in the lobby had rusted. "Are these left from the Greek-Cypriots?" I asked. "Some are; some are not," the old man replied. "I don't know."

Our coffee arrived, and as we drank, waves hit the windows of the coffee shop. I sat to speak with the woman, who said she was the old man's daughter. She had never married and had always run the hotel, now turned into a coffee shop, with her father. She told me the story of the building: "This used to be a hotel owned by a Greek-Cypriot man. After the war, Denktaş gave this hotel to my father in return for a hotel my father had left behind in the south. We started running the hotel. I was in my twenties at the time, and we got customers. But in time people began to lose interest in this part of the island, and few came to stay. So we transformed this space into a coffee shop." "Did the space look like this when you were first allocated it?" I asked. "It looked pretty much the same. We didn't change much." She pointed at the bar along one of the walls of the old hotel lobby. "Look," she said, "do you notice that this bar is in the 1970s style? That's how we found it, and that's how we left it." The layout of the lobby, as well as the furniture, was much the same as they had found in 1974 when they reached northern Cyprus as refugees from the south. "The only thing we added is my father's farm tools," said the woman. It was summertime in 2002, and I reflected on the fact that the space we were sitting in and the objects in it had been left to live their lives out over the years. The space had not been renovated or modernized. The furniture and decorations had been left un-maintained. They were rusty, worn, and torn.

As we walked out of the coffee shop, my Turkish-Cypriot friend commented on the eeriness of the place. "Can you imagine: They have left everything the way they found it in 1974," she said. "It's like going through a time tunnel and returning to a time in the 1970s, as if everything after that was frozen." She went on to reflect on the uncanniness of the cobwebbed farm tools that the old man had collected and displayed.

Collection 3

I am walking on a street in the northern part of Lefkoşa. On one side is a house and garden that appear to be overflowing with objects. Over and through the gates of the garden, I notice ten or twelve plastic baby dolls. In another corner, over the gate, I see a collection of old shoes piled on top of one another. By the entrance of the garden is a sign that says "Museum: Open between 10 and 4." An elderly Turkish-Cypriot man quietly greets me as I ask if I can visit. "Yes," he says, as he motions me in and begins to lead me through the sections of his self-styled museum. I notice that objects have been classified by type and exhibited accordingly together. Eight or ten rusty metal chairs have been placed on top of one another in one corner of the garden and old newspapers have been collected in another. In another section of the garden are old kitchen utensils, forks, knives, pots and pans. Alongside the shoe collection is an array of old clothes, classified by size and whether they are for men or women. Farther along I see books in Greek and Turkish piled on top of one another.

The old man shows me into his house. At the entrance, I notice a newspaper photo of Bülent Ecevit, the Turkish prime minister in charge of the Turkish army's invasion of northern Cyprus in 1974. The house is also filled with objects, classified according to type: blankets on one side, old pillows on another; porcelain plates in one corner, flower vases in another. The old man nods to my question of whether this is his home. It is a home space turned into a museum of objects kept in the aftermath of war.

At the back of the house, viewing one of Lefkoşa's busiest streets, the collector had created a display area. On a makeshift wooden table he had placed a number of worn shoes, old books and newspapers, and dolls. None of the objects was for sale. Beside the table was a sign with an arrow that signaled the way in to "the museum (*müze*)."

I left the old man's house-museum wondering about the significance of such objects for people who have experienced a major reshuffling of their homes and territories. Why had this man collected everything? Why had he not thrown anything away? What was the value, for him, of these old things? Why had he classified them into kinds? What was the purpose of turning his home into a "museum"? The old man had not wanted to discuss any of this. He had only told me about the difficulties he faced with the Lefkoşa municipality, which thought of his house as a dump and wanted his "museum," which overflowed into the street, to be removed. "They only allowed me to maintain it if I put high fences around my garden so the sight wouldn't disturb the neighbors or the people walking on the street."

Postwar Collections and the Tangibility of Affect

What do collections say? What do they mean? Or, what is a collection? "In the West," write John Elsner and Roger Cardinal, "the *history* of collecting objects of cultural and aesthetic virtue has tended to be presented as a sub-set of the sociology and the history of taste. The great canonical collections, with their temple-like architecture, their monumental catalogues, and their donors' names chiseled in stone, testify to the paradigm of Beauty as the exclusion of all ugliness."[17] Elsner and Cardinal argue that in the West, collectibility has been conventionally measured against waste, so that nothing discardable would be valued as collectible. Convincingly, they suggest that the predominance of curatorial traditions and museums in the West has generated a dominant notion of collections as pertaining to objects that have been not only valued but also cleaned, and therefore transformed, through curatorial practices. Such items, amassed and classified as reservoirs of knowledge, have been imagined, according to Elsner and Cardinal, against shit or the filthy.[18] The valuable objects have been kept apart for exhibition, divorced from the unwanted things, which have been packed away, thrown away, or left behind. They call for attention to be paid to unrecognized collections, what they call "the quieter, subversive voices rising out of that 'unacceptable' residue lying in culture's shadow."[19]

In this chapter, I study precisely such unnoticed, non-institutional collections and unconventional classification practices. The three Turkish-Cypriot men whose objects I have described are collectors of residue: of objects once personally valued, of things left behind in houses, villages, and open fields or in their immediate surroundings. Other Turkish-Cypriots might have put such residual objects to personal use, recycling them in their current homes. Many might have thrown them away or replaced them with modern, newly bought items. What distinguishes the relations these three collectors have forged with objects is the way they have kept them and exhibited them for public viewing. These men have gathered and retained traces of the material world around them and arranged them as personal museums. Unlike objects in Western-style museums, which are kept, dusted, and maintained, the objects in two of the collections I have described are left to deteriorate organically within their own life course. In other words, these residues are treated by their collectors as if they are living beings that give in to age. Rust is allowed to appear; dust is left to collect. The abject properties of these objects is not segregated from their desirable aspects.[20] On the contrary: That which was left behind or discarded has been found, kept, and given personal value in these unconventional collections. The abject and desirability have merged.

My next questions are: What do these objects say? What language do

they speak? And what is their significance? The conventional anthropological route, in response to these questions, would be to explore the
culturally distinct meaning the three collectors give their collected objects. This would entail an inquiry into the meanings and personal interpretations projected onto the objects. Without negating the force of such
cultural or personal interpretations, I will, here, experiment with another
path of thinking. It entails posing our questions in another way: In the
fashions in which they are kept and opened to viewing to the occasional,
haphazard visitor, what affects do the objects in these collections transmit? I argue that the remnants and residues I have described, as kept in
personal collections in northern Cyprus, carry an affect in their very
tangibility. The facts that they were collected after the war from abandoned villages and fields and that they have been left to live through their
organic life-course accumulating rust, dust, and cobwebs are part of the
objects' solid and material presence. "These objects are crying," said a
Turkish-Cypriot viewer in the house of the first collector. In turn, the
affects discharged by the objects in the second collection were described
by a Turkish-Cypriot viewer as transmitting a weird sense of eeriness. It
is a sense or knowledge of the context in which such objects were collected and put on display that mediates the affects the viewers experience
in relation to these objects, qualifying the transmission of affect and
putting it into words and meaning. For people who might have had no
idea about how such objects might have been accumulated after the war,
these tangibilities might not have produced the same affective tension. I
therefore argue that tangibilities transmit affect, but this affect is mediated and qualified by the knowledge that the people who come into
contact with them have about the context for the objects. Affect, in other
words, is tangible (not just immaterial), but it is also mediated and qualified by the specific people who experience it.

Irritability

As I argued earlier, Tarde's writings offer a quality that is rare in contemporary affect theory: His metaphors provide a qualification for affect. In
radically distancing themselves from hermeneutics and the textualism of
poststructural theory, most contemporary theorists of affect have cast
away any attempt to interpret affect or give meaning to it.[21] Likewise, we
have a proliferation of studies of object potency but no tools to under-

stand what that potency might be about or how it might be amenable to interpretation.[22] Certainly, the human subject or his or her cultural world cannot be the only source of interpretation. The question still remains: What is the quality of affect? Or, how is affect (to be) qualified? For this, Tarde has an answer. All of the metaphors he employs to study affective transmission are qualifications: the imitative, the rhythmic, the contagious, the suggestive. The "inter-mental," in Tarde, is an axis for resonating communication, for agreeable reproduction, for influenced repetition, a following. So Tarde gives us a qualification for affect. Yet the only sorts of qualification Tarde's technical terms make possible are those of harmony and resonance.

I return to my three collectors and their objects. How do we qualify the sort of affect transmitted through the atmospheres created by their collections? Recall the reflections of my Turkish-Cypriot companions while exiting the collections we were visiting. On both occasions, the Turkish-Cypriots had been irritated by what they had seen. They commented by saying they found the objects (and the whole collections) eerie, disturbing, and uncanny.

Here we are writing about a specific kind of affective transmission—not only between human subjectivities, as in Tarde's notions of "inter-mental" activity or "inter-psychology," but between objects, a general atmosphere or environment, and human subjects. This kind of transmission, not studied by Tarde, is what interests me in reflecting on my ethnographic site and material from northern Cyprus. This is akin to "the transmission of affect" as studied by Teresa Brennan in the senses evoked by an environment, as well as to studies of the agency or potency of objects by Alfred Gell, Nicholas Thomas, and Bruno Latour.[23] Therefore, I complement Tarde's attention to the "inter-mental" with an interest in the tangibility of affect.[24]

How do we qualify the affect transmitted by the three collections? An affect of eeriness, of the uncanny. An environment of objects that emits a sense of jarring. A collection that evokes disturbance or irritability in the viewer. A transmission of affect between object and subject that produces disharmony, tension, or uneasiness. A different quality for affect, a specific entanglement of sense and meaning, a distinct qualification—one that does not invoke resonance with one's surroundings, or harmony, but provokes anxious reflections about it.

And where does this qualification come from? Is it projected by the anthropologist onto the objects she has seen in her informants' collections? Is it the intended qualification of the collectors themselves? Did the collectors willingly create such atmospheres of eeriness? The answer to all these questions, I suggest, is no. Instead, I suggest that we ponder the qualifications wrought by the tangibilities themselves, the objects in the collection and their qualities: their dilapidated state, the rust, the dust, the spiders' webs that link them with one another, the decrepit state of the environment in which they are being kept, the fact that most of the collections consisted of objects collected after a war or that many of them belonged to other people who would have missed them. It is these qualities of the objects, in relation to their viewers' knowledge about their context, that evoked irritability and feelings of uneasiness among those who came into their presence. Objects and a material environment can generate affect, then, but only as they get entangled in forms of human mediation. This affect may be of a nature that evokes dis-harmony; an affect not of "suggestibility" or "contagion," as highlighted in Tarde's work, but in this instance of irritability, jarring, and disturbance.

Epilogue

THE AFFECTS ARE COMPLEX and changeable phenomena. Any apparent affect may harbor numerous differentiations within itself. Affects may also transform, metamorphose, and take new shape or color through time. This is true of the affects described in this book in relation to space, materialities, and the environment, as well as to politics, polity, and administration.

This book has made an incision into the lives of Turkish-Cypriots in northern Cyprus and beyond in a particular period. In Greek and Greek-Cypriot nationalist discourses, the Turkish-Cypriots have been represented as "peons of Turkey," as its handmaidens and accomplices in Cyprus.[1] Turkish-Cypriots have been portrayed as accidental leftovers in Cyprus in the aftermath of Ottoman imperialism or as an auxiliary to British colonialism. Likewise, in academic writing that employs the notions of nationalism and ethnicity as its main explanatory devices, Turkish-Cypriots are represented as variants within the symbolic and political world of "Turkish nationalist culture" against "the Greek."[2] It is often assumed in such works that nationalist discourses, coupled with state practices that impose it, will have unproblematic and thorough effects on populations they influence. Yet as the material put forward in this book attests, national belonging and ethnicity have little validity in analyzing the complexity of emotions a community of people might have in relation to their homeland, its past, and its future. The notion of ethnic conflict (in this case, Turkish-Cypriot versus Greek-Cypriot or Turk versus Greek) can only blind the social scientist to the possibilities of the tangled and complicated affects generated in the actual, material circumstances of war and its aftermath.[3]

Turkish-Cypriots have experienced discrimination and attacks at the hands of the Greek-Cypriot majority and have been governed by a series of administrations (and, finally, a self-declared "state") supported by Turkey. Many of them were displaced from their towns and villages in southern Cyprus and became refugees; in northern Cyprus, they significantly inhabited villages, towns, and dwellings left behind by Greek-Cypriots. In this story, conflict, war, and opposing political interests are at play, as is looting. Yet the affects generated among the Turkish-Cypriots—in being subjects of the administration that was meant to represent them; in relation to Turkey, which has purported to support them; in relation to the Republic of Cyprus, which was claimed by the Greek-Cypriots; and regarding the looting of Greek-Cypriots' belongings, in which they themselves were involved—have been complex. As illustrated in this book, Turkish-Cypriots may have been rendered subjects of the TMT and of the various administrative forms it generated to represent the Turkish-Cypriot community. But Turkish-Cypriots have produced sharp criticisms of the TMT and of the "terror," as they call it, which it spread in their community in the period of enclaves. Likewise, when I studied them, they produced constant everyday critiques of the Denktaş regime that governed them over a long period, as well as of the governments that followed it. Turkey's sovereignty over northern Cyprus has been a target of criticism from the very people for whom it was officially meant. The Turkish-Cypriots have criticized Turkey privately as well as publicly for its form of rule in northern Cyprus; they have analyzed the Denktaş regime (their own administration for more than three decades) as a handmaiden of Turkey's political, economic, and military interests on the island. While doing this, they have also generated forms of self-criticism vis-à-vis their own involvement in their administration, the civil service, and the spoils of war.

The experience of living under an unrecognized state that capitalized on the loot of war generated complex sorts of affect. Significantly, in my observations there was no triumphalism among the Turkish-Cypriots about the war Turkey claimed it fought for them, save for the expressions of some elderly members of the TMT's Fighters' Organization (Mücahitler Derneği) and its offshoots, such as the UHH (the National People's Movement), which by the late 1990s and early 2000s had been completely marginalized among the people. Instead, as my material in this ethnography attests, there was widespread criticism of militarism and its visible, tangible, poignant everyday effects among the Turkish-Cypriots. They expressed disturbance with the abundant and visible presence of nationalist flags and statues. This feeling was articulated not only in informal or

private circumstances. Turkish-Cypriots organized public demonstrations against the planting of such materialities of nationalism (such as
statues of Atatürk with spear in hand on a rearing horse) among their
everyday surroundings.

Turkish-Cypriots expressed mixed feelings about the administration
that governed them. The misgivings they expressed about their administration had something to do with the fact that transactions carried out
under its state practice had little value outside the confines of northern
Cyprus. Turkish-Cypriots have also suffered gravely from the economic
and political embargoes in place on the TRNC. On the other hand, the
Turkish-Cypriots' ambivalence vis-à-vis their state administration does
not only have to do with its unrecognized status. As they express a
sentiment of ease, comfort, and familiarity in working as civil servants in
its offices, Turkish-Cypriots also, as I demonstrated, discuss with irony
the limitations of their administration (as well as its corruption). So what
has been generated out of the ruins of war has not been completely
normalized or assimilated. Ambivalence, mixed feelings, and a critical
distance regarding a political system that was supposed to be accepted
always remained. Having experienced other forms of polity and governance, Turkish-Cypriots always had an ability to contrast their administration (and Turkey) with other state practices. And when they could,
even before the opening of checkpoints for access to the south, Turkish-
Cypriots applied for passports from the Republic of Cyprus, which gave
them access to the outside world. In turn, the Turkish-Cypriots have also
experienced discrimination and violent attacks under the Republic of
Cyprus, so that their relation with that state practice has been ambivalent
in a different way.

In the late 1990s and early 2000s, when I conducted fieldwork, Denktaş, his political regime, and Turkey were the main objects of criticism
among the Turkish-Cypriots. One of the most criticized aspects of this
state practice and sovereignty was the system and economy of loot. In
relation to the objects of postwar loot (houses, land, and personal belongings left behind by the Greek-Cypriots), Turkish-Cypriots had developed
a local moral discourse. They transformed the Ottoman-Turkish word for
loot, ganimet, into a term that implies moral criticism of those who had
obtained it, including themselves. If *ganimet* is a word employed with
military triumphalism (to refer to war booty or plunder) in Turkish nationalist (or Ottomanist) discourse, as a Turkish-Cypriot notion, ganimet

involves reflexivity as well as criticism of modes of governance (and state-craft) that support it. Turkish-Cypriots employed the term *ganimet* not only to refer to the Greek-Cypriot houses that many of them inhabited, sometimes as refugees who had lost their own belongings in the south, but also to symbolize and characterize the more general practice of the Denktaş administration under the gloss of the TRNC. They therefore expressed feelings of ambivalence (such as lack of warmth) toward the houses they had obtained through their administration's property alloca-tion system. Likewise, they expressed a sense of unease about the title deeds that were given to them in return for the Greek-Cypriot houses they were allocated or had bought or sold. The notion of Greek-Cypriot property (*Rum malı*) still signifies illegal acquisition in northern Cyprus, as this expropriation is considered illegal everywhere outside northern Cyprus, including under international law. Aware of this, the Turkish-Cypriots have used the documents of appropriation handed to them by their administration with trepidation. More broadly, they have criticized those members of their community who have turned the loot of Greek-Cypriot property into an economy, developing real-estate markets out of it. Likewise, Turkish-Cypriots have criticized their administration for facilitating disproportionate acquisition of Greek-Cypriot property, even outside the property of equal-value system, through those who were in its torpil (patronage) networks. The allocation of such property to settlers from Turkey has been even more vehemently critiqued.

More broadly, the Turkish-Cypriots lamented the loss of themselves, as a community, to their homeland. They spoke of having been turned into a minority in northern Cyprus, against the massive numbers of immi-grants from Turkey who were given allowances to settle there by the administration. This was distinct from being a minority in relation to the Greek-Cypriots on the island. What is important to note is that Turkish-Cypriots predominantly believed that people from Turkey (*Türkiyeliler*), who were brought into Cyprus through a discourse intended to work against the minoritization of the "Turks" on the island vis-à-vis the "Greeks," were favored against them, the indigenous inhabitants of the island (*Kıbrıslılar*). They thought that the TRNC administration and Tur-key preferred people from Turkey, who came from disadvantaged eco-nomic backgrounds, to the Turkish-Cypriots because they were more docile subjects of governance. Turkish-Cypriots made guesses about the numbers of their dwindling population against people from Turkey in northern Cyprus. Census practices in northern Cyprus allowed few options under nationality: "Turkish (*Türk*)," "Greek (*Rum*)," "maronite (*maronite*)," "English (*İngiliz*)," or "other (*diğeri*)." Therefore, the census blended the numbers of settlers from Turkey and Turkish-Cypriots. This was always referred to by the Turkish-Cypriots as a grave problem, a demographic play over the population on the island. Numerous Turkish-Cypriots had left Cyprus, immigrating to Turkey, England, Australia, and other countries. This was continuing as people found few prospects for themselves and their families in northern Cyprus. In turn, the Turkish-Cypriots watched as their administration continued to allow the settlement of immigrants from Turkey (whether as settlers right after the war in 1974 or as illegal workers until the present day). Turkish-Cypriots expressed concern about what they experienced as their own disappearance from the face of the island. They referred to themselves as "the last of the Mohicans." They felt that their presence on the island was devalued by their own state practice. They therefore expressed feelings of disdain toward settlers from Turkey, associating them with Turkey's rule over northern Cyprus. What the Turkish-Cypriots were expressing was their sense of a loss of themselves to their island as a community. While I lived in northern Cyprus through years of fieldwork, Turkish-Cypriots bemoaned what they saw as the spatial transformation of their surroundings, saying that Girne (Kyrenia), for example, used to "be more Cypriot" before it was "overtaken by people from Turkey."

In all of these criticisms was a subjective feeling and an affect that I studied through the notion of *maraz*—in this context, a feeling of melancholy in relation to one's life circumstances and surroundings. Although Turkish-Cypriots used the word *maraz* throughout my period of fieldwork, the designation of affect changed shape over time. Certain turning points and events transformed the maraz of the Turkish-Cypriots into organization and protest demonstrations against the Denktaş regime and Turkey. In such instances, the affect of maraz transmogrified into feelings of anger and revolt toward the government in northern Cyprus.

Turkish Cypriots' descriptions of everyday life at home and in the office, as well as in the physical surroundings of northern Cyprus, were accentuated by forms of mass mobilization against the government. In the demonstrations, rallies, and other forms of protest they organized or attended, Turkish-Cypriots related with the materiality of their everyday lives in expressly political forms. The affects of ambivalence toward their home environments and offices, of irony coupled with unease in relation to documents they had to employ, and of maraz as a more general state of subjective feeling expressed in informal circumstances took on political shape when Turkish-Cypriots took to the streets. In the numerous demonstrations and rallies I attended in 2000 and 2001, Turkish-Cypriots expressed anger toward the Denktaş regime, making explicit demands on the government to stop working through commands from Turkey, to end its repression of the opposition, and to open the border with the Greek side.

The border's sudden opening on the 23 April 2003 led to rejoicing. Many analysts interpreted the opening as a result of the antigovernment protests attended by thousands in the last months of 2002 and in early 2003.[4] On each side of the divide, Turkish-Cypriots and Greek-Cypriots gathered on foot or in cars, waiting in long queues, to have their identity papers or passports checked by border police.

The first destination of most crossers was their ancestral homes. Turkish-Cypriots who inhabited Greek-Cypriot property waited for the owners of their homes, whom they called "our landlords (ev sahiplerimiz)," to show up. When the Greek-Cypriot owners arrived, on most occasions the Turkish-Cypriots invited them in to view their homes. Some Turkish-Cypriots returned precious items and personal effects they had kept in safe rooms over the years, especially family albums. The owners and the new inhabitants had conversations about the troubles and about the turns their lives had taken in the aftermath of the conflict. Lemonade was prepared by Turkish-Cypriots in anticipation of further visits in the weeks that followed the opening. Coffee and homemade fruit preserves were offered to Greek-Cypriots during such visits. Greek-Cypriot owners were invited to pick fruit from trees on their land and in their old gardens. Tension and conflict emerged in some encounters, while other visits grew into friendships.

Turkish-Cypriots who were refugees from the south in turn took their families to visit their ancestral towns and villages in southern Cyprus. Parents recounted childhood memories to their children who had never seen the Limasol (Limassol), Larnaka (Larnaca), or Baf (Paphos) regions of Cyprus before the opening. Traces of homes and spaces once dwelled in were sought out, at times to be found and at others, not.

In the border crossings, Greek and Turkish-Cypriots found that their homes and properties, as well as the more general spatial surroundings, had changed shape. Many lamented the state of their belongings when being in their proximity rekindled feelings of loss. Crossers gave detailed descriptions of the state in which they found their homes, land, and trees. On most occasions, the accounts told of disappointment. Looting and decay was noted on both sides. But what was most significant was the near absence of physical violence between the two communities of crossers.[5]

The opening of checkpoints to the Greek side led to a significant reshuffling of sociality and affects in northern Cyprus. Turkish-Cypriots acquired identity cards from the Republic of Cyprus, applied for passports, and acquired jobs (mainly in construction) in the south. Some of them began to send their children to school on the Greek side, escorting them with passports across the checkpoints every day. Through these face-to-face and everyday encounters of a type that had been banned between 1974 and 2003, the Turkish-Cypriots re-evaluated their position and relation with the Greek-Cypriots. As old friends were found and new friendships emerged, Turkish-Cypriots also faced discriminatory attitudes on the Greek side.

In 2004, a solution for the Cyprus problem, developed by the United Nations and named the Annan Plan, was put to a referendum on both sides of the political divide in Cyprus. Favoring reconciliation with the south, and with the prospect of membership in the European Union and better economic opportunities if the island unified, the Turkish-Cypriots predominantly voted in the plan's favor. Greek-Cypriots, however, under the incitement of their leader Tassos Papadopoulos evaluated the referendum as "pro-Turkey" and as protecting mainly the interests of the Turkish-Cypriots and predominantly voted against it. The Greek-Cypriots' rejection rendered the Annan Plan defunct. The island has remained divided, although checkpoints remain in place. To this day, the Cyprus problem is officially unresolved.

The opening of checkpoints was one turning point. The results of the referendum represented another. The Greek-Cypriots' "no" gravely disconcerted the Turkish-Cypriots, triggering a shifting of political stances and structures. In spite of this, the Turkish-Cypriots elected Mehmet Ali Talat, a former member of the CTP, president in 2005 to replace, for the first time, Denktaş. However, the CTP, which was now the ruling party in government, soon began to mimic the governing style of the previous nationalist regime. Its base of supporters declined massively. In time, Turkish-Cypriots reconfigured their politics. With cynical stances about any prospects for the resolution of the Cyprus problem, many returned to voting for the DP and the UBP. The Greek-Cypriot "no," as well as disappointment with the CTP government, pushed Turkish-Cypriots to pragmatic political stances in the north. In hopes of securing jobs and prospects for their families under parties that represent the established regime in northern Cyprus, many realigned themselves with the UBP.[6]

The material for this book was observed and recorded through fieldwork in northern Cyprus between 1998 and 2003. The analyses produced in it, however, have a bearing on developments in the aftermath of this period. All of the administrative and material structures I described, based on my fieldwork, remain in place in northern Cyprus. The sentiments expressed by Turkish-Cypriots in the period before checkpoints opened, and their actions and protests during that time, were primary reference points for events that ensued. Although derived from research in a specific period, the conceptual terms produced in this book are also intended for conversations and analyses that range outside and beyond a circumscribed territory in a period of time. The situatedness of ethnography and its historical specificity is therefore an invitation, here, to compare and conceptualize contexts and experiences across time.

Notes

Preface

1. This attack was apparently according to the Acritas Plan, which Tassos Papadopoulos, the former president of the Republic of Cyprus, was also involved in designing.

2. The "disappeared" refers to the missing people of Cyprus. In Cyprus, there are people who were made to disappear in the events of 1963 and 1974. In 1963, a number of Turkish-Cypriots were made to disappear, never to be found by their families. In 1974, numerous Greek-Cypriots disappeared, as did some Turkish-Cypriots. For an ethnography on the missing people of Cyprus, see Sant-Cassia, *Bodies of Evidence*. For an excellent account based on interviews with witnesses, see Uludağ, *İncisini Kaybeden İstiridyeler*.

3. For a masterly account of the 6–7 September events in Istanbul, see Vryonis, *The Mechanism of Catastrophe*. See also Bali, *6–7 Eylül 1955 Olayları*; Fahri Çoker Arşivi, *6–7 Eylül Olayları*; Güven 2005. The film *Güz Sancısı* (Pain of Autumn), directed by Tomris Giritlioğlu, is one of the few Turkish-made films about the 6–7 September events: Tomris Giritlioğlu, dir., *Güz Sancısı*, Yapım Filmcilik Produksiyon, Istanbul, 2009. Kıbrıs Türktür Cemiyeti (Cyprus Is Turkish Association) was directly linked with this pogrom on the Greek community of Istanbul in particular. However, it was later revealed that the Turkish government had been aware of and involved in planning these attacks. For an assessment of the links between the events in Cyprus's and Turkey's policies vis-à-vis its Greek minority, see Demir and Akar, *Istanbul'un Son Sürgünleri*, chaps. 1–3.

4. For a full historical account of the deportation of Istanbul's Greek citizens in 1964, see Demir and Akar.

5. When my grandfather was born, Didimoticho was Ottoman. It then was briefly held by the Bulgarians (1913–19), until it devolved into a possession of Greece under the Treaty of Neige (27 November 1919).

6. For an account in the form of oral history and memoirs of the departure of the Greeks of Büyükada (Prinkipo) and their subsequent life in Athens, see Tanrıverdi, *Atina'daki Büyükada*; Tanrıverdi, *Hoşçakal Prinkipo*.

7. In later years, Israel's actions against the Palestinians would have similar re-

percussions in Turkey. Every major attack by Israel (the bombing of Lebanon, the war on Gaza, the Mavi Marmara event) would produce anti-Semitic slogans in demonstrations in Turkey that addressed and targeted Turkey's own Jewish community.

8. "Minority" is not a taken-for-granted category. It is as a result of a historical event, the Lausanne Treaty of 1923, when Turkey's non-Muslims (the Jews, Greeks, and Armenians) were given the official status of "minority" (azınlık in Turkish) in the newly established Republic of Turkey: see Clark, *Twice a Stranger*. Under the Ottoman Empire, non-Muslims were classified as "religious communities" according to the *millet* system.

9. For a study of Turkey's Jews in the course of the twentieth century, see Bali, *Musa'nın Evlatları Cumhuriyet'in Yurttaşları*.

10. Dimitriu and Vlahos, *İhanete Uğramış Ayaklanma*, 56.

11. Ibid.

12. Ibid.

13. "Deep state (*derin devlet*)" is an idiomatic term developed in Turkey to refer to underground links between Turkey's statesmen, militaries, and the far-right-wing mafia. Informally, the Turkish-Cypriots linked Adalı's murder with Turkey's deep state. In the early 2000s, an underground army-state-mafia network operating under the code name Ergenekon was revealed in Turkey, and several people were brought to court as suspect members of the ring.

14. Dimitriu and Vlahos, *İhanete Uğramış Ayaklanma*, 57.

15. Ibid., 58.

16. Ibid., 62.

17. For an excellent account of this period of demonstrations, see Ilıcan, "The Making of Sovereignty through Changing Property/Land Rights and the Contestation of Authority in Cyprus," chap. 7. For a problematic account that misinterprets the motives behind the protests and miscontextualizes them, see Hatay and Bryant, "The Jasmine Scent of Nicosia."

18. Ilıcan, "The Making of Sovereignty through Changing Property/Land Rights and the Contestation of Authority in Cyprus," 195.

19. See Dimitriu and Vlahos, *İhanete Uğramış Ayaklanma*.

20. The CTP at the time was one of the organizations that had formed the This Country Is Ours Platform.

21. The feeling of protest continued in northern Cyprus until the election of Mehmet Ali Talat (formerly of the CTP) as president of the TRNC in place of Denktaş in 2005.

22. The Green Line refers to the ceasefire line between northern and southern Cyprus determined after Turkey's invasion of the north. Turkish-Cypriots refer to the line as "the border (*sınır*)" while Greek-Cypriots usually prefer to call it the Green Line in order not to appear to be granting sovereignty to the administration in the north. For studies of the eventful crossing and its aftermath, see Demetriou, "Freedom Square"; Demetriou, "To Cross or Not to Cross?"; Dikom-

itis, "A *Moving* Field"; Dikomitis, "Three Readings of a Border"; Hadjipavlou, " 'I Grow in Different Ways Every Time I Cross."

Introduction

1. "Turkish Republic of Northern Cyprus" is placed in quotation marks in most sources outside northern Cyprus and Turkey. I put it in quotation marks here but refrain from doing so in most of the rest of the book, which attempts to place the TRNC conceptually as a case comparable with other (including legally recognized) states.

2. Throughout the book, I identify Turkish-Cypriots and Greek-Cypriots with a dash between the references to so-called ethnicity and nationality, or vice versa thereof. This is to emphasize the "Cypriot" quality of identities and social relations in Cyprus in the period when I conducted my field research. In the Turkish-Cypriot dialect of the Turkish language, the term of ascription used for Turkish-Cypriots has recently been *Kıbrıslı Türkler*. Turkish-Cypriot (with a dash) is the best English rendering of that. In the Turkish language, the reference for citizens of Greece is *Yunan*, while that for Greek-Cypriots is *Rum*. My use of the term "Greek-Cypriot" throughout the book also helps in differentiating members of this community from citizens of Greece. Likewise, the term "Turkish-Cypriots" differentiates members of this community from citizens of Turkey. "Turkish-Cypriot" and "Greek-Cypriot" renders, as well, how members of these two communities, separated by war and partition, differentiate between one another.

3. Giray, *K.K.T.C. Coğrafi İsimler Katalogu (Cilt-III). Girne İlçesi*, i–iii.

4. Copeaux and Mauss-Copeaux have also studied toponymic changes in northern Cyprus: see Copeaux and Mauss-Copeaux, *Taksim!*, 74–78. The distinction of my account is its attention to the administrative practice (the bureaucracy) that went into the geographical name changes and the theoretical conceptualization I derive from this. For a comprehensive glossary of old (Armenian, Greek, Syriac, Kurdish, Arabic, Georgian, Circassian, Laz) and new (all Turkish) geographical names in Turkey, see Nişanyan, *Adını Unutan Ülke*. The name-changing practices in northern Cyprus would have followed and modeled themselves on similar such earlier practices in Turkey. For a study of toponymic changes in Turkey, see Öktem, "The Nation's Imprint."

5. See, e.g., Anderson, *Imagined Communities*.

6. See, e.g., Henare et al., *Thinking through Things*; Latour and Weibel, *Making Things Public*.

7. Since the publication of Benedict Anderson's *Imagined Communities*, the inventiveness that goes into the establishment of nation-states has been widely explored. For an elaboration of a specific use of the phantasmatic, which implies the imaginary in Anderson's, Castoriadis's, and Lacan's senses of the term, see Ivy, *Discourses of the Vanishing*, 4. In my earlier work, I distinguished the work of fantasy from that of discourses in a political arena, arguing that the term "fan-

tasy" (by reference to Lacan and Žižek) better captures psychical attachments to power than "discourses," which can be deconstructed: see Navaro-Yashin, *Faces of the State*. In turn, rather than appearing in the guise of a psychic glue for the imagination, the phantasmatic emerges in this book in tangible material shape and in the form of actual social practices.

8. For a comparable account, see Killoran, "Time, Space and National Identities in Cyprus."

9. Many Greek-Cypriots prefer to refer to the border that separates northern and southern Cyprus as the Green Line, because the notion of a border might imply granting separate sovereignty to the northern Cypriot regime.

10. EOKA was a guerrilla unit that fought the British defending the union of Cyprus with Greece (*enosis*). In the process of anti-colonial resistance, EOKA targeted many members of the Turkish-Cypriot community, as well.

11. For comparison and to consider British colonial projects for partition elsewhere, see Butalia, *The Other Side of Silence*.

12. Perry Anderson, "The Divisions of Cyprus."

13. Volkan, *Cyprus*.

14. Navaro-Yashin, "Fantasy and the Real in the Work of Begoña Aretxaga."

15. There was a historical precedent for the exchange of populations between northern and southern Cyprus. The internal displacement of Greek-Cypriots to the south and Turkish-Cypriots to the north of Cyprus was the materialization of a reference point to an earlier and major exchange of populations between Greece and Turkey in 1922. The pushing of Turks and Greeks into separate enclaves between 1963 and 1974 and the absolute partition along ethnically defined lines from 1974 could be interpreted as a repetition of an earlier such event of enforced separate habitation. For studies of the exchange of populations between Greece and Turkey in 1922, see Hirschon, *Heirs of the Greek Catastrophe*; Hirschon, *Crossing the Aegean*; Yıldırım, *Diplomacy and Displacement*.

16. Bryant, *Imagining the Modern*; Yashin, *Step-Mothertongue*.

17. *Linobambaki* means literally the bringing together of linen and cotton and refers to syncretism between two religious frameworks. For a more detailed account, see Yashin, *Step-Mothertongue*.

18. Ibid.

19. See Volkan, *Cyprus*, for a detailed account of the period of enclaves.

20. Loizos, *Heart Grown Bitter*.

21. It must be noted that the TMT and EOKA targeted not just members of the other community in the intercommunal conflict but also those within their own communities who were identified as left-wing or communist, including anyone who was working for coexistence between the communities of Cyprus. Therefore, protection was not unproblematic for many left-wing Turkish and Greek-Cypriots in the areas administered by the guerrilla forces representing their respective ethnic groups.

22. A comparable study of south Cyprus, by reference to the absent Turkish-

Cypriots in the spaces they once inhabited is yet to be done. The present ethnographic project focuses on northern Cyprus, but the analyses it produces could very well be of use for thinking about south Cyprus (and other comparative postwar locations) too.

23. Latour, *We Have Never Been Modern*.

24. Here, I refer to Turks rather than Turkish-Cypriots because the north of the island was subsequently also opened for the settlement of migrants from Turkey who were classified as "Turks" by the northern Cypriot administration (even if they might not have been so because they were of Laz, Kurdish, or Arab origin).

25. In this book, I study the aftermath of 1974 until 2003, when checkpoints between north and south were opened for the first time for mutual crossing. The reference to the bodily absence of Greek-Cypriots from the north refers to the period between 1974 and 2003. After the checkpoints opened in 2003, many Greek-Cypriots crossed to the north to visit their ancestral homes and villages. For studies of the aftermath of 2003, see Bryant, *The Past in Pieces*; Demetriou, "Freedom Square"; Demetriou, "To Cross or Not to Cross?"; Dikomitis, "A *Moving Field*"; Dikomitis, "Three Readings of a Border"; Hadjipavlou, "I Grow in Different Ways Every Time I Cross."

26. Mete Hatay and Rebecca Bryant, working on northern Cyprus, have tended to normalize what I call the phantasmatic, representing modernity under the TRNC as undifferentiated from globalizing modernities elsewhere and therefore reiterating the line and framework of nationalist ideologies in northern Cyprus: see Hatay and Bryant, "The Jasmine Scent of Nicosia."

27. For an extensive study of the plight of missing people on both sides of the divide conducted by a Turkish-Cypriot journalist and writer, see Uludağ, *İncisini Kaybeden İstiridyeler*.

28. In *Faces of the State*, I employed the notion of fantasy to refer to psychical attachments to power that exceeded deconstruction. My use of the phantasmatic in this book is different, as it incorporates materiality.

29. Here I therefore differ from Henare et al., *Thinking through Things*, as well as from Latour and Weibel, *Making Things Public*, works that want to dissociate the material from the imaginary to emphasize its separate ontological agency and potency.

30. Brennan, *The Transmission of Affect*.

31. Gordon, *Ghostly Matters*. For other anthropological studies of ghostly presences, see Aretxaga, *States of Terror*; Carsten, *Ghosts of Memory*; Kwon, *After the Massacre*.

32. Derrida, *Specters of Marx*, 10, 12.

33. Ibid., 10.

34. Ibid., 37. See also Negri, "The Specter's Smile."

35. Derrida, *Writing and Difference*.

36. I have not come across Turkish-Cypriot references to seeing or suspecting apparitions of Greek-Cypriots. This aspect of my ethnography is different from

the material on apparitions documented by Heonik Kwon in postwar Vietnam: see Kwon, *After the Massacre*.

37. Ibid.

38. In an instructive comparison from the same region, Orhan Miroğlu describes the apparition of *djins* to the Kurds of Mardin and Midyat in contemporary Turkey in the aftermath of the massacres committed against the local Syriac-Christians and the expropriation of their properties: see Miroğlu, *Affet Bizi Marin*.

39. Henare et al., *Thinking through Things*; Latour, *Reassembling the Social*; Massumi, *Parables for the Virtual*; Thrift, *Non-Representational Theory*.

40. See Latour and Weibel, *Making Things Public*.

41. Brennan, *The Transmission of Affect*, 1.

42. Ibid., 24–25.

43. Ibid., 19.

44. Ibid., 6.

45. I propose that this approach could challenge human-centered conceptualizations of subjectivity as referring to interiority, as in Biehl et al., *Subjectivity*; Das et al., *Violence and Subjectivity*; Kleinman et al., *Social Suffering*.

46. See also Strathern, *Property, Substance, and Effect*.

47. See Brennan, *The Transmission of Affect*, 6.

48. Ibid., 8.

49. Bennett, *The Enchantment of Modern Life*, 1–2, 8.

50. Ibid., 11. See also Connolly, *Why I Am Not a Secularist?*

51. Bennett, *The Enchantment of Modern Life*, 14.

52. Ibid., 3.

53. Ibid., 4–5.

54. Ibid., 3.

55. Ibid., 12–13.

56. Tarde, *On Communication and Social Influence*.

57. Blackman, "Reinventing Psychological Matters."

58. The materialism of ethnography and the surprise elements that it harbors are what distinguish an anthropologist's approach to affect from that of a cultural theorist or a philosopher. In this sense, I would also distinguish the present study from geographers' works on affect, which lack proper ethnographic methodologies and remain mostly Eurocentric: see, e.g., Anderson, "Becoming and Being Hopeful"; McCormack, "An Event of Geographical Ethics in Spaces of Affect"; Thrift, *Non-Representational Theory*.

59. Anderson, *The Powers of Distance*.

60. Stewart, *Ordinary Affects*, 3, 10, 12.

61. Ibid. See also Green, *Notes from the Balkans*.

62. For a key anthropological text that takes this approach to subjectivity, associating it singularly with the interiority of human beings, see Biehl et al., *Subjectivity*.

63. Freud, "The Unconscious." For a critique of the notion of the psyche as

invented by the psychological (*psy*) disciplines, see Rose, *Governing the Soul*; Rose, *Inventing Our Selves*.

64. Born, "Anthropology, Kleinian Psychoanalysis, and the Subject in Culture"; Jacobus, *The Poetics of Psychoanalysis*; Klein, *The Psycho-Analysis of Children*; Mitchell, *The Selected Melanie Klein*.

65. Lacan, *The Four Fundamental Concepts of Psychoanalysis*.

66. Borch-Jacobsen, *The Emotional Tie*.

67. Rose, *Governing the Soul*; Rose, *Inventing Our Selves*.

68. João Biehl, Byron Good, and Arthur Kleinman mention that "the current understanding of subjectivity as a synonym for inner life processes and affective states is of relatively recent origin": Biehl et al., *Subjectivity*, 6. However, having historically situated the concept of subjectivity in a Western tradition, Biehl and his colleagues still proceed to employ it unproblematically as the core analytical category for their project.

69. Freud, "The Unconscious."

70. Brennan, *The Transmission of Affect*, 19.

71. Deleuze, *Foucault*.

72. See Butler, *The Psychic Life of Power*.

73. This, in fact, is what Nikolas Rose argues in *Governing the Soul* and *Inventing Our Selves*.

74. Foucault, *The Order of Things*; Latour, *We Have Never Been Modern*; Latour and Weibel, *Making Things Public*.

75. Amiria Henare, Martin Holbraad, and Sari Wastell have combined Latour's insights with those of Alfred Gell, Eduardo Viveiros de Castro, and Marilyn Strathern to enhance this new materialism that privileges the ontology of the object: see Henare et al. *Thinking through Things*; Gell, *Art and Agency*; Strathern, *Property, Substance, and Effect*; Viveiros de Castro, 1998.

76. Latour, "On Recalling ANT," 23.

77. Henare et al., *Thinking through Things*; Latour and Weibel, *Making Things Public*.

78. Here, I refer to Lisa Blackman's work, which, as I found out in the final editorial stages of this book, takes a similar cue vis-à-vis the inside and the outside. She develops the notion of suggestibility, via Tarde, arguing that affective contagion moves through "porous" and "permeable" boundaries: Blackman, "Reinventing Psychological Matters," 39–41.

79. See, e.g., Mageo, *Power and the Self*. Most of this work follows from the origins of the American anthropological tradition, specifically the "culture and personality school." There has subsequently been a special interest in merging culturalist and psychological approaches in American anthropology. The early work of students of Franz Boas (Margaret Mead, Ruth Benedict, and others) was followed by Clifford Geertz and his students in orienting anthropological queries to the symbolic interpretation of selfhood: see Biehl at al., *Subjectivity*, 6–7. Both Catherine Lutz and Lila Abu-Lughod and Biehl and his colleagues could be consid-

ered heirs of this tradition: see Lutz and Abu-Lughod, *Language and the Politics of Emotion*; Biehl et al., *Subjectivity*. In turn, British social anthropology has conventionally distanced itself from studies of psychology (or the self), as well as culture. This can be traced back to a well-known article by Edmund Leach that clearly differentiates the project of social anthropology from psychology: see Leach, "Magical Hair." For a critique of Leach's gatekeeping by someone who arguably spans both national traditions in anthropology, see Obeyesekere, *Medusa's Hair*.

80. See Lutz, *Unnatural Emotions*.

81. Lutz and Abu-Lughod, *Language and the Politics of Emotion*.

82. See, e.g., Rosaldo, *Knowledge and Passion*.

83. See Latour, *Reassembling the Social* for a critique of the category of the social that could be productively extended to the notion of the cultural.

84. See, e.g., Biehl et al., *Subjectivity*; Das et al., *Violence and Subjectivity*; Kleinman et al., *Social Suffering*; Kleinman and Good, *Culture and Depression*.

85. Kleinman et al., *Social Suffering*, 1.

86. Ibid., 1–2.

87. Ibid., 5, 8, 10.

88. See, e.g., ibid., 5.

89. Spinoza, *Ethics*, 68–69.

90. Ibid., 69.

91. See Gupta and Ferguson, *Anthropological Locations*.

92. *North Cyprus Almanack*, 1–2.

93. See Green, *Notes from the Balkans*, for an ethnography of maps and numbers.

94. *North Cyprus Almanack*, 20–21.

95. Ibid., 21.

96. Ibid., 22.

97. Ibid., 24–72.

98. Ibid., 73–186.

99. Ibid., 36.

100. See Stoler, *Along the Archival Grain*.

101. Weber, "Bureaucracy."

102. On audit cultures, see Strathern, *Audit Cultures*. On organizations, see Wright, *Anthropology of Organisations*. On documentary practices, see Riles, *Documents*. On industry, see Born, *Rationalizing Culture*; Corsin-Jimenez, "Industry Going Public."

103. See, e.g., Navaro-Yashin, *Faces of the State*.

104. See, e.g., Aretxaga, *Shattering Silence*; Aretxaga, *States of Terror*; Navaro-Yashin, *Faces of the State*; Stoler, "Affective States"; Stoler, *Along the Archival Grain*.

105. See Barry et al., *Foucault and Political Reason*; Burchell et al., *The Foucault Effect*; Cruikshank, *The Will to Empower*.

106. Deutsch, *The Nerves of Government*.

107. Amanda Anderson has introduced the concept of detachment as an exemplary motif and methodology left by the Enlightenment tradition. Anderson

propagates this approach, which she calls "the cultivation of detachment," as one that human scientists might take on from the natural scientists: Anderson, *The Powers of Distance*. In turn, in this work I critique precisely such attempts to resuscitate the Enlightenment tradition of positivism and objectivity by arguing that detachment is an affect in its own right, one that is induced and produced by specific modes of governance. I argue, as well, against a certain Weberian association of bureaucracies with detachment. Instead, I propose that bureaucracies themselves are affective entities, detachment being one kind of affectivity they might transmit, produce, or inflict.

108. Herzfeld, *The Social Production of Indifference*.

109. See also Patel, "Imagining Risk, Care, and Security."

110. This project may ring bells with those of psychologists and other scholars in organizational behavior and management on "emotion in organizations": Fineman, *Emotion in Organizations*. However, a distinction must be drawn between scholarship that would address the role of the emotions in organizations to provide consultancy and solutions for it in organizational management and the approach developed in this book about administrative practices as inducing and producing affect in and of themselves.

1. The Materiality of Sovereignty

1. A *dönüm* is a land measure of 1,000 square meters.

2. See, e.g., Bender and Winer, *Contested Landscapes*; Hirsch and O'Hanlon, *The Anthropology of Landscape*.

3. See, e.g., Weiner, *The Empty Place*.

4. Hirsch, "Introduction," 5, 22–23.

5. Hetherington, "In Place of Geometry," 188–89.

6. Ibid., 183–84.

7. Ibid., 184, 187.

8. Agamben, *Homo Sacer*; Schmitt, *The Concept of the Political*.

9. See, e.g., Strathern, *The Gender of the Gift*.

10. I employ the term "Turkey-fying" instead of "Turkifying" here because the Maps Department also changed the names of villages and towns in the Cypriot dialect of the Turkish language, giving them names that resonate more with Turkey and its standard official Turkish language.

11. This specific kind of mosque architecture is recognized by the Turkish-Cypriots as different from the traditional mosques they used to have in Cyprus. The old mosques of Cyprus are smaller and have short minarets, while the new ones built under the sponsorship of the Turkish army are much more prominent and dominant in size and shape. Some Turkish-Cypriots comment that this new kind of mosque has been designed and implanted in northern Cyprus as a message of Turkish sovereignty in the north against the material presence of domineering Greek Orthodox churches in the south.

12. Hirst, *Space and Power*, 3.

13. Weizman, *Hollow Land*, 5.

14. Segal and Weizman, *A Civilian Occupation*, 2003.

15. For an account of mapmaking practices in Cyprus in the British colonial period, see Ilıcan, "The Making of Sovereignty through Changing Property / Land Rights and the Contestation of Authority in Cyprus."

16. On "cultural intimacy," see Herzfeld, *Cultural Intimacy*.

2. Repopulating a Territory

1. See, e.g., Joseph, "International Dimensions of the Cyprus Problem"; Volkan and Itzkowitz, *Turks and Greeks*.

2. See, e.g., Bryant, *Imagining the Modern*; Bryant, "The Purity of Spirit and the Power of Blood"; Volkan, *Cyprus*.

3. Until the development of nationalism in Cyprus, the term "Turkish-Cypriot" did not exist as such. People identified as Muslims or as Ottomans: Ateşin, *Kıbrıslı "Müslüman"ların "Türk"leşme ve "Laik"leşme Serüveni*. For the development of Turkish-Cypriot identity during the colonial period, see Bryant, *Imagining the Modern*. For studies of syncretic practices in Cyprus, see Yashin, *Step-Mother-tongue*; Yashin, *Kozmopoetika*.

4. It is interesting to note that Greek-Cypriots also refer to themselves as Cypriots to distinguish themselves from Greeks of Greece. However, Greek-Cypriots often also employ this term to distinguish themselves from the Turkish-Cypriots.

5. This view is problematically assumed in certain studies of Turkish nationalism, as well: see, e.g., Bryant, "The Purity of Spirit and the Power of Blood."

6. Rauf Denktaş, quoted in Belge, "Kıbrıslı Var Mıdır?"

7. Ibid.

8. This chapter is not a comprehensive study of settlers from Turkey; it is a study only of Turkish-Cypriots' perceptions of their difference from settlers from Turkey. Mete Hatay has developed a completely different perspective on Turkish-Cypriots' relations with immigrants from Turkey, studying it simply as xenophobia: see Hatay, *Beyond Numbers*.

9. Turkish-Cypriots do not refer to the settlers as "settlers" or as "immigrants." The term they ordinarily use is "people from Turkey." Turkish-Cypriots distinguish between themselves and people from Turkey by employing several mechanisms of othering. This distinction goes against the official claims to kinship between Turkish-Cypriots and people from Turkey, all of whom are classified as Turks by Turkey and the TRNC. Until the turn in governmental power and the assumption of the presidency of the TRNC by Mehmet Ali Talat in 2005, after decades of rule by Denktaş, officials of the administration in northern Cyprus did not use the term "people from Turkey" while on duty, as it would have countered the integrationist policies of Turkey and the Denktaş regime. Instead, they employed the term "the motherlanders (*anavatanlılar*)," glossing implications of internal difference among

Turks with metaphors of kinship between motherland (*anavatan*) Turkey and infant-land (*yavruvatan*) TRNC, thereby constructing a symbolic parental relationship between people from Turkey and Turkish-Cypriots.

10. Since access was allowed across the border in 2003, the economy of northern Nicosia, and of northern Cyprus more generally, has begun to address Greek-Cypriot shoppers and international tourists, as well as the rising Turkish-Cypriot middle class.

11. Cynthia Enloe has studied similar features of militarization: see Enloe, *Bananas, Beaches, and Bases.*

12. Turkish-Cypriots use the term "the Turkish soldier (*Türk askeri*)" to refer exclusively to soldiers from Turkey and not to Turkish-Cypriot soldiers. The latter are called "*mücahitler*" in reference to fighters of the TMT in the period of intercommunal conflict.

13. The use of the term "*fellah*" in the Turkish vernacular of Cyprus is different from its use in the Turkish vernaculars of Turkey and its meaning in Arabic. On this, see, e.g., Türk Dil Kurumu, *Türkçe Sözlük*, 493. In Arabic, "fellah" means "peasant": see Fahmy, *All the Pasha's Men.* In contrast, in the Turkish vernacular of Cyprus, "fellah" is used interchangeably with "*cingâne*" to refer metaphorically to gypsies or dispossessed people: see Hakeri, *Kıbrıs'ta Halk Ağzından Derlenmiş Sözcükler Sözlüğü*, 27. "Fellah" in the contemporary Turkish-Cypriot vernacular does not include a reference to Arabs. In fact, many Turkish-Cypriots, and especially those originally from the Famagusta (Mağusa) region, claim Arab backgrounds and kinship, explicitly referring to their Arab (sometimes Egyptian) ancestors with pride. "Fellah" is an othering, as well as a derogatory, term that Turkish-Cypriots use to refer specifically to settlers from Turkey in northern Cyprus. For a study of different uses of the Turkish language (or multiple Turkishes), with specific reference to the Turkish-Cypriot dialect, see Yashin, *Step-Mothertongue*; Yashin, *Kozmopoetika.*

14. Under-the-table workers from Turkey work and live in the most difficult conditions and without working permits from the TRNC. Such workers do not have the rights granted to the officially approved settlers in northern Cyprus who have acquired citizenship of the TRNC.

15. Bourdieu, *Distinction.*

16. Women's veiling in Turkey has been constructed as a central marker of class and culture: Göle, *Forbidden Modern*; Navaro-Yashin, *Faces of the State.* Turkish-Cypriots are aware of such distinctions in Turkey in a removed manner, mainly through television but also through visits to Turkey and temporary residence there for study and work. However, the associations that Turkish-Cypriots make with veiling must be studied in their own context without being confused with internal cultural politics in Turkey. For Turkish-Cypriots in the contemporary period, veiling is one marker, among many, of the cultural transformation of Cyprus through the administration's population policies.

17. Such attempts by the settlers are not always successful.

18. The distinction of "Turkey-fication" from "Turkification" is necessary here because the policies of the administration in northern Cyprus are geared to assimilate the Turkish-Cypriot language into that of Turkey. There are official attempts to make proper "Turks" out of the Turkish-Cypriots by teaching the Turkish vernacular of Turkey in schools and discouraging the use of the Turkish-Cypriot dialect; by changing place names in Cyprus (not only of Greek-Cypriot locations but also of old Turkish-Cypriot villages) to names that recall place names in Turkey; and by presenting the culture of Turkey as that of Turkish-Cypriots.

19. Statistics are politically charged in northern Cyprus, and no one is sure about the population of Turkish-Cypriots compared with that of settlers because the censuses conducted by the administration registers all as "Turkish" in nationality, regardless of origin or background.

3. Affects of Spatial Confinement

1. The *Avrupa* (later *Afrika*) newspaper spearheaded this movement with daily publications criticizing the Denktaş regime, as did several trade unions and other organizations that had joined forces on this platform. To this day, *Afrika* publishes regular articles that call Turkey's presence in northern Cyprus an "occupation."

2. This is how this study differs from social psychology of the 1930s and 1940s that argued that populations were brainwashed by the polities of which they were subjects: see, e.g., Adorno, "Freudian Theory and the Pattern of Fascist Propaganda."

3. Akkurt, *Kutsal Kavgaların Korkusuz Neferi Dr. Niyazi Manyera*, 35; Tansu, *Aslında Hiç Kimse Uyumuyordu*, 27–29.

4. With the term "culture of politics," I refer to a whole set of experiences inscribed in collective memory, a network of common political reference points, an enduring political system with a specific style of government, and an unarticulated and unconscious experience of the political shared by a group of people who have been subjects of a specific kind of polity under a specific historical contingency.

5. Yiannis Papadakis has written ethnographically about the Greek side of this border area: see Papadakis, *Echoes from the Dead Zone*.

6. Rebecca Bryant has written about the metaphor of blood in Turkish-Cypriot nationalism: see Bryant, "The Purity of Spirit and the Power of Blood." However, very problematically, she has assumed that Turkish nationalists' uses of "blood" and "martyr" symbolism reflect a general tendency or sentiment among Turkish-Cypriots (and even, as a more general category, among Turks). In my decade of ethnographic research in northern Cyprus, I never once met a Turkish-Cypriot who legitimized his or her autochthony on the island by referring to "the blood of martyrs." This was characterized (and ridiculed) by the Turkish-Cypriots as the recognizably ideological discourse of the Denktaş administration and its support-

ers. It is hugely problematic for an anthropologist to take nationalist discourses as representative of a culture, as Bryant claims the "blood" metaphor to be for the Turkish-Cypriots and the "spirit" metaphor for the Greek-Cypriots. It is also ethnographically incorrect.

7. Such permissions were sometimes, though rarely, granted to attend bi-communal meetings at Ledra Palace in the buffer zone controlled by the United Nations or for hospital treatment on the Greek side in cases of major health emergency.

8. After the opening of checkpoints in 2003, the park started to be frequented only by settlers and soldiers from Turkey who were not allowed to cross to the Greek side. Nationals of Turkey, including settlers in northern Cyprus, have not been given permission to cross to the Greek side of Cyprus. At the same time, Turkish-Cypriots, having obtained the permission to cross, abandoned their visits to the Zafer Burcu park. They could now view the park from the Greek side, walking alongside the old city walls on top of which it was built.

9. The Lokmacı barricade was not opened for crossing in 2003, when check-points at Ledra Palace and Metehan-Kermiya/Ayios Demetios were. In fact, the opening of this centermost barricade for pedestrians in the heart of the divided city took much longer and engendered controversy between the two sides of the divide.

10. Young people in northern Cyprus—those called the "'74 generation"—have never experienced anything but the post-1974 reality of northern Cyprus.

11. I take the notion of hidden injury from Sennett and Cobb, *The Hidden Injuries of Class*. Wendy Brown has used the notion of injury in relation to her analysis of power in late modernity: Brown, *States of Injury*.

4. Administration and Affect

1. For a study of cynical reverence for the state in Turkey, see Navaro-Yashin, *Faces of the State*.

2. See, e.g., Barry and Slater, *The Technological Economy*; Shore and Wright, *Anthropology of Policy*; Strathern, "Introduction," *Audit Cultures*; Wright, *Anthropology of Organisations*.

3. Here I think in line with Stoler, "Affective States"; Stoler, *Along the Archival Grain*.

4. Michael Herzfeld has studied the bureaucratic production of "indifference": see Herzfeld, *The Social Production of Indifference*. Ann Laura Stoler has studied the affective nature of state practices: see Stoler, "Affective States"; Stoler, *Along the Archival Grain*. See also Graham, "Emotional Bureaucracies."

5. Arendt, *The Origins of Totalitarianism*; Bauman, *Modernity and the Holocaust*.

6. Agamben, *Homo Sacer*.

7. This feeling changed to a considerable extent after the period studied in this chapter due to the electoral wins of the CTP, the previous opposition party. But

through the CTP's term in government, similar reflections in turn began to be made about the CTP's abuse of its power in the administration.

8. Patrick, *Political Geography and the Cyprus Conflict*, 34.

9. Separate municipalities for Turkish-Cypriots and Greek-Cypriots in Nicosia had already been granted by the British in the colonial period.

10. Hakkı, *Kıbrıs'ta Statükonun Sonu*, 40–41.

11. Patrick, *Political Geography and the Cyprus Conflict*, 49.

12. Plümer, *Anılar*, 100.

13. Hakkı, *Kıbrıs'ta Statükonun Sonu*, 45.

14. See also Patrick, *Political Geography and the Cyprus Conflict*, 82.

15. Ibid., 106–8.

16. Ibid., 110.

17. Mapolar, *Kıbrıs Güncesi*, 332.

18. Patrick, *Political Geography and the Cyprus Conflict*, 84.

19. Mapolar, *Kıbrıs Güncesi*, 332–33.

20. By 2001–2, Turkish-Cypriots no longer felt the fear they remembered feeling in relation to their state administration during the period of enclaves, even though they knew, and pointed to the fact that, the TRNC was an extension of the fighters' regime. By the time I conducted my fieldwork, the regime had been normalized, and its authoritarian tendencies were treated with caution and reserve (rather than fear) among civil servants and other subjects.

21. For references to Turkish-Cypriots' tendency to prefer civil service positions in the 1940s and under the British administration, see Attalides, "The Turkish-Cypriots"; Gürkan, *Bir Zamanlar Kıbrıs'ta*, 135–43.

22. See Attalides, "The Turkish-Cypriots," 78–86; Calotychos, *Cyprus and Its People*, 6–9; Fehmi, *Kuzey Kıbrıs Türk Cumhuriyeti'nin El Kitabı*; Gürkan, *Bir Zamanlar Kıbrıs'ta*, 134–57; *North Cyprus Almanack*.

23. Even Turkey does not properly recognize the TRNC as a state and refrains from inviting Turkish-Cypriot administrators to international conventions held in Turkey.

24. Calotychos, *Cyprus and Its People*.

25. On the issue of recognition in Cyprus, see Constantinou and Papadakis, "The Cypriot State(s) in Situ."

26. Gupta, "Blurred Boundaries." See also Abrams, "Notes on the Difficulty of Studying the State"; Mitchell, "The Limits of the State"; Navaro-Yashin, *Faces of the State*; Taussig, "Maleficium."

27. See, e.g., Navaro-Yashin, *Faces of the State*.

28. Abrams, "Notes on the Difficulty of Studying the State."

29. Such punitive measures refer to the period of the Denktaş regime, before the turnover of government to the CTP in 2002.

30. Aziz Nesin is one of Turkey's best-known authors.

31. See Uğural and Soyer, *Şükran Ekonomisi*.

32. For Foucauldian analyses of Western European organizations and institu-

tions, see Barry et al., *Foucault and Political Reason*; Shore and Wright, *Anthropology of Policy*. Northern Cyprus cannot be studied outside the bounds of economic "calculability," in Michel Callon's terms, or "measurement," in Andrew Barry's terms: see Callon in Barry and Slater, *The Technological Economy*; and Barry in Barry and Slater, *The Technological Economy*.

33. Strathern, "Introduction," *Audit Cultures*.

34. This saying is used by the Turkish-Cypriots to refer to state practice under a "Muslim" polity. Turkish-Cypriots told me that a similar term was once employed to refer to Ottoman administration in Cyprus.

35. Butler, *The Psychic Life of Power*, 1, 3.

36. Benjamin, "Critique of Violence."

5. The Affective Life of Documents

1. Navaro-Yashin, *Faces of the State*; Taussig, "Maleficium."

2. Douzinas and Warrington, *Justice Miscarried*, 17.

3. For studies of other such devices in documentary practices, see Riles, *Documents*.

4. The absence of quotation marks in references to the Republic of Cyprus in international law and practice could be magnified as anthropological objects, too.

5. See, e.g., Papadakis, "Greek Cypriot Narratives of History and Collective Identity."

6. There are, of course, precedents for this. Richard Wilson has suggested that "the numbers of anthropologists actively researching transnational legal processes is relatively small": Wilson, *Human Rights, Culture, and Context*, 1. What I attempt to do here is different from the project, as outlined by Wilson, of studying the reception of transnational legal discourses in local contexts, or of "the tension between global and local formulations of human rights": ibid., 23. I think the objective, as defined by Wilson, does not really challenge anthropology's conventional project of studying the local, if in its assimilation or response to the global. Nor does it really, despite Wilson's claims, move very far beyond the universalism–relativism debate that has kept anthropologists from analyzing more radically the discourses and politics of modern legal systems.

7. See, e.g., Ferguson, *The Anti-Politics Machine*; Malkki, *Purity and Exile*; Shore and Wright, "Policy."

8. Resolution 541 (1983), quoted in Press and Information Office, "Resolutions Adopted by the United Nations on the Cyprus Problem," 87–88.

9. Resolution 550 (1984), quoted ibid., 90.

10. See Malkki, "Citizens of Humanity."

11. Derrida, "Force of Law," 36.

12. Press and Information Office, "Turkish Policy on Cyprus and Efforts to Solve the Cyprus Problem," 16–17.

13. It is only since the checkpoints opened across the Green Line in 2003 that

Republic of Cyprus institutions such as the border police have taken TRNC identity cards and drivers licenses as proof of identity for Turkish-Cypriots.

14. Nejatigil, *Turkish Republic of Northern Cyprus in Perspective*, 3.

15. Please note that I have changed the name of the person concerned, as well as
the details of his story, to retain confidentiality. The person concerned has already attained asylum in the United Kingdom and lives with recognized papers,
now, in that country. Home Office documents are public documents and can be
quoted from as long as the confidentiality of the asylum claimant or appellant is
protected.

16. A legal representative who acts for asylum seekers observed, in an interview
I conducted with her on 8 March 2001, that immigration adjudicators in the
United Kingdom are not able to comprehend persecution on the basis of one's
political ideas, even though this is one of the criteria sought in a "proper" refugee
under the Geneva Convention: see Tuitt, *False Images*, 11–12. According to the
representative, immigration officers have a much easier time comprehending
persecution on the basis of ethnicity or race.

17. But one had to seek advice from the right community centers. Social work-
ers who affiliated with the TRNC did not assist their clients in applying for
Republic of Cyprus passports, because TRNC authorities do not recognize the
Republic of Cyprus.

18. This is according to Önder Konuloğlu, who was the president of the Türk-
Sen trade union at the time of my fieldwork.

19. See Hitchens, *Hostage to History*.

20. Derrida, *Writing and Difference*, 281.

21. Das, "Documentary Practices"; Derrida, "Force of Law."

22. Messick, "On the Question of Lithography," 162, 164.

23. Douzinas and Warrington, *Justice Miscarried*, 211–13.

24. Ibid.

25. Hackney is a part of London that has been especially inhabited by immigrants from Turkey and Cyprus, as well as the Caribbean.

26. In recent anthropological work on policy documents and their implementations, organizations, networks, and audit cultures have been studied as forms of
rationalized practice: see, e.g.. Riles, *The Network Inside Out*; Shore and Wright,
"Policy"; Strathern, *Audit Cultures*; Wright, *Anthropology of Organisations*.

27. See Aretxaga, *States of Terror*; Navaro-Yashin, *Faces of the State*.

28. For examples of studies of other groups caught between several regimes, see
Das and Poole, *Anthropology in the Margins of the State*.

29. See also Navaro-Yashin, *Faces of the State*.

30. For a study of law and writing, see Messick, *The Calligraphic State*.

31. For an analysis of such zones of familiarity studied through the terms,
respectively, of "indifference" and "cultural intimacy," see Herzfeld, *The Social
Production of Indifference*; Herzfeld, *Cultural Intimacy*.

32. R. Kyriakides, "Turkish Cypriot Passport Applications Soar," *Cyprus Mail*, 2
September 2001.

33. For this, see http://www.tumgazeteler.com/fc/ln.cgi?cat=33&a=811475 (last accessed March 2006).

34. "Sahte Kimlik ve Pasaport Şebekesi," *Yeni Düzen*, 26 January 2006, 1.

35. H. Sadrazam, "Sahte Vatandaşlık," 2003. http://arifler.mycyprus.net/turk ish/yazarlar/HSadrazam/sahtevatandaslik.htm (last accessed March 2006).

36. Aretxaga, *States of Terror*, 201–3.

37. Ibid., 202.

38. *Oxford Advanced Learners Dictionary*, 1328.

39. Riles, "Law as Object."

40. Riles, *The Network Inside Out*, 21.

41. Ibid., 73.

42. Ibid., 78.

43. I develop the argument about the "transmission of energy" through inspiration from Brennan, *The Transmission of Affect*.

44. In work in a similar spirit, Ann Laura Stoler studies colonial states and their governance of affect: see Stoler, "Affective States." However, Stoler studies affect as governmentalized, whereas I argue that governmentality itself is affectively charged.

6. Abjected Spaces, Debris of War

1. Green, *The Fabric of Affect in Psychoanalytic Discourse*, 6.

2. "This relation between subjective quality and quantity of instinctive energy (quality and quantity has often led to a confusion between the quota of affect and cathectic energy). Moreover, in an article written in French, 'Quelques considér-ations pour une étude comparative des paralysies motrices organiques et hystéri-ques' (1893, Freud translated *Affektbetrag* by '*valuer affective*'). By a relaxation of psychoanalytic language, one speaks indifferently of an activity being 'laden with affect' or 'cathected'. In their *Language of Psycho-Analysis*, Laplanche and Pontalis give the following definition of 'cathectic energy': 'Substratum of energy postulated as the quantitative factor in the working of the psychical apparatus', without further commentary. Thus cathectic energy relates to a quantity of energy in play in an operation, whereas a quota of affect refers only to the quantitative aspect of energy bound up with the qualitative subjective aspect, which 'qualifies' the affect, as it were. So, although every affect refers to the quantitative aspect of cathectic energy corresponding to it, every quantity of energy is not necessarily related to affect": ibid., 6–7.

3. See, e.g., Abu-Lughod, *Veiled Sentiments*; Lutz, *Unnatural Emotions*; Myers, *Pintupi Country, Pintupi Self*; Rosaldo, *Knowledge and Passion*; Wikan, *Managing Turbulent Hearts*.

4. See, e.g., Lutz and Abu-Lughod, *Language and the Politics of Emotion*.

5. Adorno, "Freudian Theory and the Pattern of Fascist Propaganda"; Canetti, *Crowds and Power*.

6. Berlant, *The Queen of America Goes to Washington City*; Hendler 2001.

7. Berlant, *Compassion*.

8. Brennan, *The Transmission of Affect*, 1.

9. Ibid., 2.

10. For a similar argument, see Blackman, "Affect, Relationality, and the 'Problem of Personality.'"

11. Ibid., 3.

12. Ibid., 8.

13. Murataǧa and Sandallar are villages in which there were Greek-Cypriot atrocities against Turkish-Cypriots and where mass graves of Turkish-Cypriots were found. This site has been turned into a commemoration space for "martyrs" by the TRNC administration.

14. Kristeva, *Powers of Horror*, 1.

15. Ibid., 1–2.

16. Ibid., 3–4.

17. Ibid., 66.

18. Ibid., 66–67.

19. Stallybrass and White, *The Politics and Poetics of Transgression*, 3.

20. Ibid., 202.

21. See also Cohen, "Introduction," xiv.

22. Bataille, *Visions of Excess*.

23. Cohen, "Introduction," xvi–xvii.

24. Botting and Wilson, *Bataille*, 9.

25. Bataille, *Visions of Excess*, 51.

26. Botting and Wilson, *Bataille*, 11.

27. Benjamin, "Critique of Violence."

28. Derrida, "Force of Law," 42.

29. Ibid., 40.

30. Ibid., 47

31. There was also massive looting in southern Cyprus of Turkish-Cypriots' belongings by Greek-Cypriots. Numerous Turkish-Cypriot properties stand in ruins in southern Cyprus, as well.

32. Political negotiations between the Turkish-Cypriots and the Greek-Cypriots have focused on the fate of material properties: see also Ilıcan,"The Making of Sovereignty through Changing Property/Land Rights and the Contestation of Authority in Cyprus."

33. Brennan, *The Transmission of Affect*.

7. Affective Spaces, Melancholic Objects

1. Middle-class Turkish-Cypriots, better versed in the language of the psychological disciplines, spoke of "depression (*bunalım*)."

2. Paul Sant-Cassia has explored melancholia in a different way in his work in (mainly south) Cyprus: Sant-Cassia, *Bodies of Evidence*.

3. Latour, *We Have Never Been Modern*.

4. Latour, "From *Realpolitik* to *Dingpolitik*," 15.

5. Ibid., 23.

6. Latour and Weibel, *Making Things Public*, 943. See also Henare et al., *Thinking Through through Things*.

7. Latour, "From *Realpolitik* to *Dingpolitik*," 16.

8. See Latour, *Reassembling the Social*, 165–72.

9. Agamben, *Homo Sacer*; Agamben, *State of Exception*.

10. Strathern, "Cutting the Network."

11. Ibid., 522–23.

12. See, e.g., Latour, *Reassembling the Social*, 11.

13. See also Thrift, "Afterwords," 215.

14. Ibid., 215.

15. Clough, *The Affective Turn*; Massumi, *Parables for the Virtual*; Thrift, *Non-Representational Theory*.

16. Thrift, "Afterwords," *Non-Representational Theory*.

17. Thrift, "Afterwords," 219.

18. Latour, "On Recalling ANT," 23.

19. Spinoza, *Ethics*, 70. See also Connolly, "Brain Waves, Transcendental Fields, and Techniques of Thought"; Connolly, "Europe."

20. Žižek, *Organs without Bodies*, 34–35.

21. Deleuze, quoted in Thrift, "Afterwords," 219.

22. Massumi, *Parables for the Virtual*.

23. See Deleuze and Guattari, *A Thousand Plateaus*, 13.

24. Guattari, "Ritornellos and Existential Affects," 159.

25. Ibid., 160.

26. Ibid., 158.

27. Ibid., 160.

28. Ibid., 162.

29. Ibid., 169.

30. Deleuze and Guattari, *A Thousand Plateaus*, 5.

31. Ibid., 7.

32. Ibid., 13.

33. Ibid., 12.

34. Ibid., 24.

35. Ibid., 220.

36. Freud, "Mourning and Melancholia."

37. Ibid., 243–44.

38. Ibid., 245.

39. Butler, *The Psychic Life of Power*, 140.

40. Ibid., 142–43.

41. Ibid., 143.

242 NOTES TO CHAPTER EIGHT

8. Home, Law, and the Uncanny

1. Even before 1974, the name of the village of Dohni (Dochni) in southern Cyprus had been changed to Taşkent by Turkish-Cypriot administrators of the enclave period. The name Taşkent was then to be assigned to the village of Vouno in the north, where the Turkish-Cypriots of Dohni were settled. However, Turkish-Cypriots always referred to their original village in the south as Dohni. The Greek name for Dohni is Tochni. Dohni is known to Turkish-Cypriots as one of the major sites of atrocities against them by the Greek-Cypriots. In the village of Taşkent (Vouno) in the north, where the widows of Dohni were settled as refugees from the south, there are two monuments to the Turkish-Cypriot men of Dohni who were murdered by Greek-Cypriots. One of the monuments was funded by the Turkish-Cypriot administration in northern Cyprus and lists the names of all of the deceased. The other monument was made inside a small Greek Orthodox church in Taşkent (Vouno) by a villager of Dohni who lost his father and two elder brothers in the Dohni massacre. That memorial includes photographs of all of the deceased. For a study of the widows of the men of Dohni whose bodies mostly disappeared after the massacre, see Sant-Cassia, *Bodies of Evidence*. Also see Uludağ, *İncisini Kaybeden İstiridyeler*, for a thorough study of the missing people of Cyprus.

2. Miller, *Home Possessions*, 4. For an example of an anthropological analysis of the cultural constructions of the house, see Carsten and Hugh-Jones, *About the House*.

3. Miller, *Home Possessions*, 107–20. Surprisingly, Miller does not socially differentiate the degree of alienation felt by an inheritor of a grand estate, and his imaginings of the ghosts of his ancestors, and an inhabitant of a council estate, who has been granted temporary cheap housing by the state. When presented as such, his theory of agency as generated out of material objects is limited in its social and political theorization.

4. See, e.g., Gell, *Art and Agency*; Henare et al., *Thinking through Things*; Latour, *We Have Never Been Modern*; Strathern, *Property, Substance, and Effect*.

5. Cf. Strathern, *Property, Substance, and Effect*.

6. Latour, *We Have Never Been Modern*.

7. Freud, *The Uncanny*.

8. Ibid., 124.

9. Vidler, *The Architectural Uncanny*, 37.

10. Freud, *The Uncanny*, 124.

11. Ibid., 127–28.

12. Ibid., 133.

13. Ibid., 125.

14. Ibid., 148.

15. In this sense, the items in Latife Hanım's home resemble objects studied by the contributors to Appadurai, *The Social Life of Things*, and to "Objects on the Loose," special issue, *Ethnos* 65, no. 2 (1999).

16. Freud, *The Uncanny*, 134.

17. Anthony Vidler stresses the ways in which Freud collapsed the unhomely with the homely: "For Freud's purposes, the multiple significations and affiliations of the German word unheimlich were more promising. They served at once to clarify the operations of the uncanny as a systematic principle as well as to situate its domain firmly in the domestic and the homely, thence to permit its decipherment in individual experience as the unconscious product of a family romance. To this end, Freud deliberately approached the definition of unheimlich by way of that of its apparent opposite, heimlich, thereby exposing the disturbing affiliation between the two and constituting the one as a direct outgrowth of the other": Vidler, *The Architectural Uncanny*, 23.

18. Ibid., 124.

19. Note that this essay was published in 1919, long before Freud and his family had to evacuate their family home in Vienna with the arrival of the Nazis in 1938. Had he been able to write about the uncanny after the war, would his notion of the heimlich have been different? When I visited both Freud's original family home in Vienna and the house his family moved to in Hampstead, London, in 2004, I thought both were uncanny in different ways.

20. Freud, *The Uncanny*, 156.

21. Viveiros de Castro, "Cosmological Deixis and Amerindian Perspectivism."

22. Freud, *The Uncanny*, 127.

23. The Güzelyurt (Morphou) region where Nezih's adopted village was located has been subject to several negotiation procedures between the Turkish-Cypriot and Greek-Cypriot administrations over the years. In all of these negotiations, none of which was finalized as an agreement between the two sides, the Güzelyurt region was proposed for return to Greek-Cypriots. Not all regions invaded by the Turkish army and settled by Turkish-Cypriot refugees or Turkish immigrants were subject to negotiations in this way. In the Güzelyurt region, Turkish-Cypriot refugees related to their dwellings in a particularly tentative manner.

24. For a series of full ethnographic manuscripts on the Greek-Cypriot villagers of Argaki (renamed Akçay), a village close to the one I study here, see Loizos, *Greek Gift*; Loizos, *Heart Grown Bitter*; Loizos, *Iron in the Soul*.

25. When the checkpoints were opened in 2003, Christina appeared, along with her husband, at her marital home where Nezih and his family had been living since 1974. Nezih took out the photographs he had kept for them in the basement of the house. Since then, the two families have visited each other regularly on both sides of the border. No negotiation has yet reached a solution between the two administrations in Cyprus, and Nezih and his family still live in Christina's home.

26. I borrow the term "psychic state" from Bachelard, *The Poetics of Space*.

27. Ibid., 3.

28. Ibid., 30.

29. Ibid., 15.

30. Ibid., 8, 22, 33, 38, 72.

31. Ibid., 4.

32. Ibid., 7.

33. Carsten and Hugh-Jones, *About the House*, 2.

34. Gell, *Art and Agency*, 252.

35. Ibid., 253.

36. Gordon, *Ghostly Matters*; Kwon, *After the Massacre*.

37. For a detailed study of this law, see Ilıcan, "The Making of Sovereignty through Changing Property/Land Rights and the Contestation of Authority in Cyprus."

38. See Benjamin, "Critique of Violence."

39. Julie Scott has also studied how social networks (*torpil*) were involved in the allocation of property in northern Cyprus: see Scott, "Property Values."

40. For a study of the property regime of the Republic of Cyprus compared with that of the TRNC in historical context, see Ilıcan, "The Making of Sovereignty through Changing Property/Land Rights and the Contestation of Authority in Cyprus."

41. Freud, *The Uncanny*.

42. See, e.g., Kelley, *The Uncanny*; Vidler. *The Architectural Uncanny*.

43. Kristeva, *Strangers to Ourselves*.

44. Welchman, "On the Uncanny in Visual Culture," 43.

45. Vidler, *The Architectural Uncanny*.

9. Collectibles of War

1. For an insightful comparison, see Slyomovics, *The Object of Memory*, on Palestinians' relations to their "objects of memory."

2. See Freud, "The Unconscious."

3. See Borch-Jacobsen, *The Emotional Tie*.

4. Durkheim, *The Elementary Forms of the Religious Life*, 242, 245.

5. Ibid., 249–50.

6. Gell, *Art and Agency*; Latour, *We Have Never Been Modern*; Strathern, "The Tangible and Intangible." See also Henare et al., *Thinking through Things*.

7. See, e.g., Henare et al., *Thinking through Things*.

8. See, e.g., Massumi, *Parables for the Virtual*.

9. The exceptions are Blackman, "Affect, Relationality and the 'Problem of Personality'"; Blackman "Reinventing Psychological Matters"; Thrift, *Non-Representational Theory*.

10. Following Latour, *Reassembling the Social*; See Candea, *The Social after Gabriel Tarde*.

11. Blackman, "Reinventing Psychological Matters," 576.

12. See Barry and Thrift, "Gabriel Tarde," 511.

13. Latour, *Reassembling the Social*.

14. Toews, "The New Tarde," 86.

15. Clark, "Introduction," 16.

16. This is the impression given by the recent Tardean turn in Actor-Network Theory, following Latour's rereading and reintroduction of Tarde's work: see Barry and Thrift, "Gabriel Tarde"; Candea, *The Social after Gabriel Tarde*; Latour, *Reassembling the Social*.

17. Elsner and Cardinal, *The Cultures of Collecting*, 4.

18. Ibid., 5.

19. Ibid.

20. See Kristeva, *Powers of Horror*.

21. The best examples of this are the Deleuzian works of Connolly, *Neuropolitics*; Massumi, *Parables for the Virtual*; Thrift, *Non-Representational Theory*. None, however, qualifies affect.

22. See, e.g., Henare et al., *Thinking through Things*; Thomas, *Entangled Objects*.

23. Brennan, *The Transmission of Affect*; Gell, *Art and Agency*; Latour, *Reassembling the Social*; Thomas, *Entangled Objects*.

24. Strathern, "The Tangible and Intangible."

Epilogue

1. For a critique of such Greek and Greek-Cypriot nationalist representations of the Turkish-Cypriots, see Dimitriu and Vlahos, *İhanete Uğramış Ayaklanma*, ix.

2. See, e.g., Bryant, *Imagining the Modern*; Bryant, "The Purity of Spirit and the Power of Blood."

3. A good example of work that assumes the contradistinction of Turks and Greeks is Volkan and Itzkowitz, *Turks and Greeks*. But this notion of ethnic conflict imbues academic scholarship (as it does public and political analyses) in and beyond Cyprus, Greece, and Turkey.

4. See, e.g., Dimitriu and Vlahos, *İhanete Uğramış Ayaklanma*; Ilıcan 2010.

5. For detailed ethnographic studies of the crossing, see Bryant, *The Past in Pieces*; Demetriou, "Freedom Square"; Demetriou, "To Cross or Not to Cross?"; Dikomitis, "A *Moving* Field"; Dikomitis, "Three Readings of a Border"; Hadjipavlou, "I Grow in Different Ways Every Time I Cross."

6. It must be noted that the UBP also earned its success in the most recent elections in northern Cyprus through the predominating presence of settlers from Turkey registered as citizens (and therefore as voters) under the TRNC.

Works Cited

Abrams, Philip. "Notes on the Difficulty of Studying the State." *Journal of Historical Sociology* 1, no. 1 (1988), 58–89.

Abou El-Haj, Nadia. *Facts on the Ground: Archaeological Practice and Territorial Self-Fashioning in Israeli Society*. Chicago: University of Chicago Press, 2001.

Abu-Lughod, Lila. *Veiled Sentiments: Honor and Poetry in a Bedouin Society*. Berkeley: University of California Press, 1986.

Adorno, Theodor W. "Freudian Theory and the Pattern of Fascist Propaganda." *The Essential Frankfurt School Reader*, ed. Andrew Arato and Eike Gebhardt, 118–37. New York: Continuum, 1998.

Agamben, Giorgio. *Homo Sacer: Sovereign Power and Bare Life*, trans. Daniel Heller-Roazen. Stanford: Stanford University Press, 1998.

———. *State of Exception*, trans. Kevin Attell. Chicago: University of Chicago Press, 2005.

Akkurt, Aydın. *Kutsal Kavgaların Korkusuz Neferi Dr. Niyazi Manyera*. Lefkoşa: Akdeniz Haber Ajansı Yayınları, 2000.

Anderson, Amanda. *The Powers of Distance: Cosmopolitanism and the Cultivation of Detachment*. Princeton: Princeton University Press, 2001.

Anderson, Ben. "Becoming and Being Hopeful: Towards a Theory of Affect." *Environment and Planning D: Society and Space* 24, no. 5 (2006), 733–52.

Anderson, Benedict. *Imagined Communities: Reflections on the Origin and Spread of Nationalism*. London: Verso, 1983.

Anderson, Perry. "The Divisions of Cyprus." *London Review of Books* 30, no. 8 (2008), 7–16.

Appadurai, Arjun, ed. *The Social Life of Things: Commodities in Cultural Perspective*. Cambridge: Cambridge University Press, 1986.

Arendt, Hannah. *The Origins of Totalitarianism*. San Diego: Harvest, 1976.

Aretxaga, Begoña. *Shattering Silence: Women, Nationalism, and Political Subjectivity in Northern Ireland*. Princeton: Princeton University Press, 1997.

———. *States of Terror: Begoña Aretxaga's Essays*, ed. Joseba Zulaika. Reno: Center for Basque Studies, University of Nevada, 2005.

Attalides, Michael A. "The Turkish-Cypriots: Their Relations to Greek-Cypriots in

Perspective." *Cyprus Reviewed*, ed. Michael A. Attalides, 71–97. Nicosia: Jus Cypri Association, 1977.

Ateşin, Hüseyin Mehmet. *Kıbrıslı "Müslüman"ların "Türk"leşme ve "Laik"leşme Serüveni (1925–1975)*. Istanbul: Marifet Yayınları, 1999.

Bachelard, Gaston. *The Poetics of Space*. Boston: Beacon, 1994.

Bali, Rıfat N. *Musa'nın Evlatları Cumhuriyet'in Yurttaşları*. Istanbul: İletişim Yayınları, 2001.

Bali, Rıfat N., ed. *6–7 Eylül 1955 Olayları: Tanıklar-Hatıralar*. Istanbul: Libra Kitap, 2010.

Barry, Andrew, Tom Osborne, and Nikolas Rose, eds. *Foucault and Political Reason*. London: Routledge, 1996.

Barry, Andrew, and Don Slater, eds. *The Technological Economy*. London: Routledge, 2005.

Barry, Andrew, and Nigel Thrift. "Gabriel Tarde: Imitation, Invention, and Economy." *Economy and Society* 36, no. 4 (2007), 509–25.

Bataille, Georges. *Visions of Excess: Selected Writings, 1927–1939*. Minneapolis: University of Minnesota Press, 1985.

Bauman, Zygmunt. *Modernity and the Holocaust*. Ithaca: Cornell University Press, 1991.

Belge, Murat. "Kıbrıslı Var Mıdır?" *Radikal*, 2 July 2002, 9.

Bender, Barbara, and Margot Winer. eds. *Contested Landscapes: Movement, Exile, and Place*. Oxford: Berg, 2001.

Benjamin, Walter. "Critique of Violence." *One-Way Street and Other Writings*, 132–56. London: Verso, 1998.

———. "Theses on the Philosophy of History." *Illuminations*, ed. Hannah Arendt, 245–55. London: Fontana, 1992.

Bennett, Jane. *The Enchantment of Modern Life: Attachments, Crossings, and Ethics*. Princeton: Princeton University Press, 2001.

Benvenisti, Meron. *Sacred Landscape: The Buried History of the Holy Land since 1948*. Berkeley: University of California Press, 2000.

Berlant, Lauren. *The Queen of America Goes to Washington City: Essays on Sex and Citizenship*. Durham: Duke University Press, 1997.

Berlant, Lauren, ed. *Compassion: The Culture and Politics of an Emotion*. New York: Routledge, 2004.

Biehl, João, Byron Good, and Arthur Kleinman, eds. *Subjectivity: Ethnographic Investigations*. Berkeley: University of California Press, 2007.

Blackman, Lisa. "Affect, Relationality, and the 'Problem of Personality.'" *Theory, Culture, and Society* 25, no. 1 (2008), 23–47.

———. "Reinventing Psychological Matters: The Importance of the Suggestive Realm of Tarde's Ontology." *Economy and Society* 36, no. 4 (2007), 574–96.

Bloch, Maurice, and Jonathan Parry, eds. *Death and the Regeneration of Life*. Cambridge: Cambridge University Press, 1982.

Borch-Jacobsen, Mikkel. *The Emotional Tie: Psychoanalysis, Mimesis, and Affect*. Stanford: Stanford University Press, 1992.

Born, Georgina. "Anthropology, Kleinian Psychoanalysis, and the Subject in Culture." *American Anthropologist* 100, no. 2 (1998), 373–86.

——. *Rationalizing Culture: IRCAM, Boulez, and the Institutionalization of the Musical Avant-Garde*. Berkeley: University of California Press, 1995.

Botting, Fred, and Scott Wilson. *Bataille: A Critical Reader*. Oxford: Blackwell, 1998.

Bourdieu, Pierre. *Distinction: A Social Critique of the Judgment of Taste*. London: Routledge, 1984.

Brennan, Teresa. *The Transmission of Affect*. Ithaca: Cornell University Press, 2004.

Brown, Wendy. *States of Injury: Power and Freedom in Late Modernity*. Princeton: Princeton University Press, 1995.

Bryant, Rebecca. *Imagining the Modern: The Cultures of Nationalism in Cyprus*. London: I. B. Tauris, 2004.

——. *The Past in Pieces: Belonging in the New Cyprus*. Philadelphia: University of Pennsylvania Press, 2010.

——. "The Purity of Spirit and the Power of Blood: A Comparative Perspective on Nation, Gender, and Kinship in Cyprus." *Journal of the Royal Anthropological Institute* 8, no. 3 (2002), 509–30.

Burchell, Graham, Colin Gordon, and Peter Miller, eds. *The Foucault Effect: Studies in Governmentality*. London: Harvester Wheatsheaf, 1991.

Butalia, Urvashi. *The Other Side of Silence: Voices from the Partition of India*. London: Hurst, 2000.

Butler, Judith. *The Psychic Life of Power: Theories in Subjection*. Stanford: Stanford University Press, 1997.

Callon, Michel, "Technology, Politics, and the Market: An Interview with Michel Callon." *The Technological Economy*, ed. Andrew Barry and Don Slater, 101–21. London: Routledge, 2005.

Calotychos, Vangelis, ed. *Cyprus and Its People: Nation, Identity, and Experience in an Unimaginable Community*. Boulder: Westview, 1998.

Candea, Matei, ed. *The Social after Gabriel Tarde: Debates and Assessments*. London: Routledge, 2009.

Canetti, Elias. *Crowds and Power*. Harmondsworth: Penguin, 1973.

Carsten, Janet, ed. *Ghosts of Memory: Essays on Remembrance and Relatedness*. Oxford: Blackwell, 2007.

Carsten, Janet, and Stephen Hugh-Jones, eds. *About the House: Lévi-Strauss and Beyond*. Cambridge: Cambridge University Press, 1995.

Clark, Bruce. *Twice a Stranger: How Mass Expulsion Forged Modern Greece and Turkey*. London: Granta, 2007.

Clark, Terry N. Introduction to *On Communication and Social Influence*, by Gabriel Tarde, ed. Terry N. Clark. Chicago: University of Chicago Press, 1969.

Clough, Patricia Ticineto, with Jean Halley, eds. *The Affective Turn: Theorizing the Social*. Durham: Duke University Press, 2007.

Cohen, William A. "Introduction: Locating Filth." *Filth: Dirt, Disgust, and Modern*

Life, ed. William A. Cohen and Ryan Johnson, vii–xxxvii. Minneapolis: University of Minnesota Press, 2005.

Connolly, William, E. "Brain Waves, Transcendental Fields, and Techniques of Thought." *Radical Philosophy* 94 (1999), 19–28.

——. "Europe: A Minor Tradition." *Powers of the Secular Modern: Talal Asad and His Interlocutors*, ed. David Scott and Charles Hirschkind, 75–92. Stanford: Stanford University Press, 2006.

——. *Neuropolitics: Thinking, Culture, Speed*. Minneapolis: University of Minnesota Press, 2002.

——. *Why I Am Not a Secularist*. Minneapolis: University of Minnesota Press, 1999.

Constantinou, Costas M., and Yiannis Papadakis. "The Cypriot State(s) in Situ: Cross-ethnic Contact and the Discourse of Recognition." *Global Society* 15, no. 2 (2001), 125–48.

Copeaux, Etienne, and Claire Mauss-Copeaux. *Taksim! Chypre Divisée, 1964–2005*. Lyon: Aedelsa, 2005.

Corsin-Jimenez, Alberto. "Industry Going Public: Rethinking Knowledge and Administration." *Anthropology and Science*, ed. Peter Wade, Jeanette Edwards, and Penny Harvey. Oxford: Berg, 2007.

Cruikshank, Barbara. *The Will to Empower: Democratic Citizens and Other Subjects*. Ithaca: Cornell University Press, 1999.

Das, Veena. "Documentary Practices: State and Everyday Life on the Peripheries." Paper presented as the South Asia Centre Annual Lecture, School of Oriental and African Studies, University of London, 22 February 2001.

Das, Veena, Arthur Kleinman, Mamphela Ramphele, and Pamela Reynolds, eds. *Violence and Subjectivity*. Berkeley: University of California Press, 2000.

Das, Veena, and Deborah Poole, eds. *Anthropology in the Margins of the State*. Santa Fe: School of American Research Press, 2004.

Deleuze, Gilles. *Foucault*. Minneapolis: University of Minnesota Press, 1998.

Deleuze, Gilles, and Felix Guattari. *A Thousand Plateaus: Capitalism and Schizophrenia*. London: Continuum, 2004.

Demetriou, Olga. "Freedom Square: The Unspoken Reunification of a Divided City." *Hagar: Studies in Culture, Polity and Identities* 7, no. 1 (2006), 55–77.

——. "To Cross or Not to Cross?: Subjectivization and the Absent State in Cyprus." *Journal of the Royal Anthropological Institute* 13 (2007), 987–1006.

Demir, Hülya, and Rıdvan Akar. *Istanbul'un Son Sürgünleri: 1964'te Rumların Sınırdışı Edilmesi*. Istanbul: İletişim, 1994.

Derrida, Jacques. "Force of Law: The 'Mystical Foundation of Authority.'" *Deconstruction and the Possibility of Justice*, ed. Drucilla Cornell, Michel Rosenfeld, and David Gray Carlson, 3–67. New York: Routledge, 1992.

——. *Specters of Marx: The State of Debt, the Work of Mourning, and the New International*. London: Routledge, 1994.

——. *Writing and Difference*, trans. Alan Bass. Chicago: University of Chicago Press, 1978.

Deutsch, Karl Wolfgang. *The Nerves of Government: Models of Political Communication and Control*. New York: Free Press, 1966.

Dikomitis, Lisa. "A *Moving* Field: Greek-Cypriot Refugees Returning Home." *Durham Anthropology Journal* 12, no. 1 (2004), 7–20.

——. "Three Readings of a Border: Greek Cypriots Crossing the Green Line in Cyprus." *Anthropology Today* 21, no. 5 (2005), 7–12.

Dimitriu, Themos, and Sotiris Vlahos. *İhanete Uğramış Ayaklanma*. Ankara: Arkadaş Yayınları, 2009.

Dirks, Nick, ed. *In Near Ruins: Cultural Theory at the End of the Century*. Minneapolis: University of Minnesota Press, 1998.

Douglas, Mary. *Purity and Danger: An Analysis of Concepts of Pollution and Taboo*. London: Routledge and Kegan Paul, 1966.

Douzinas, Costas, and Ronnie Warrington. *Justice Miscarried: Ethics, Aesthetics, and the Law*. New York: Harvester Wheatsheaf, 1994.

Durkheim, Emile. *The Elementary Forms of the Religious Life*. New York: Free Press, 1965.

Elsner, John, and Roger Cardinal. *The Cultures of Collecting*. London: Reaktion, 1994.

Enloe, Cynthia. *Bananas, Beaches, and Bases: Making Feminist Sense of International Politics*. London: Pandora, 1989.

Fabian, Johannes. *Time and the Other: How Anthropology Makes Its Object*. New York: Columbia University Press, 1983.

Fahmy, Khaled. *All the Pasha's Men: Mehmet Ali, His Army, and the Making of Modern Egypt*. Cambridge: Cambridge University Press, 1997.

Fahri Çoker Arşivi. *6–7 Eylül Olayları: Fotoğraflar-Belgeler*. Istanbul: Tarih Vakfı Yurt Yayınları, 2005.

Fehmi, Hasan. *Kuzey Kıbrıs Türk Cumhuriyeti'nin El Kitabı*. Nicosia: Gelişim Off-Set, 1987.

Ferguson, James. *The Anti-Politics Machine: "Development," Depoliticization, and Bureaucratic Power in Lesotho*. Cambridge: Cambridge University Press, 1990.

Fineman, Stephen, ed. *Emotion in Organizations*. London: Sage, 2000.

Foucault, Michel. 1972. *Archaeology of Knowledge*, trans. A. M. Sheridan Smith. London: Tavistock.

——. "Governmentality." *The Foucault Effect*, ed. Graham Burchell, Colin Gordon, and Peter Miller, 87–104. Hemel Hempstead: Harvester Wheatsheaf, 1991.

——. *The Order of Things: An Archaeology of the Human Sciences*. London: Tavistock, 1970.

Freud, Sigmund. *Group Psychology and the Analysis of the Ego*, trans. and ed. James Strachey. New York: W. W. Norton. 1990.

——. "Mourning and Melancholia" (1917). *The Standard Edition of the Complete Psychological Works of Sigmund Freud*. London: Vintage, 2001.

——. *The Uncanny* (1919). London: Penguin, 2003.

——. "The Unconscious." *The Standard Edition of the Complete Psychological Works* of *Sigmund Freud: On the History of the Psycho-Analytic Movement, Papers on Metapsychology and Other Works*, Volume 14. London: Vintage, 2001.

Geertz, Clifford. "'From the Native's Point of View': On the Nature of Anthropological Understanding." *Local Knowledge: Further Essays in Interpretive Anthropology*, 55–72. New York: Basic, 1983.

Gell, Alfred. *Art and Agency: An Anthropological Theory*. Oxford: Clarendon Press, 1998.

Giray, Halil. "Önsöz." *K.K.T.C. Coğrafi İsimler Katalogu (Cilt-III). Girne İlçesi.* Lefkoşa: Devlet Basımevi, 1999.

Göle, Nilüfer. *Forbidden Modern: Civilization and Veiling*. Ann Arbor: University of Michigan Press, 1996.

Gordon, Avery. *Ghostly Matters: Haunting and the Sociological Imagination*. Minneapolis: University of Minnesota Press, 1997.

Graham, Mark. "Emotional Bureaucracies: Emotions, Civil Servants, and Immigrants in the Swedish Welfare State." *Ethos* 30, no. 3 (2002), 199–226.

Green, André. *The Fabric of Affect in Psychoanalytic Discourse*. New York: Routledge, 1999.

Green, Sarah. *Notes from the Balkans: Locating Marginality and Ambiguity on the Greek-Albanian Border*. Princeton: Princeton University Press, 2005.

Guattari, Felix. "Ritornellos and Existential Affects." *The Guattari Reader / Pierre Felix Guattari*, ed. G. Genosko, 158–71. Oxford: Blackwell, 1996.

Gupta, Akhil. "Blurred Boundaries: The Discourse of Corruption, the Culture of Politics, and the Imagined State." *American Ethnologist* 22, no. 2 (1995): 375–402.

Gupta, Akhil, and James Ferguson. *Anthropological Locations: Boundaries and Grounds of a Field Science*. Berkeley: University of California Press, 1997.

Gürkan, Haşmet M. *Bir Zamanlar Kıbrıs'ta: Tarih Yazıları (1860–1945)*. Nicosia: CYREP Yayınları, 1986.

Güven, Dilek. *Cumhuriyet Dönemi Azınlık Politikaları ve Stratejileri Bağlamında 6–7 Eylül Olayları*. Istanbul: İletişim, 2005.

Hadjipavlou, Maria. "'I Grow in Different Ways Every Time I Cross': Multiple Stories: The 'Crossings' as Part of Citizens' Reconciliation Efforts in Cyprus?" *The Cyprus Conflict: Looking Ahead*, ed. Ahmet Sözen, 193–223. Famagusta: Eastern Mediterranean University Printing House, 2008.

Hakeri, Bener Hakkı. *Kıbrıs'ta Halk Ağzından Derlenmiş Sözcükler Sözlüğü*. Gazimağusa: Hakeri Yayınları, 1981.

Hakkı, Murat Metin. *Kıbrıs'ta Statükonun Sonu*. Istanbul: Naos Yayınları, 2004.

Hatay, Mete. *Beyond Numbers: An Inquiry into the Political Integration of the Turkish "Settlers" in Northern Cyprus*. Nicosia: Peace Research Institute in Oslo Cyprus Centre, 2005.

Hatay, Mete, and Rebecca Bryant. "The Jasmine Scent of Nicosia: Of Returns, Revolutions, and the Longing for Forbidden Pasts." *Journal of Modern Greek Studies* 26, no. 2 (2008): 423–49.

Henare, Amiria, Martin Holbraad, and Sari Wastell, eds. *Thinking Through Things: Theorising Artefacts Ethnographically*. London: Routledge, 2007.

Hendler, Glenn. *Public Sentiments: Structures of Feeling in Nineteenth-Century American Literature*. Chapel Hill: University of North Carolina Press, 2001.

Herzfeld, Michael. *Cultural Intimacy: Social Poetics in the Nation-State*. New York: Routledge, 1997.

——. *The Social Production of Indifference: Exploring the Symbolic Roots of Western Bureaucracy*. Chicago: University of Chicago Press, 1992.

Hetherington, Kevin. "In Place of Geometry: The Materiality of Place." *Ideas of Difference*, ed. Kevin Hetherington and Rolland Munro, 183–99. Oxford: Blackwell, 1997.

Hirsch, Eric. "Landscape: Between Place and Space." *The Anthropology of Landscape: Perspectives on Place and Space*, ed. Eric Hirsch and Michael O'Hanlon, 1–30. Oxford: Clarendon, 1995.

Hirsch, Eric, and Michael O'Hanlon, eds. *The Anthropology of Landscape: Perspectives on Place and Space*. Oxford: Clarendon, 1995.

Hirschon, Renee. *Heirs of the Greek Catastrophe: The Social Life of Asia Minor Refugees in Piraeus*. New York: Berghahn, 1998.

Hirschon, Renee, ed. *Crossing the Aegean: An Appraisal of the 1923 Compulsory Population Exchange between Greece and Turkey*. New York: Berghahn, 2003.

Hirst, Paul. *Space and Power: Politics, War and Architecture*. Cambridge: Polity, 2005.

Hitchens, Christopher. *Hostage to History: Cyprus from the Ottomans to Kissinger*. London: Verso, 1999.

Humphrey, Caroline, and Altanhuu Hürelbaatar. "Regret as a Political Intervention: An Essay in the Historical Anthropology of the Early Mongols." *Past and Present* 186 (2005), 3–45.

Ilıcan, Murat Erdal. "The Making of Sovereignty through Changing Property/ Land Rights and the Contestation of Authority in Cyprus." Ph.D. diss., Oxford University, 2010.

Ivy, Marilyn. *Discourses of the Vanishing: Modernity, Phantasm, Japan*. Chicago: University of Chicago Press, 1995.

Jacobus, Mary. *The Poetics of Psychoanalysis: In the Wake of Klein*. Oxford: Oxford University Press, 2005.

Joseph, Joseph S. "International Dimensions of the Cyprus Problem." *Cyprus Review* 2, no. 2 (1990): 15–39.

Kelley, Mike. *The Uncanny*. Cologne: Verlag der Buchhandlung Walther König, 2004.

Killoran, Moira. "Time, Space, and National Identities in Cyprus." *Step-Mother-tongue: From Nationalism to Multiculturalism the Literatures of Cyprus, Greece, and Turkey*, ed. Mehmet Yashin, 129–46. London: Middlesex University Press, 2000.

Klein, Melanie. *The Psycho-Analysis of Children*. New York: Vintage, 1997.

——. *The Selected Melanie Klein*, ed. Juliet Mitchell. New York: Free Press, 1997.

Kleinman, Arthur, Veena Das, and Margaret Lock. *Social Suffering*. Berkeley: University of California Press, 1997.

Kleinman, Arthur, and Byron Good. *Culture and Depression: Studies in the Anthropology and Cross-Cultural Psychiatry of Affect and Disorder*. Berkeley: University of California Press, 1985.

Kristeva, Julia. *Powers of Horror: An Essay on Abjection*. New York: Columbia University Press, 1982.

——. *Strangers to Ourselves*. New York: Columbia University Press, 1991.

Kuhn, Thomas S. *The Structure of Scientific Revolutions*. Chicago: University of Chicago Press, 1970.

Kuzey Kıbrıs Türk Cumhuriyeti. *K. K. T. C. Coğrafi İsimler Katalogu. Cilt-III. Girne İlçesi*. Ankara: Devlet Basımevi, 1999.

Kwon, Heonik. *After the Massacre: Commemoration and Consolation in Ha My and My Lai*. Berkeley: University of California Press, 2006.

Lacan, Jacques. *The Four Fundamental Concepts of Psychoanalysis*. Harmondsworth: Penguin, 1991.

Laporte, Dominique. *History of Shit*. Cambridge: MIT Press, 2000.

Latour, Bruno. "From *Realpolitik* to *Dingpolitik*, or How to Make Things Public." *Making Things Public: Atmospheres of Democracy*, ed. Bruno Latour and Peter Weibel, 14–41. Cambridge: MIT Press, 2005.

——. "On Recalling ANT." *Actor-Network Theory and After*, ed. John Law and John Hassard, 15–25. Oxford: Blackwell, 1999.

——. *Reassembling the Social: An Introduction to Actor-Network Theory*. Oxford: Oxford University Press, 2005.

——. *We Have Never Been Modern*. Hemel Hampstead: Harvester Wheatsheaf, 1993.

Latour, Bruno, and Peter Weibel, eds. *Making Things Public: Atmospheres of Democracy*. Cambridge: MIT Press, 2005.

Leach, Edmund. "Magical Hair" (1958). *The Essential Edmund Leach*, ed. Stephen Hugh-Jones and James Laidlaw, 177–201. New Haven: Yale University Press, 2000.

Loizos, Peter. *Greek Gift: Politics in a Cypriot Village*. Oxford: Blackwell, 1975.

——. *Heart Grown Bitter: A Chronicle of Cypriot War Refugees*. Cambridge: Cambridge University Press, 1981.

——. *Iron in the Soul: Displacement, Livelihood, and Health in Cyprus*. Oxford: Berghahn, 2008.

Lutz, Catherine A. *Unnatural Emotions: Everyday Sentiments on a Micronesian Atoll and Their Challenge to Western Theory*. Chicago: University of Chicago Press, 1988.

Lutz, Catherine, and Lila Abu-Lughod, eds. *Language and the Politics of Emotion*. Cambridge: Cambridge University Press, 1990.

Mageo, Jeanette, ed. *Power and the Self*. Cambridge: Cambridge University Press, 2002.

Malkki, Lisa. "Citizens of Humanity: Internationalism and the Imagined Community of Nations." *Diaspora* 3, no. 1 (1994), 41–68.

———. *Purity and Exile: Violence, Memory and National Cosmology among Hutu Refugees in Tanzania*. Chicago: University of Chicago Press, 1995.

Mapolar, Hikmet Afif. *Kıbrıs Güncesi: 40 Yılın Anıları 2*. Nicosia: Galeri Kültür Yayınları, 2002.

Massumi, Brian. *Parables for the Virtual: Movement, Affect, Sensation*. Durham: Duke University Press, 2002.

McCormack, Derek. "An Event of Geographical Ethics in Spaces of Affect." *Transactions of the Institute of British Geographers* 28, no. 4 (2003): 488–507.

Messick, Brinkley. *The Calligraphic State: Textual Domination in a Muslim Society*. Berkeley: University of California Press, 1993.

———. "On the Question of Lithography." *Culture and History* 16 (1997): 158–76.

Miller, Daniel, ed. *Home Possessions*. Oxford: Berg, 2001.

Miroğlu, Orhan. *Affet Bizi Marin*. Istanbul: Everest, 2009.

Mitchell, Timothy. "The Limits of the State: Beyond Statist Approaches and Their Critics." *American Political Science Review* 85, no. 1 (1991): 77–96.

———. *Rule of Experts: Egypt, Techno-Politics, Modernity*. Berkeley: University of California Press, 2002.

Myers, Fred. *Pintupi Country, Pintupi Self: Sentiment, Place, and Politics among Western Desert Aborigines*. Washington: Smithsonian Institution Press, 1986.

Navaro-Yashin, Yael. "De-Ethnicizing the Ethnography of Cyprus: Political and Social Conflict between Turkish-Cypriots and Settlers from Turkey." *Divided Cyprus: Modernity and an Island in Conflict*, ed. Yiannis Papadakis, Nicos Peristianis, and Gisela Welz, 84–99. Bloomington: Indiana University Press, 2006.

———. *Faces of the State: Secularism and Public Life in Turkey*. Princeton: Princeton University Press, 2002.

———. "Fantasy and the Real in the Work of Begoña Aretxaga." *Anthropological Theory* 7, no. 1 (2007): 5–8.

Negri, Antonio. "The Specter's Smile." *Ghostly Demarcations: A Symposium on Jacques Derrida*, ed. Michael Sprinker, 5–16. London: Verso, 1999.

Nejatigil, Zaim M. *Turkish Republic of Northern Cyprus in Perspective*. Nicosia: n.p., 1983.

Nesin, Aziz. *Yaşar Ne Yaşar Ne Yaşamaz*. Istanbul: Adam Yayınları, 1995.

Nişanyan, Sevan. *Adını Unutan Ülke: Türkiye'de Adı Değiştirilen Yerler Sözlüğü*. Istanbul: Everest, 2010.

North Cyprus Almanack. London: K. Rustem and Brother, 1987.

Obeyesekere, Gananath. *Medusa's Hair: An Essay on Personal Symbols and Religious Experience*. Chicago: University of Chicago Press, 1981.

Öktem, Kerem. "The Nation's Imprint: Demographic Engineering and the Change of Toponymes in Republican Turkey." *European Journal of Turkish Studies* 7 (2008).

Oxford Advanced Learners Dictionary. Oxford: Oxford University Press, 2004.

Papadakis, Yiannis. *Echoes from the Dead Zone: Across the Cyprus Divide*. London: I. B. Tauris, 2005.

——. "Greek Cypriot Narratives of History and Collective Identity: Nationalism as a Contested Process." *American Ethnologist* 25, no. 2 (1998): 149–65.

Patel, Geeta. "Imagining Risk, Care, and Security: Insurance and Fantasy." *Anthropological Theory* 7, no. 1 (2007): 99–118.

Patrick, Richard. *Political Geography and the Cyprus Conflict, 1963–1971*. Faculty of Environmental Studies publication. Waterloo, Ont.: Department of Geography, University of Waterloo, 1976.

Plümer, Fazıl. *Anılar: Toplum Hizmetinde Bir Ömür*. Nicosia: CYREP, 2001.

Press and Information Office, Republic of Cyprus. "Resolutions Adopted by the United Nations on the Cyprus Problem, 1964–1999." Booklet. Nicosia.

——. 1996. "Turkish Policy on Cyprus and Efforts to Solve the Cyprus Problem." Press release. Nicosia.

Riles, Annelise, ed. *Documents: Artifacts of Modern Knowledge*. Ann Arbor: University of Michigan Press, 2006.

——. "Law as Object." *Law and Empire in the Pacific*, ed. Sally Engle Merry and Donald Brenneis, 187–212. Santa Fe: School of American Research Press, 2004.

——. *The Network Inside Out*. Ann Arbor: University of Michigan Press, 2000.

Rosaldo, Michelle. *Knowledge and Passion: Ilongot Notions of Self and Social Life*. Cambridge: Cambridge University Press, 1980.

Rose, Nikolas. *Governing the Soul: The Shaping of the Private Self*. London: Free Association Books, 1999.

——. *Inventing Our Selves: Psychology, Power, and Personhood*. Cambridge: Cambridge University Press, 1998.

Sant-Cassia, Paul, 2005. *Bodies of Evidence: Burial, Memory and the Recovery of Missing Persons in Cyprus*. New York: Berghahn.

Schmitt, Carl. *The Concept of the Political*. Chicago: University of Chicago Press, 1996.

——. *Political Theology: Four Chapters on the Concept of Sovereignty*, trans. George Schwab. Cambridge: MIT Press, 1985.

Scott, Julie. "Property Values: Ownership, Legitimacy, and Land Markets in Northern Cyprus." *Property Relations: Renewing the Anthropological Tradition*, ed. Chris M. Hann, 142–59. Cambridge: Cambridge University Press, 1998.

Segal, Rafi, and Eyal Weizman, eds. *A Civilian Occupation: The Politics of Israeli Architecture*. London: Verso, 2003.

Sennett, Richard, and Jonathan Cobb. *The Hidden Injuries of Class*. Cambridge: Cambridge University Press, 1977.

Shore, Chris, and Susan Wright, eds. *Anthropology of Policy: Critical Perspectives on Governance and Power*. London: Routledge, 1997.

——. "Policy: A New Field of Anthropology." *Anthropology of Policy: Critical Perspectives on Governance and Power*, ed. Chris Shore and Susan Wright, 3–30. London: Routledge, 1997.

Slyomovics, Susan. *The Object of Memory: Arab and Jew Narrate the Palestinian Village*. Philadelphia: University of Pennsylvania Press, 1998.

Spinoza, Benedict de. *Ethics*. London: Penguin, 1996.

Stallybrass, Peter, and Allon White. *The Politics and Poetics of Transgression*. Ithaca: Cornell University Press, 1986.

Starn, Orin. "Missing the Revolution: Anthropologists and the War in Peru." *Cultural Anthropology* 6, no. 1 (1991): 63–91.

Stewart, Kathleen. *Ordinary Affects*. Durham: Duke University Press, 2007.

Stoler, Ann Laura. "Affective States." *A Companion to the Anthropology of Politics*, ed. David Nugent and Joan Vincent, 4–20. Oxford: Blackwell, 2004.

——. *Along the Archival Grain: Epistemic Anxieties and Colonial Common Sense*. Princeton: Princeton University Press, 2009.

Strathern, Marilyn. "Afterword: Accountability . . . and Ethnography." *Audit Cultures: Anthropological Studies in Accountability, Ethics and the Academy*, ed. Marilyn Strathern, 279–304. London: Routledge, 2000.

——. "An Awkward Relationship: The Case of Feminism and Anthropology." *Signs* 12, no. 2 (1987): 276–92.

——. "Cutting the Network." *Journal of the Royal Anthropological Institute* 2, no. 3 (1996): 517–35.

——. *The Gender of the Gift: Problems with Women and Problems with Society in Melanesia*. Berkeley: University of California Press, 1988.

——. "New Accountabilities." *Audit Cultures: Anthropological Studies in Accountability, Ethics and the Academy*, 1–18. London: Routledge, 2000.

——. *Property, Substance, and Effect: Anthropological Essays on Persons and Things*. London: Athlone, 1999.

——. "The Tangible and Intangible: A Holistic Analysis?" *Memorial Volume for Daniel de Coppet*, ed. André Iteanu. Paris: MHS, 2007.

Strathern, Marilyn, ed. *Audit Cultures: Anthropological Studies in Accountability, Ethics, and the Academy*. London: Routledge, 2000.

Tanrıverdi, Fıstık Ahmet. *Atina'daki Büyükada*. Istanbul: Adalı Yayınları, 2007.

——. *Hoşçakal Prinkipo: Bir Rüyaydı Unut Gitsin*. Istanbul: Literatür Yayıncılık, 2004.

Tansu, Ismail. *Aslında Hiç Kimse Uyumuyordu*. Ankara: Minpa Matbaacılık, 2001.

Tarde, Gabriel. *On Communication and Social Influence*, ed. Terry N. Clark. Chicago: University of Chicago Press, 1969.

——. *Psychologie economique*. Paris: F. Alcan, 1902.

Taussig, Michael. "Maleficium: State Fetishism." *The Nervous System*, 111–40. London: Routledge, 1992.

Thomas, Nicholas. *Entangled Objects: Exchange, Material Culture, and Colonialism in the Pacific*. Cambridge: Harvard University Press, 1991.

Thrift, Nigel. "Afterwords." *Environment and Planning D: Society and Space* 18 (2000): 213–55.

——. *Non-Representational Theory: Space/Politics/Affect*. London: Routledge, 2008.

Toews, David. "The New Tarde: Sociology after the End of the Social." *Theory, Culture, and Society* 20, no. 5 (2003): 81–98.

Torpey, John. *The Invention of the Passport: Surveillance, Citizenship, and the State.* Cambridge: Cambridge University Press, 2000.

Tuitt, Patricia. *False Images: Law's Construction of the Refugee.* London: Pluto, 1996.

Türk Dil Kurumu (Turkish Language Association). *Türkçe Sözlük,* vol. 1. Ankara: Türk Tarih Kurumu Basımevi, 1988.

Uğural, Çetin, and Ferdi Sabit Soyer. *Şükran Ekonomisi: Üzerimizdeki İpotek (Kuzey Kıbrıs Ekonomisi Bütçe Analizleri).* Nicosia: Naci Talat Vakfı Yayınları, 1998.

Uludağ, Sevgül. *İncisini Kaybeden İstiridyeler: Kıbrıs'ta Kayıplar, Toplu Mezarlar, Ölümün Kıyısından Dönenler.* Nicosia: IKME, Socio-Political Studies Institute and Bilban Bilgi Bankası, 2006.

Vidler, Anthony. *The Architectural Uncanny: Essays in the Modern Unhomely.* Cambridge: MIT Press, 1992.

Viveiros de Castro, Eduardo. "Cosmological Deixis and Amerindian Perspectivism." *Journal of the Royal Anthropological Institute* 4, no. 3 (1998): 469–88.

Volkan, Vamık D. *Cyprus—War and Adaptation : A Psychoanalytic History of Two Ethnic Groups in Conflict.* Charlottesville: University Press of Virginia, 1979.

Volkan, Vamık D., and Norman Itzkowitz. *Turks and Greeks: Neighbours in Conflict.* Hemingford Grey: Eothen, 1994.

Vryonis, Speros, Jr. *The Mechanism of Catastrophe: The Turkish Pogrom of September 6–7, 1955, and the Destruction of the Greek Community of Istanbul.* New York: Greekworks, 2005.

Weber, Max. "Bureaucracy." *From Max Weber,* ed. H. H. Gerth and C. Wright Mills. New York: Oxford University Press, 1972.

Weiner, James. *The Empty Place: Poetry, Space, and Being among the Foi of Papua New Guinea.* Bloomington: Indiana University Press, 1991.

Weizman, Eyal. *Hollow Land: Israel's Architecture of Occupation.* London: Verso, 2007.

Welchman, John C. "On the Uncanny in Visual Culture." In Mike Kelley, *The Uncanny,* 39–56. Cologne: Verlag der Buchhandlung Walther König, 2004.

Wikan, Unni. *Managing Turbulent Hearts: A Balinese Formula for Living.* Chicago: University of Chicago Press, 1990.

Wilson, Richard A., ed. *Human Rights, Culture, and Context: Anthropological Perspectives.* London: Pluto, 1997.

Wright, Susan. *Anthropology of Organisations.* London: Routledge, 1994.

Yashin (Yaşın), Mehmet. *Kozmopoetika: Yazılar, Söyleşiler, Değiniler (1978–2001).* Istanbul: Yapı Kredi Yayınları, 2002.

——. *Toplu Yazılar (1978–2005).* Istanbul: Everest Yayınları, 2007.

Yashin (Yaşın), Mehmet, ed. *Step-Mothertongue: From Nationalism to Multiculturalism: the Literatures of Cyprus, Greece and Turkey.* London: Middlesex University Press, 2000.

Yıldırım, Onur. *Diplomacy and Displacement: Reconsidering the Turco-Greek Ex-change of Populations, 1922–1934.* London: Routledge, 2006.

Žižek, Slavoj. *Organs without Bodies: On Deleuze and Consequences.* New York: Routledge, 2004.

———. *The Sublime Object of Ideology.* London: Verso, 1989.

Index

268 INDEX

root, the 169–72
Rose, Nikolas, 22
ruination, 162, 170–75
ruins: as abject spaces, 152–60, 174–75;
bullet holes in, 152, 158–59, 170–71.
See also debris
Rüstem, Kemal, 27

Sacred Landscape (Benvenisti), 47
Sampson, Nikos, x
Sant-Cassia, Paul, 240n2
Schmitt, Carl, 42
Segal, Rafi, 47
senses of governance. *See* administration of TRNC
settlers from Turkey, 51–53, 227n24,
232n8; causes of migrations of, 57–
58; citizenship of, 57, 118–19, 122–
23, 245n6; conflation of, with soldiers, 55–56; housing allocations for,
143, 197–98; identification of, with
Turkey, 54–55, 60–61, 232n9, 233n17;
in Lefkoşa's border area, 130–32, 137,
140–41, 143, 146; majority status of,
218–19; othering terms used for, 56–
57, 58, 146, 151, 232n9, 233n13; passports of, 108–9; power relationships
of, 58–60, 233n17; prohibition on,
from crossing Green Line, 235n8;
social and economic status of,
233n14; symbolic markers of, 58,
233n16
'74 generation, 76–77, 235n10
Seylani, Ali, 92
simulacra, 16–17
social constructionist concepts, 5–6;
anthropocentrism of, 164; contextualized readings of space in, 17–
18, 41–42; Durkheim's notion of
affect in, 202–6
Social Suffering (Das and Kleinman),
25–26
soldiers. *See* military occupation
sovereignty, 41–43; Agamben's theory
of, 42, 44, 94, 96; colonial past of,
47–48; distributed agency in, 43;
political intention in, 43, 47–50; tangibility of, 47–48; Turkey-fication in,
44–47, 231nn10–11

space, xiv, 6–11; Bachelard's imaginary
of, 188–90; engagement with landscape in, 41–43; expressions of confinement in, 68–77; hauntology of,
15–17; making of abject in, 147–60;
political constructions of sovereignty in, 47–48; resonance of, on
affect, 17–21, 228n45, 228n58; settlers' perceptions of, 54–55; in
Thrift's non-representational theory
of affect, 168; uncanny in, 182, 199–
201. *See also* confinement; inside–
outside positions; make-believe
spatial melancholia, 174
Specters of Marx (Derrida), 15–17
Spinoza, Benedict de, 26–27, 168
Stallybrass, Peter, 149, 150
"state, the," as term, 97–100, 237n4.
See also administration of TRNC
Stewart, Kathleen, 20–21
Stoler, Ann Laura, 33, 235n4, 239n44
Strathern, Marilyn, 94, 163, 203,
229n75
subjectivity, 21–27, 229n68; in abjection,
147–52; in affect-subjectivity continuum, 24–27, 132–33, 229n68, 239n2;
anthropological study of, 25–26;
Deleuze's views on, 167–70; as interiority of human subject, 167–68; in
making of place, 41–43. *See also* affect
suggestibility, 204–5
syncretism, 11, 226n17

Talat, Mehmet Ali, 221, 232n9
tangible. *See* materiality
Tarde, Gabriel, 20, 204–6, 229n78; on
inter-mental relationality, 204–5; on
quality of affect, 213–14
Taussig, Michael, 97
Thinking through Things (Henare et al.),
227n29
This Country Is Ours Platform, xvii–
xviii, 62–63, 67, 224n20, 234n1
Thomas, Nicholas, 213
Thousand Plateaus, A (Deleueze and
Guattari), 169–70
Thrift, Nigel, 18, 165; on cartographic
imagination, 170; non-representa-
tional theory of, 167–68

YAEL NAVARO-YASHIN is a senior lecturer in social
anthropology at the University of Cambridge and a fellow
of Newnham College. She is the author of *Faces of the State:
Secularism and Public Life in Turkey* (2002).

Library of Congress Cataloging-in-Publication Data
Navaro-Yashin, Yael, 1969–
The make-believe space : affective geography in a postwar
polity / Yael Navaro-Yashin.
p. cm.
Includes bibliographical references and index.
ISBN 978-0-8223-5193-1 (cloth : alk. paper)
ISBN 978-0-8223-5204-4 (pbk. : alk. paper)
1. Cyprus—History—Cyprus Crisis, 1974— —Public opinion.
2. War and society—Cyprus. 3. War—Psychological aspects.
I. Title.
DS54.9.N38 2012
956.9304—dc23
2011036575